Refugee Resettlement in the United States

Full details of all our publications can be found on http://www.multilingual-matters.com, or by writing to Multilingual Matters, St Nicholas House, 31-34 High Street, Bristol BS1 2AW, UK.

Refugee Resettlement in the United States

Language, Policy, Pedagogy

Edited by
**Emily M. Feuerherm and
Vaidehi Ramanathan**

MULTILINGUAL MATTERS
Bristol • Buffalo • Toronto

Library of Congress Cataloging in Publication Data
A catalog record for this book is available from the Library of Congress.
Refugee Resettlement in the United States: Language, Policy, Pedagogy/Edited by Emily M. Feuerherm and Vaidehi Ramanathan.
Includes bibliographical references and index.
1. Language and languages—Political aspects—United States. 2. Language policy—United States. 3. Refugees—United States. 4. Refugees—Education—United States. 5. Linguistic minorities—Education—United States. I. Feuerherm, Emily M., editor. II. Ramanathan, Vaidehi, editor.
P119.32.U6R44 2015
362.870973–dc23 2015023405

British Library Cataloguing in Publication Data
A catalogue entry for this book is available from the British Library.

ISBN-13: 978-1-78309-457-8 (hbk)
ISBN-13: 978-1-78309-456-1 (pbk)

Multilingual Matters
UK: St Nicholas House, 31-34 High Street, Bristol BS1 2AW, UK.
USA: UTP, 2250 Military Road, Tonawanda, NY 14150, USA.
Canada: UTP, 5201 Dufferin Street, North York, Ontario M3H 5T8, Canada.

Website: www.multilingual-matters.com
Twitter: Multi_Ling_Mat
Facebook: https://www.facebook.com/multilingualmatters
Blog: www.channelviewpublications.wordpress.com

The policy of Multilingual Matters/Channel View Publications is to use papers that are natural, renewable and recyclable products, made from wood grown in sustainable forests. In the manufacturing process of our books, and to further support our policy, preference is given to printers that have FSC and PEFC Chain of Custody certification. The FSC and/or PEFC logos will appear on those books where full certification has been granted to the printer concerned.

Typeset by Deanta Global Publishing Services Limited.
Printed and bound in Great Britain by Short Run Press Ltd.

To the families of the contributors, for their support.

To all the families discussed in this volume, thank you for sharing your stories.

Contents

Acknowledgments

First of all, we would like to thank the contributors to this volume for their insightful work and enthusiastic responses to the volume's focus on refugees. Each contributor was a pleasure to work with and it was a joy to read her contributions at each stage of the process. Special thanks go to Kim Eggleton, our editor at Multilingual Matters, who made our path to publication so smooth and easy. To our blind reviewer, a very heartfelt thank you for the thoughtful feedback and suggestions.

Contributors

Diana M.J. Camps is a PhD research fellow at the University of Oslo's Center for Multilingualism in Society across the Lifespan: a Center of Excellence financed by the Research Council of Norway. She holds an MA in teaching English as a second language (TESL) from the University of Texas in San Antonio and a BA in international studies from Texas A&M University. Her main research interests are language and migration, minority languages, language policy and the role of language in social differentiation. She is presently working on a chapter for an edited volume entitled *Standardizing Minority Languages: Competing Ideologies of Authority and Authenticity in the Global Periphery*, to be published in the Routledge Critical Studies in Multilingualism series.

Emily M. Feuerherm is an assistant professor of linguistics in the English Department at the University of Michigan, Flint. She received her PhD in linguistics from the University of California, Davis, where her research focused on the community-based program she founded in Sacramento called the Refugee Health and Employment Attainment Program (RHEAP). She is currently constructing a bridge program at UM-Flint for international students, with her research in program building continuing in this new social and geographical location. Her research interests integrate policy, curriculum design, TESOL pedagogies and (dis)citizenship in English teaching and learning. She has published in the *CATESOL Journal* and has a chapter in the edited volume *Language Policies and (Dis)Citizenship: Rights, Access, Pedagogies.*

Daisy E. Fredricks is an assistant clinical professor of TESOL and the TESOL program coordinator in the Department of Teaching and Learning, Policy and Leadership in the College of Education at the University of Maryland, College Park. Daisy holds a PhD in applied linguistics from Arizona State University and she served as an elementary and middle school classroom teacher in the states of Michigan, Texas and Arizona. Her general research interests include English language learner (ELL) education, pre-service teacher education, (restrictive) language education policy and qualitative research methods. Her current research focuses on how current theories of language and literacy translate into the daily instructional practices of pre-service ESOL teachers throughout their teaching internship experiences – and how ELL youth respond to such practices. Her work has appeared in the *International Multilingual Research Journal* and the *CATESOL Journal*.

Cassie D. Leymarie (PhD applied linguistics) is a visiting lecturer in the Department of Applied Linguistics at Georgia State University. She also serves as the educational program specialist for the Somali American Community Center in Clarkston, Georgia, and is an advocate at large for the refugee communities in the greater Atlanta area. Her research focuses on Somali refugee women's perceptions of and experiences with language and literacy in their daily lives and the consequent implications on community participation. Leymarie's other research interests include the linguistic landscape and the role of textual mediation in multilingual communities and issues related to language and human rights.

Ariel Loring holds a PhD in linguistics from the University of California, Davis. She is currently a lecturer in the Anthropology Department of California State University, Sacramento, and a writing specialist at UC Davis. Her dissertation is concerned with discursive and semiotic interpretations of citizenship policy and practice in the US. She has several forthcoming publications in the *Journal of Language, Identity, and Education*; *Critical Inquiry in Language Studies*; and the *Journal of Social Science Education*, as well as a co-edited volume on the legal and linguistic issues of immigration and naturalization. Her current research interests are situated in language politics, policies and discourses; immigration; and language ideologies.

Bernadette Ludwig is an assistant professor in the Sociology Department at Wagner College in Staten Island, New York. She received her PhD from the Graduate Center of the City University of New York. Her research focuses on the Liberian refugee community in Staten Island. In her work, Bernadette Ludwig focuses on the intersection of immigration, gender and race, specifically how refugees and immigrants assert their agency to respond to imposed racial and gender hierarchies and refugee (resettlement) policies. Some of her publications include 'Wiping the refugee dust from my feet': Advantages and burdens of refugee status and the refugee label (*International Migration*) and Liberians: Continued struggles for refugee families (in *One Out of Three: Immigrant New York in the Twenty-First Century* by Nancy Foner [ed.]). She is also the co-founder and a board member of Culture Connect Inc., an organization working with refugees and immigrants in Atlanta, Georgia.

Vaidehi Ramanathan is professor of applied sociolinguistics in the Linguistics Department at the University of California, Davis. Her research interests span all domains of literacy, including teacher education, minority languages and language policies, as well as concerns about aging, health and disability studies. Her publications include *Language, Body and Health* (co-edited, 2011, Mouton de Gruyter); *Bodies and Language: Health, Ailments, Disabilities*; *The English-Vernacular Divide: Postcolonial Language Politics and Practice*; *The Politics of TESOL Education: Writing, Knowledge, Critical Pedagogy*; and *Alzheimer's Discourse: Some Sociolinguistic Dimensions*.

Shawna Shapiro is an assistant professor of writing and linguistics at Middlebury College, where she teaches courses in composition, sociolinguistics and education. Dr Shapiro's research looks at the experiences of multilingual students (including both immigrant and international populations) in US colleges and universities, focusing on issues such as academic integration, curricular innovation and institutional policy. Her current research project focuses on refugee students transitioning to higher education in Vermont. She also writes frequently about how the college curriculum can promote linguistic diversity and global citizenship for all students. Dr Shapiro's work has appeared in a number of journals, including *Research in the Teaching of English*, *TESOL Quarterly* and *Teaching and Teacher Education*, as well as in many peer-reviewed book collections. Her co-authored book, entitled *Fostering International Student Success in Higher Education* (TESOL Press), was published in 2014.

Tina Shrestha is a postdoctoral fellow in the International Institute for Asian Studies (IIAS) at Leiden University, the Netherlands. She received her PhD in cultural anthropology from Cornell University in 2014. Her research focuses on the contemporary US immigration and asylum processes, anthropological theories of the state and bureaucracy, critical humanitarianism and compassion. She is currently working on her dissertation-based book-manuscript on the co-production of asylum testimonials as a useful analytical site for an investigation into the relationship between suffering and migrant integration practices.

Nora Tyeklar is a PhD student in linguistic anthropology at the University of Texas at Austin. She holds a master's in applied linguistics from the University of Massachusetts at Boston. Having worked in US refugee resettlement as an ESL tutor for several years, she analyzes how reportage in the media, the public activities of powerful state actors and the institutional discourses as shaped by the politico-economic relations between sending and receiving countries regularly disrupt the advocacy work of resettlement organizations. Her work focuses on the ways in which the scaffolding structures of resettlement, despite the aforementioned top-down disruptions, function to promote language acquisition as a social practice; facilitate the entrance of newcomers into communities that foster advocacy, care and coping; and create responsive affective atmospheres to mitigate institutional pressures and past traumas.

Doris Warriner is an associate professor in the Department of English at Arizona State University. In her scholarship and teaching, she examines processes of transnationalism, refugee resettlement, migration and literacy development with a focus on the complicated ways that communicative practices and social processes are interconnected, the material consequences associated with those connections and the possibilities for fostering fuller membership and participation among marginalized learners of English. Drawing on the theories and approaches of linguistic anthropology and educational linguistics, Warriner uses ethnographic methods to examine questions and concerns of interest to applied linguists, educational researchers and literacy scholars. She has published in a number of edited volumes and encyclopedias as well as in journals such as *Anthropology and Education Quarterly*; *Linguistics and Education*; the *International Multilingual Research Journal*; the *Journal of Language, Identity, and Education*; and *Women's Studies Quarterly*.

1 Introduction to Refugee Resettlement in the United States: Language, Policies, Pedagogies

Emily M. Feuerherm and
Vaidehi Ramanathan

Situating Discourses of Refugee Resettlement

This volume brings together some leading female scholars writing about refugee resettlement, focusing on discourses of the lived, local experiences of refugees and asylum seekers as they are resettled in countries of asylum. Each chapter unravels the complex discursive constructions that position refugees as needy and burdens upon local and state resources, while questioning and analyzing the assumptions upon which such constructions are based. Such discursive practices have serious effects on several aspects of resettlement: upon refugees' experiences of resettlement and their ability to adapt to the country of asylum; upon the policies which guide and provide resources for resettlement; and upon the ways in which educational resources are developed and administered. This collection is centered on how language is used *by*, *for* and *about* refugees by authors from various disciplines. Such an interdisciplinary investigation serves to broaden our understandings of what *refugee* and *resettlement* mean.

Research about refugees in applied linguistics has focused on several specific orientations: language use in the asylum-seeking process, positionings in the media and the educational experiences of refugees in or from particular geographical locations. For example, Blommaert (2009), Eades (2005, 2009) and Maryns (2005) each discuss how asylum seekers' linguistic background is used in the asylum-seeking process, often resulting in limited access to refugee status. Gabrielatos and Baker (2008), KhosraviNik (2010) and Leudar *et al.* (2008) show the ways that refugees in the UK are positioned in relation to other groups of immigrants, finding regular themes of hostility, misidentification and other negative discourses. The educational needs and experiences of refugees are perhaps the most well researched (e.g. Cranitch, 2010; Delgado-Gaitan, 1994; Dooley & Thangaperumal, 2011; Elmeroth, 2003; Finn, 2010; Fridland & Dalle, 2002; Kanno & Varghese, 2010; Naidoo, 2011; Stevenson & Willot, 2007; Tollefson, 1989; Watkins *et al.*, 2012; Windle & Miller, 2012). Such work is increasingly beneficial as the number of refugees worldwide climbs, and the populations seeking asylum continue to change. According to the United Nations High Commissioner for Refugees' (UNHCR) 2014 report, 13.9 million people were newly displaced in 2014 due to conflict or persecution, 51% of whom were under 18 years old (UNHCR Global Trends, 2015). As of 2014, 59.5 million people worldwide have been displaced, a 40% increase within a span of just three years (UNHCR Global Trends, 2015: 5). Such violent displacement of people around the world affects our understanding of traditional concepts of *home, identity* and *citizenship* (Feuerherm, 2013). Critical scholarship is needed to understand the causes and effects of such global flows of asylum seekers. This volume highlights the unique human flows of displacement and the resources and expectations these immigrants have as they seek asylum and a new home. In this volume, particular attention is paid to the ways that policies and pedagogies constrain or make room for resettlements of different kinds.

The chapters in this volume contribute to established scholarship regarding the educational needs and best pedagogical practices for local communities of refugees (Due & Riggs, 2009; Finn, 2010; Kanno & Varghese, 2010; Watkins *et al.*, 2012; Woods, 2009), and they also contribute to interdisciplinary understandings of what it means to be a refugee as seen through the policies affecting their resettlement (Blommaert, 2009; Eades, 2009; Ricento, 2013). The discourse used in the media regarding refugees and the language policies which affect resettlement mold communities' perceptions of refugees (Gale, 2004; Leudar *et al.*, 2008). Refugees themselves may react in different ways to the label *refugee*, either choosing to disassociate themselves from the term to avoid negative associations and connotations, or identifying themselves with the label in order to access legal rights or resources. Language is at the crux of these issues, and each of the chapters that follow highlight the linguistic issues as they relate to refugee resettlement policies, practices and pedagogies.

Why Focus on Refugees?

Refugees are a very specific group of political immigrants, and the policies around their resettlement are complex. They are distinct from other immigrants for a confluence of reasons: (1) they are not voluntary or economic immigrants.[1] Refugees are forced to flee from their homes because of persecution and are resettled in countries and cities based on allowances and services, not personal choice. (2) Refugees have legal status which provides them with special services upon arrival, including funding and welfare access, as well as work permits and access to training and educational resources. (3) Refugees arrive into a country of resettlement having survived traumatic experiences, often with limited or interrupted education, and regularly suffering from severe mental and physical health issues as a result of their lives in their home countries and refugee camps.

In order to better understand the refugee resettlement process, it is important to explore several of the keywords regarding refugees. Table 1.1 outlines some of the key policies regarding resettlement, especially who has access to refugee status.

The definitions in Table 1.1 are contested and the interpretation of these labels on the ground is often unclear (Gabrielatos & Baker, 2008). Those who must flee their homes in search of asylum are essentially political beings, involved in power – or its inverse, resistance – in its most basic and physical sense (Chilton & Schaeffner, 1997). The political pressures and the context of each case influence the ways that labels are applied. Williams (1976) presents the idea that *keywords* are those terms which are difficult to define because the semantic range is broad and tied to the socio-historical context of each utterance. *Keywords*, he argues, are especially those which involve ideas and values so that any investigation of the meaning of a word goes well beyond the 'proper meaning' to the range of meanings. Critically considering their internal developments, structures, range and edges uncovers the lack of neutrality with which they are used. The chapters in this volume will critically explore the keyword *refugee*, in relation to other keywords such as *race, resettlement, self-sufficiency, support, immigrant, (dis)citizen*, among others. However, throughout each chapter, it becomes evident that many of the crucial meanings have been shaped by those in power, while those who are labeled *refugee, asylee* or *immigrant* construct semantic webs that to varying degrees reproduce or counter recognized meanings. Such work illuminates the ideologies upon which these discourses are founded.

By critically analyzing the discourses which mediate access to refugee and asylee status, relationships of power and underlying ideologies are revealed. Ideologies both define groups (e.g. who counts as a legitimate *refugee?*) and place them in complex societal structures through their relationship to other groups (e.g. who is denied access to status or services?). However, ideologies are not solely social systems, but mental representations that have cognitive functions of belief organization of which individuals may be more or less aware (van Dijk, 1997; Fairclough, 2010). It is when these ideologies dominate and oppress social groups that researchers and practitioners must intervene on the side of the dominated in order to reveal

Table 1.1 Defining refugees, asylees and IDPs

Internally displaced persons (IDPs)	Asylum seeker	Prima facie[a] refugee status	Refugee
IDPs are people who have been displaced, often because of violent circumstances, but remain in their country of origin. IDPs are not able to apply for refugee status[b]	An asylum seeker claims to be a refugee, but his or her claim has not been definitively evaluated and he or she has not been granted refugee status	Prima facie status is recognition of a large-scale exodus, when circumstances prevent determination of refugee status on an individual basis	A refugee has proven that he or she cannot return to his or her country of origin because of persecution based on race, religion, nationality, membership of a particular social group or political opinion[c]
Three bodies of law provide protection for IDPs: international human rights law; international humanitarian law; international criminal law	Refugees and asylum seekers are already outside of their country of origin, and fall under the care of the UNHCR. There are several outcomes for asylum seekers and prima facie refugees: (1) Repatriation (i.e. returning to the country of origin) (2) Local integration (3) Resettling to a third country through family reunification or on one's own (4) Resettlement by UNHCR in a third country (such as the US)		

[a]Meaning 'at first sight' until proven otherwise.
[b]The US allows some IDPs to apply for resettlement through the special immigrant visa (SIV) which in 2008 was designed in response to Iraqis who aided the US military occupation. These individuals' lives were put in danger because of their association with the US. Additionally, as of 2009, Afghans may also apply for an SIV.
[c]This definition is taken from the UNHCR's 1951 convention where 'refugee' was defined.

oppressive regimes (Fairclough, 2010; Fairclough & Wodak, 1997). In other words, ideologies mitigate between language and social structures, and when social structures are oppressive, revealing the ideologies and discourses that legitimize such structures is necessary when attempting to resist them. The chapters in this volume uncover the dialectical relationship between the discourses, policies, ideologies and power/social structures that position refugees and their process of resettlement in very particular ways, as well as local discourses of resistance.

Yet, there are gaps in research pertaining directly to the policies and pedagogies which affect refugees, particularly how ideological and discursive constructions shape their fates. Critically interpreting the policies of asylum seeking allows for a better understanding of the process of applying for refugee status in the US, particularly related to discriminatory practices and unequal treatment based on ideologies of *asylum* and *refugee*. Like Blommaert (2009), Eades (2005, 2009) and Maryns (2005), this introductory chapter presents issues of language in relation to the asylum-seeking process in order to orient the reader to some of the issues around becoming a *refugee*. However, rather than focusing on the language of the asylum claims and the beliefs about language that guide the claims' analysis as previous research has done, this introduction will focus on the political constructions of asylum and refuge in policies. The goal is to show how forces of discrimination and unequal access are legitimized through the language of policies and demonstrate why a focus on refugees is important within the field of applied linguistics.

The following section explores the political nature of labeling, taking the current example of unaccompanied Central American minors crossing the Southern US border. This is an example that demonstrates the ways in which language, policy and ideology construct refugees, asylum seekers and resettlement. The following section is intended to provide the reader with some background and context for the larger issues which influence refugee resettlement, and the role of language in the construction of who counts as a *refugee*.

Unaccompanied Minors Coming to the US

The unaccompanied minors from Central America who have been crossing the Southern US border since 2013 are being labeled variously depending on the context and political orientations of the speaker. These unaccompanied minors are fleeing unstable and violent circumstances,[2] and it seems as though they should be recognized as *prima facie refugees* (an estimated 57,000 arrived between October 2013 and July 2014), or at the very least *asylum seekers*. However, rather than being labeled as *refugees* or even *asylum seekers*, they are more commonly referred to in the media as *children, minors* or *kids* who are *unaccompanied, undocumented, immigrant, migrant* or *illegal*[3] – the latter being the most problematic (see Wiley [2013] for a discussion of this). Such labeling erases the violence from which they fled and the potential for violence if they are repatriated, and focuses on their immediate status in the US through analogy to other immigrants.

United States immigration policy requires that asylum seekers must enter the country first, and then file the necessary documents to apply for asylum, regardless of age or ability. The application is only in English, spans at least nine pages and requires an interview where persecution and abuse are recounted in detail.

Furthermore, children – like adults – who have been apprehended are not provided with legal aid to navigate this process, unless they have the wherewithal to hire a lawyer or a pro bono legal service offers help. Congress directed the department of Health and Human Services (HHS) to ensure that the unaccompanied children would have counsel 'to the greatest extent practicable' but also they should 'make every effort to utilize the services of pro bono counsel who agree to provide representation to such children without charge' (American Immigration Council 2015). And yet, as of April 2015, over 38,000 children's cases remained unrepresented, leaving these children to navigate the asylum process and the immigration court legal defense by themselves (American Immigration Council 2015). The Department of Homeland Security (DHS), on the other hand, has a lawyer trained in immigration law present at every case. Such discriminatory treatment of these cases is founded on economic and linguistic inequality, and undermines the international policies meant to protect all people, and especially children, from persecution and dangerous repatriation. Access to and participation in the rights of a nation or state is the foundation of *citizenship*. Thus, *dis-citizenship* is the exclusion of rights and participation to some based on illegitimate hierarchies (Devlin & Pothier, 2006; Ramanathan, 2013a, 2013b). In this case, through the use of paperwork provided only in English while providing no legal counsel to defend potential asylum seekers, these children are global dis-citizens, whose rights to asylum are jeopardized by the practices and policies of the HHS and DHS.

Although policies are in place to provide for unaccompanied minors when they are found by border authorities, the long-term fate of these children is being caught up in larger debates about immigration. Here, the language of the policies outlines who counts as valid asylum seekers/ refugees versus voluntary immigrants. Central American minors are held for no more than 72 hours by border patrol, given a notice to appear in court and they are then placed in the Health and Human Services Department's custody – the same department that houses the Office of Refugee Resettlement. However, Mexican minors who cross the border and are apprehended by border authorities can be deported immediately, despite the fact that the UNHCR found that they had an equal percentage of viable claims for asylum as their Southern neighbors (UNHCR Children on the Run, 2014). This policy is outlined in the William Wilberforce Trafficking Victims Protection Action Act, which President Bush signed into law in 2008. Because of this law, children from Central America are not deported immediately upon being found by border authorities and have the ability to apply for asylum, while Mexican minors are excluded from this right to apply for asylum and are deported immediately. In this context, Mexican immigrants are global *dis-citizens* (Devlin & Pothier, 2006; Ramanathan, 2013a, 2013b) who are excluded from opportunity and participation from the instant they cross the US border. In other words, who counts as a potential asylum seeker is outlined in the policy based on international politics and ideology – not need.

The difference between asylum seekers and refugees is one of timing: in each case, an individual must prove that he or she has a reasonable fear of persecution in his or her home country and must be outside of his or her country of origin upon application for refugee status; however, refugees have completed the process while asylum seekers are still navigating the policies. Eades (2005, 2009) describes the importance of linguistic analysis in refugees' claims for asylum, and shows that ideological understandings about language can influence the analysis of these claims (see also Blommaert, 2009; Maryns, 2005). The asylum seekers focused on in this chapter are applying for refugee status directly to the US. Unlike those entering the US as refugees, the Central American asylees have not applied to the UNHCR for permanent resettlement. This makes them particularly vulnerable to US-based ideological attitudes regarding their country of origin, the validity of their claim for asylum and the perceived burden they would be on the state.

In response to the surge in unaccompanied minors crossing the border, on July 8, 2014, President Obama called for 3.7 billion dollars in emergency funding for medical care, legal aid and education. In response, policymakers in the House and Senate proposed bills for policy changes to expedite either the process of deportation or the process of gaining asylum/ refugee status. The bill analyzed below is evidence of how ideologies about asylum and refugees both construct and are reflected through discourse (Blackledge, 2005; Fairclough, 2010; van Dijk, 1997; Weiss & Wodak, 2003). This bill was chosen for analysis because it was one of the first responses at policy level to the recent increase in unaccompanied minors crossing the border.

Policy and unaccompanied minors: Constructing criminals

The bill proposed to the senate by McCain and Flake (Republican senators from Arizona[4]), Provisions of Legislation to Address Crisis at the Border (July 10, 2014), proposes that policy changes be made in order to 'increase' the 'expedited removal' and repatriation of all undocumented immigrants. Below are the major points of the bill, as listed on McCain's press release website, though explanations in the original document have been omitted here in the interest of brevity.

(1) Amend the Trafficking Victims Prevention Act (TVPA) to increase repatriation of undocumented children from non-contiguous countries.

(2) Allow for expedited removal of all undocumented immigrants that are stopped at the border attempting to enter the United States illegally, allowing law enforcement to return them to their home countries within a matter of hours or days as opposed to the months or years removal currently takes in most cases.

(3) Require mandatory detention or the mandatory use of 'alternatives to detention' like ankle monitors to ensure individuals waiting for their court dates actually appear to court.

(4) Increase the number of immigration judges to hear cases and create a separate immigration docket to hear the cases of juveniles.

(5) Increase the number of refugee visas by 5000 for each of El Salvador, Honduras and Guatemala.

(6) Condition foreign aid on countries' efforts to secure their borders and deter smuggling of children to the United States. (McCain and Flake to Address Border Crisis, 2014)

The universality of the proposed bill in dealing with individuals from a range of countries, situations and backgrounds iconizes them and erases their histories and the situations from which they have fled (Irvine & Gal, 2000). In the second point, the bill states that it currently takes months or years to return undocumented immigrants to their home countries. This point erases the fact that approximately 58% of these children have valid claims for asylum and are in need of international protection (UNHCR Children on the Run, 2014), while iconizing them all as undocumented immigrants.

In addition, the treatment of these 'undocumented children', as the bill identifies them in the first point, calls into question humanitarian and children's rights. In a UNHCR (2008) report on children's repatriation to Honduras, it was found that the country lacked any agency that could be responsible for repatriated children and depended on family members to pick the child up upon arrival, and a more recent report states that there are significant gaps in protection mechanisms, the extent of which is still unknown (UNHCR Children on the Run, 2014). Because the children have fled the violence of their home countries and there is a distinct lack of government services for these children, it would seem that sending them back would breach basic humanitarian rights of non-refoulment. The UNHCR definition of *refugee* is such that asylum seekers cannot be sent back to their home countries if there are no protections from their governments against persecution. These undocumented minors from Central America (and Mexico) would seem to fall under such a definition, as their governments offer them little or no protection upon their return. Furthermore, universal repatriation would be in direct violation of the 1990 UNHCR Convention of the Rights of the Child, which states that 'In all actions concerning children, whether undertaken by public or private social welfare institutions, courts of law, administrative authorities or legislative bodies, the best interests of the child should be a primary consideration' (Article 3, Section 1). How, then, could such a blatant disregard for children's rights be proposed at the highest level of US policy?

The content of McCain and Flake's bill validates its orientation to undocumented minors by discursively constructing the unaccompanied minors as criminals. The bill uses the following terms in order to criminalize those who would otherwise be seen as authentic and lawful asylum seeking[5]: *undocumented* ('2); *illegally*; *law enforcement*; *mandatory detention*; *alternatives to detention*; *ankle monitors*; *court dates*; *court*; *judges*; *cases* ('2); *smuggling of children*. That these minors should be detained and monitored until their court date suggests that they pose a very real threat to society, even though some are as young as five years old (Isacson & Meyer, 2014). The third point in the bill requires 'mandatory detention' or 'ankle monitors to ensure individuals waiting for their court dates *actually* appear to court' (my emphasis). The use of *actually* implies that the minors are willfully avoiding immigration procedures, and should be treated as though they are breaking the law while they await an immigration hearing. The bill does not account for the fact that these children may be preliterate, may not speak English (the asylum forms are all and only in English) and may not have the cultural competence or even the maturity to understand the immigration and asylum process. For these reasons the minors may not in fact be willfully avoiding immigration hearings, and the lack of legal counsel for these minors is a striking omission (though the bill advocates increasing the number of immigration judges). Not only are undocumented minors criminalized in the language of this bill through analogy to *detention* and *monitoring*, but also their rights to seek asylum and apply for refugee status once they are in the US are denied through a lack of services.

The sixth point of the bill states that the US should 'condition foreign aid on countries' efforts to secure their borders and deter smuggling of children to the United States'. The use of the term *smuggling* again criminalizes the act of crossing the border. However, it also indicates that there may be human trafficking in children, a clear violation of US and international law against human trafficking. However, rather than offering aid to these countries to provide resources for repatriated minors or for suppressing the gang violence that has been the impetus for escape, this bill suggests that aid should be contingent upon secure borders. The language of this bill criminalizes the minors *and their nations* while removing accountability from the receiving country (the US) and rendering the causes for their flight invisible.

The bill does not entirely ignore the possibility of refugee status, but does so by recommending the 'increase [of] the number of refugee visas by 5,000 for each of El Salvador, Honduras, and Guatemala'. However, the bill does not account for the fact that applications for refugee status must be made to the UNHCR from outside the country of origin, and that the 5000 visas for each of these countries would go through the UNHCR, not necessarily helping those who may already be in the US and have valid claims for asylum. Although no policy currently stands, provisions could be made for applications for asylum to be made in the country of origin, but the bill fails to make accommodations for this. Furthermore, if 57,000 children have arrived in less than a year, a total of 15,000 visas for refugees would hardly be sufficient. Through omission of the technicalities of asylum seeking, and by discursively constructing the unaccompanied minors and their nations as criminal, the bill appears to be a reasonable proposal.

What this example shows is that refugee and asylum policies are complex and intensely political. The criminalization of victimhood is legitimized through erasure and ideological orientations to countries of origin. Furthermore, the discourses around *refugee* and *asylum* are highly contested, variously interpreted and set apart from other discourses around immigration through policies which control global human flows. Policies and practices that position refugees are deserving of a great deal more reflection by applied linguistics than has currently been done, and this volume attempts to address that gap.

Overview of the Chapters

Each of the chapters in this volume addresses the interrelations between language, policy and education as they relate to refugees. The chapters that follow are examples of localized articulations of refugee resettlement policy and represent very different perspectives from a variety of geographic contexts in the US. They are organized into two parts focusing broadly on (1) defining refugees through policy and practice (with Ludwig, Loring and Camps) and (2) education and refugee resettlement practices (with Feuerherm, Shrestha, Shapiro, Fredericks and Warriner, Tyeklar and Leymarie). In some sense, the division of the volume into these two parts is arbitrary as many of the chapters overlap in their integrated focus on language, policies and education. Nevertheless, we have chosen to organize it in this way to first provide necessary background on refugee resettlement politics and policies, then redirect the focus to localized investigations of the effects such policies have on education and resettlement. Thus, as we conceive it, the volume begins with a focus on defining refugees through *de jure* and *de facto* policies in order to set up a solid background upon which to discuss resettlement pedagogies. What follows are brief summaries of each of the chapters with some additional contextualization to their ordering.

Part 1: Defining Refugees through Policy and Practice

The part begins with Loring defining the key term *refugee* in Chapter 2. Loring draws distinctions between the terms *refugee, alien* and *immigrant* through a corpus analysis of media articles. She depicts the ways in which refugees are constructed through Immigration and Nationality Act policies for immigration and asylum, then juxtaposes their positionings in the policies with media representations. This chapter shows that groups of immigrants are portrayed differently, according to immigration policy and public opinion. Importantly, this chapter orients the reader to *de facto* policies evident through media representations, highlighting the metaphors and collocations which shape public understanding of refugees.

Chapter 3, written by Ludwig, further explores the various meanings of the word *refugee* by situating the term within New York's Liberian refugee community. Importantly, she distinguishes between legal refugee status, the informal refugee label, internally displaced persons (IDPs), asylees and other individuals such as those on deferred enforced departure, thus further orienting the reader to more of the legal terms and processes involved in refugee resettlement. Contextualized in the Liberian refugee community of New York, Ludwig peels away layers of meaning, showing that *refugee* may be associated with positive discourses of escape from refugee camps and new opportunities, or alternatively, with discourses of victimhood, suffering and a lack of agency. Viewed from outside the community, issues of aid, refugee status and race may be conflated, thus complicating the definition of *refugee* through the positionality of the viewer. The voices of the Liberian refugee community that are documented in this chapter show that an essentialized definition of *refugee* is neither possible nor preferable to those who identify with the label. Rather, it is a tool that can be used to index particular associations.

The last chapter in Part 1, written by Camps, critically analyses the policies of language acquisition across different scales. Chapter 4 untangles the often contradictory discourses that surround refugee policies, particularly as they relate to language learning and teaching. Using a discourse analytic approach, Camps demonstrates how policies entextualize particular perspectives through various scales, resulting in a hybrid discourse that frames the teaching of English as a second language (ESL) to adults.

She shows that language education policies are interdiscursively linked through issues of language acquisition and self-sufficiency, underscoring language learning for employment purposes. Additionally, she outlines how contradictions in language education policy counteract explicit goals, further limiting services to refugees and marginalizing their identities and social positions. She advocates awareness of such discourses and framing policies so that educators and refugee advocates can counteract exclusionary and marginalizing practices.

Thus, this part moves from *de facto* policies as represented in the media (Loring), to local interpretations of *asylum* and *refugee* (Ludwig) and ends with Camps, whose dual focus on policy and adult ESL education prepares the reader for the chapters in Part 2 of the volume, setting the stage for analyses of resettlement policy, pedagogy and curriculum design in refugee-directed education.

Part 2: Resettlement Practices and Effects on Education

Part 2 begins with a focus on education and the language of policies that guide instruction. Bridging the discussion on resettlement policy from the previous section, and education in this section, the first two chapters focus on adult education (Feuerherm and Shrestha). This is followed by studies located in higher education (Shapiro) and elementary school (Fredericks and Warriner). The chapters then return to a situated analysis of the resettlement process by addressing issues found in the discursive constructions of the agencies responsible for resettlement, and the pedagogical orientations that can be used in the classroom to counteract subordinating practices. These last two chapters (by Tyeklar and Leymarie) describe resettlement agencies' roles in resettlement, of which education is a key feature.

The first chapter in Part 2, Chapter 5, chronicles the development of a participatory ESL program for Iraqi refugee women and families. Feuerherm advocates community-based participatory research for action and participatory ESL program and curriculum building that is conducted with the community of learners. To demonstrate participatory program development, she tells the story of the Refugee Health and Employment Attainment Program (RHEAP), highlighting themes, developments and struggles throughout the process of developing a voluntary program for Iraqi refugees. Through each iteration of the program, she shows how challenges were met and to what extent the program was truly community-led and participatory. She concludes with the observation that the more ownership the refugee participants had of the program, the more successful it was and the better the program was able to respond to participants' needs while addressing underlying social inequalities.

In Chapter 6, Shrestha presents her ethnographic research of an ESL class for Nepali refugee women. She documents her own initial assumptions about these students and their reasons for attending the ESL class she teaches. Her students' desire/need to learn English is problematized in the classroom, as she discovers that many of her students find employment through their ability to speak Hindi, rather than English. Nevertheless, speaking 'good English' is, for them, connected to 'better jobs', although they continue to be subordinated and racialized through language. She shows how her students both acknowledge and anticipate their continued participation in the racialized labor market. They continue to pursue learning 'good English' despite their full acknowledgment that they will continue in their marginalized reality.

Moving away from voluntary adult education programs to higher education is the chapter by Shapiro, Chapter 7. Shapiro presents educators' perspectives about what appropriate support for refugee students in higher education should entail. Through interviews with faculty and staff who teach and support refugee-background college students, she presents two distinct perspectives regarding academic support: (1) that more support is better for refugee students and, alternatively, (2) that more support may be a detriment to students' long-term success or compromise the institutions' rigor. These points of divergence about what academic support should entail highlight ideological constructs about the needs of refugee students and the role of education in their futures. She shows that educators' perceptions about what counts as success versus failure for refugee-background students may not be aligned with students' own views. She advocates for stronger lines of communication among faculty, staff and students where students have more opportunities to discuss their goals and are better informed about when special accommodations are made on their behalf.

In Chapter 8, Fredericks and Warriner explore the ways in which language policies and ideologies influence the choices made by refugee youth in English language development (ELD) and mainstream classrooms. In this ethnographic study, everyday interactions demonstrate the ways that refugee-background students in an elementary school in Arizona reproduce or contest deficit discourses of multilingualism. This is shown especially by instances of language policing by refugee students themselves. They show that the students both reflect and shape local practices and policies.

Chapter 9, by Tyeklar, explores the way that refugees are positioned by the agencies responsible for their first months in the US. As in the previous chapters, Tyeklar explores the legal definition of *refugee*, but then contextualizes the term through a critical discourse analysis of two voluntary resettlement agency websites. Specifically, she shows that the voluntary agencies position refugees as foreign, vulnerable and in need of their aid in order to become *self-sufficient*. The term *self-sufficiency* becomes a hypernym for several components of survival, most of which are focused on employment and economics. She advocates for empowering pedagogies tailored to the particular needs of refugee communities that counter negative discourses – even when those negative discourses are coming from the agencies responsible for helping refugees resettle.

Chapter 10 presents a case study which documents the untapped resources that established refugee communities could offer voluntary resettlement agencies and educational services. Here, Leymarie theorizes the case study of Mama Rita, a Somali refugee, community leader and activist. Although Somalis are often depicted as pirates, criminals or victims in the media, and – as Tyeklar shows – refugees are generally positioned as dependent upon government services, this chapter counters such positionings by describing the resourcefulness of Mama Rita. Leymarie describes the funds of knowledge cultivated by Mama Rita that enable her to become a bridge between the newly resettled refugee communities and established residents of a small town in Georgia. Through direct engagement with politicians and community and religious leaders, Mama Rita develops multiple lines of resources that she uses to become an agent of change in and for her community. Leymarie concludes with suggestions for restructuring voluntary agencies and language teaching pedagogies aimed at refugee resettlement, making them more dynamic and engaged with local refugee activists.

Notes

(1)   While this is technically true according to the definition of *refugee*, it does not presuppose that refugees have no economic pressures or incentives for migrating. Rather, because they must *prove* that they are being persecuted and cannot return to their country, and because they do not choose where they are resettled, they are considered involuntary migrants.

(2)   Many reports are positing that these minors are fleeing economic crises, but a UNHCR report, Children on the Run (2014), shows that this is rarely the case; more often they are fleeing violence from gangs or family members.

(3)   This is based on a Google alert of various media from July 15 to July 31, 2014.

(4)   McCain and Flake come from a notoriously conservative state regarding immigration policy, which applied linguists have explored in relation to language policy and education (e.g. McCarty, 2004; Moore, 2014; Schmidt, 2000).

(5)   The UNHCR report, Children on the Run (2014), estimates that over half of the unaccompanied minors have valid claims for asylum, under international law.

References

American Immigration Council (June, 2015). A Guide to Children Arriving At The Border: Laws, Policies And Responses. See http://immigrationpolicy.org/sites/default/files/docs/a_guide_to_children_arriving_at_the_border_and_the_laws_and_policies_governing_our_response.pdf (retrieved 10 July 2015).

Blackledge, A. (2005) *Discourse and Power in a Multilingual World*. Amsterdam: John Benjamins.

Blommaert, J. (2009) Language, asylum, and the national order. *Current Anthropology* 50 (4), 415–441.

Chilton, P. and Schaeffner, C. (1997) Discourse and politics. In T.A. van Dijk (ed.) *Discourse as Social Interaction* (pp. 206–230). London: Sage.

Cranitch, M. (2010) Developing language and literacy skills to support refugee students in the transition from primary to secondary school. *Australian Journal of Language & Literacy* 33 (3), 255–267.

Delgado-Gaitan, C. (1994) Russian refugee families: Accommodating aspirations through education. *Anthropology & Education Quarterly* 25 (2), 137–155.

Devlin, R. and Pothier, D. (2006) *Critical Disability Theory.* Vancouver: UBC Press.

Dooley, K.T. and Thangaperumal, P. (2011) Pedagogy and participation: Literacy education for low-literate refugee students of African origin in a western school system. *Language and Education* 25 (5), 385–397.

Due, C. and Riggs, D. (2009) Moving beyond English as a requirement to 'fit in': Considering refugee and migrant education in South Australia. *Refuge* 26 (2), 55–64.

Eadas, D. (2005) Applied linguistics and language analysis in asylum seeker cases. *Applied Linguistics* 26 (4), 503–526.

Eades, D. (2009) Testing the claims of asylum seekers: The role of language analysis. *Language Assessment Quarterly* 6 (1), 30–40.

Elmeroth, E. (2003) From refugee camp to solitary confinement: Illiterate adults learn Swedish as a second language. *Scandinavian Journal of Educational Research* 47 (4), 431–449.

Fairclough, N. (2010) *Critical Discourse Analysis: The Critical Study of Language* (2nd edn). New York: Longman.

Fairclough, N. and Wodak, R. (1997) Critical discourse analysis. In T.A. van Dijk (ed.) *Discourse as Social Interaction* (pp. 258–284). London: Sage.

Feuerherm, E. (2013) Keywords in refugee accounts: Implications for language policies. In V. Ramanathan (ed.) *Language Policies and (Dis)Citizenship: Rights, Access, Pedagogies* (pp. 52–72). Bristol: Multilingual Matters.

Finn, H.B. (2010) Overcoming barriers: Adult refugee trauma survivors in a learning community. *TESOL Quarterly* 44 (3), 586–596.

Fridland, G. and Dalle, T. (2002) Start with what they know; build with what they have: Survival skills for refugee women. In E. Auerbach (ed.) *Community Partnerships* (pp. 27–40). Alexandria, VA: TESOL Publishing.

Gabrielatos, B. and Baker, P. (2008) Fleeing, sneaking, flooding: A corpus analysis of discursive constructions of refugees and asylum seekers in the UK press, 1996–2005. *Journal of English Linguistics* 36 (1), 5–38.

Gale, P. (2004) The refugee crisis and fear: Populist politics and media discourse. *Journal of Sociology* 40 (4), 321–340.

Irvine, J.T. and Gal, S. (2000) Language ideology and linguistic differentiation. In P. Kroskrity (ed.) *Regimes of Language: Ideologies, Polities, and Identities* (pp. 35–84). Santa Fe, NM: School of American Research Press.

Isacson, A. and Meyer, M. (2014) Are unaccompanied minors fleeing violence, or just poverty, in Central America? Border Fact Check: Separating Rhetoric from Reality. See http://www.borderfactcheck.org/?gclid=Cj0KEQjwr-KeBRCMh92 Ax9rNgJ8BEiQA1OVm-Ppy9wwcgdrrN51nKAImUGjJ-G2fYgzaA8xi DJZa0UQaAmUa8P8HAQ (accessed 10 July 2015).

Kanno, Y. and Varghese, M.M. (2010) Immigrant and refugee ESL students' challenges to accessing four-year college education: From language policy to educational policy. *Journal of Language, Identity, and Education* 9 (5), 310–328.

KhosraviNik, M. (2010) The representation of refugees, asylum seekers and immigrants in British newspapers: A critical discourse analysis. *Journal of Language and Politics* 9 (1), 1–28.

Leudar, I., Hayes, J., Nekvapil, J. and Turner, J. (2008) Hostility themes in the media, community and refugee narratives. *Discourse Society* 19 (2), 187–221.

Maryns, K. (2005) Monolingual language ideologies and code choice in the Belgian asylum procedure. *Language and Communication* 25 (3), 299–314.

McCain, J. and Flake, J. (July 10, 2014) Summary: Provisions of Legislation to Address Crisis at the Border. See http://www.mccain.senate.gov/public/index.cfm/2014/7/mccain-and-flake-to-introduce-bill-to-address-humanitarian-crisis-at-us-mexico-border (accessed 10 July 2015).

McCarty, T. (2004) Dangerous difference: A critical-historical analysis of language education policies in the United States. In J.W. Tollefson and B.M. Tsui (eds) *Medium of Instruction Policies: Which Agenda? Whose Agenda?* (pp. 71–93). Mahwah, NJ: Lawrence Erlbaum Associates.

Moore, S.C.K. (2014) *Language Policy, Processes and Consequences: Arizona Case Studies.* Bristol: Multilingual Matters.

Naidoo, L. (2011) What works? A program of best practice for supporting the literacy needs of refugee high school students. *Literacy Learning: The Middle Years* 19 (1), 29–38.

Ramanathan, V. (2013a) Language policies and (dis)citizenship: Rights, access, pedagogies. In V. Ramanathan (ed.) *Language Policies and (Dis)Citizenship: Rights, Access, Pedagogies* (pp. 1–16). Bristol: Multilingual Matters.

Ramanathan, V. (2013b) Language policies and (dis)citizenship: Who belongs? who is a guest? who is deported? *Journal of Language, Identity and Education* 12 (3), 162–166.

Ricento, T. (2013) Dis-citizenship for refugees in Canada: The case of Fernando. *Journal of Language, Identity, & Education* 12 (3), 184–188.

Schmidt, R. (2000) *Language Policy & Identity in the U.S.* Philadelphia, PA: Temple University Press.

Stevenson, J. and Willott, J. (2007) The aspiration and access to higher education of teenage refugees in the UK. *Compare: A Journal of Comparative Education* 37(5), 671–687.

Tollefson, J. (1989) *Alien Winds: The Reeducation of America's Indochinese Refugees.* New York: Praeger.

UNHCR (September 2, 1990) Convention on the Rights of the Child. See http://www.unhcr.org/50f941fe9.html (accessed 10 July 2015).

UNHCR (October, 2008) The International Protection of Unaccompanied or Separated Children Along the Southern Border of Mexico. See http://www.unhcr.org/cgi-bin/texis/vtx/home/opendocPDFViewer.html?docid=4cbeb6a96&query=unaccompanied%20minors (accessed 10 July 2015).

UNHCR (June 20, 2014) Global Trends 2013. See http://www.unhcr.org/5399a14f9.html.

UNHCR (March 12, 2014) Children on the Run: Unaccompanied Children Leaving Central America and Mexico and the Need for International Protection. http://www.unhcrwashington.org/sites/default/files/1_UAC_Children%20on%20the%20Run_Full%20Report.pdf (accessed 10 July 2015).

UNHCR (June 18, 2015) Global Trends: Forced Displacement in 2014. See http://unhcr.org/556/25e69.html (accessed 7 July 2015).

van Dijk, T.A. (1997) Discourse as interaction in society. In T.A. van Dijk (ed.) *Discourse as Social Interaction* (pp. 1–37). London: Sage.

Watkins, P.G., Razee, H. and Richters, J. (2012) 'I'm telling you...the language barrier is the most, the biggest challenge': Barriers to education among Karen refugee women in Australia. *Australian Journal of Education* 56 (2), 126–141.

Weiss, G. and Wodak, R. (2003) Introduction: Theory, interdisciplinarity and critical discourse analysis. In G. Weiss and R. Wodak (eds) *Critical Discourse Analysis: Theory and Interdisciplinarity* (pp. 1–34). New York: Palgrave Macmillan.

Wiley, T. (2013) Constructing and deconstructing 'illegal' children. *Journal of Language, Identity, & Education* 12 (3), 167–172.

Williams, R. (1976) *Keywords: A Vocabulary of Culture and Society.* London: Collins.

Windle, J. and Miller, J. (2012) Approaches to teaching low literacy refugee-background students. *Australian Journal of Language and Literacy* 35 (3), 317–333.

Woods, A. (2009) Learning to be literate: Issues of pedagogy for recently arrived refugee youth in Australia. *Critical Inquiry in Language Studies* 6 (1), 81–101.

Part 1

Defining Refugees through Policy and Practice

2 Positionings of Refugees, Aliens and Immigrants in the Media

Ariel Loring

Introduction

This chapter analyzes the discursive representation of refugees, aliens and immigrants in the US news media as it pertains to issues of citizenship and naturalization. This research transpires at a time when the number of immigrants in the US continues to rise (Office of Immigration Statistics, 2012) and national discourse increasingly revolves around matters of national identity and exclusion (McNamara & Shohamy, 2008). In the 2013 fiscal year, 503,104 immigrants became US citizens, contributing to the 6.8 million who have become naturalized in the last decade (Naturalization Fact Sheet, 2013). Globally, according to the United Nations High Commissioner for Refugees (UNHCR), 'during the past decade, 1.1 million refugees around the world became citizens in their country of asylum' (Local Integration, n.d.). In 2012, President Obama enacted Deferred Action for Childhood Arrivals (DACA) for undocumented young adults who were brought to the US as children, and in 2013, the US Congress continued to discuss a comprehensive immigration policy, which has yet to be passed into law. Obama expanded the DACA eligible population in 2014 by allowing parents of US citizens and permanent residents to apply for deferred action and employment authorization themselves. Before the policy's implementation in 2015, a federal judge issued a temporary injunction of the executive action.

In discussing the multifaceted positionings of refugees, aliens and immigrants, I rely on the US Immigration and Nationality Act's (INA) legal definition of the three groups, as provided in INA Section 101. An abbreviated definition of *refugee* is: any person who is 'unable or unwilling to return to' a country due to 'persecution or a well-founded fear of persecution on account of race, religion, nationality, membership in a particular social group, or political opinion'. The term *alien* is used to represent 'any person not a citizen or national of the United States'. An *immigrant* is 'every alien except an alien who is within one of the following classes of nonimmigrant aliens', which includes ambassadors, international organization employees and family, crewmen, bona fide foreign press representatives and bona fide students. Thus, most immigrants are also aliens, and refugees can also be called aliens because they are neither citizens nor nationals of their country of residence. This chapter will use the word *alien* to refer to refugees and immigrants in a general sense.

The objective of this chapter is to demonstrate that within the realm of citizenship, the terms *refugees, aliens* and *immigrants* are different discursive constructions which appear in various domains. This goal is guided by the following research question: how are refugees, aliens and immigrants portrayed in policy discourse and the news media, and through which rhetorical devices? Certain themes from INA policy are reiterated in the news media, but news articles deviate in their use of metaphorical expressions and collocations. Regardless of the linguistic domain, these depictions are related to underlying attitudes about refugees and immigrants, which are often covert and couched in 'common-sense' ideologies.

Review of Policy and News Discourse

This section summarizes current literature and government policy concerning the path from immigration and refugeehood to naturalization. Citizenship can be bestowed through the principle of *jus soli* (birth within a country's borders), *jus sanguinis* (blood descent) or naturalization.[1] Countries choose to enact these three principles in varying combinations and to different extents. For example, in the US and Mexico, anyone born within the country is automatically a citizen, regardless of parental citizenship status (Becerra Ramirez, 2000).[2] However, in South Africa, the principle of *jus soli* does not apply if the child is born to temporary residents or undocumented parents (Klaaren, 2000). Although *jus soli* citizenship is restricted, *jus sanguinis* citizenship in South Africa can be transferred indefinitely (Klaaren, 2000). Countries such as the US, Australia, Canada and Mexico also tend to limit the extent to which citizenship can be transmitted through *jus sanguinis* when no residency ties have been established generationally (Klusmeyer, 2000). While the rigor of naturalization requirements varies internationally, they generally necessitate country-specific knowledge, language abilities, moral character, residency, loyalty and acculturation.

Naturalization in US government policy

All of the above facets (except perhaps acculturation) are dictated in US naturalization policy. INA Section 312 stipulates that naturalization applicants must demonstrate (1) 'a knowledge and understanding of the fundamentals of the history, and of the principles and form of government, of the United States'. In addition they must be able to (2) 'read, write, and speak words in ordinary usage in the English language'.[3] Applicants must have (3) good moral character, which in Section 313 is defined as *not* being an advocate, teacher, member or affiliate of the communist or other totalitarian party. The first two requirements are satisfied through a naturalization interview; the third is met by passing a background check. Before applying, the residency requirement mandates five years of continuous residence as a permanent resident (INA Section 316). Refugees and asylum seekers can apply for permanent resident status after one year of US residence. The loyalty component of naturalization is stipulated in INA Section 337 and involves reciting the oath of allegiance to the US after completing the naturalization interview.

In particular, the INA documents regarding refugees exemplify a certain type of discourse. Emphasized and repeated are phrases such as 'burden of proof' and words that indicate the necessity of 'evidence' and 'documentation', especially in INA Section 208, entitled 'Authority to apply for asylum' (Table 2.1).

Often a factor in the 'burden of proof' discourse is language proficiency (Blommaert, 2009; Eades, 2009), which conflates language and nationhood as static and singular (Piller, 2011). In this policy section, the terms *alien* and *applicant* are used exclusively; *refugee* and *asylum seeker* are never used, presumably because these titles are not conferred until after authorization has been granted.

In INA Section 412, entitled 'Authorization for programs for domestic resettlement of and assistance to refugees', the label *alien* has been replaced by *refugee*; determining eligibility for refugeehood is not the focus of this act. Repeated phrases in INA Section 412 indicate a discourse of limited, temporary monetary assistance, centered on a goal of economic self-sufficiency. Table 2.2 illustrates this discourse.

How refugees are positioned in US governmental discourse is strikingly different from that of other aliens. Immigrants who apply for permanent residence are not discussed in the same terms of proving nationality and applicability, and reliance on government assistance. This *de jure* policy can

Table 2.1 Refugee discourse in INA Section 208

Source	Quote
INA 208	'the burden of proof is on the applicant to establish that the applicant is a refugee'
INA 208	'clear and convincing evidence'
INA 208	'sufficient facts sufficient to demonstrate that the applicant is a refugee'
INA 208	'credibility determination'

Table 2.2 Refugee discourse in INA Section 412

Source	Quote
INA 412	'in order to achieve economic self-sufficiency among refugees as quickly as possible'
INA 412	'temporary care of refugees in the United States in emergency circumstances'
INA 412	'efforts to reduce welfare dependency among refugees resettled by that agency'
INA 412	'in allocating resources'

affect how refugees and immigrants are then represented in the media and other popular discourses.

Naturalization in the media

In reporting on political events, media discourse transmits certain political rhetoric to its constituents, who then translate it into everyday conversations (van Leeuwen & Wodak, 1999). News media also offers a window into the language attitudes of the general population, because not only does the media affect public opinion (Bell, 1991; Gabrielatos & Baker, 2008; Garrett & Bell, 1998), but it also reflects the sentiments of its readers who often subscribe to newspapers that share their worldviews (Crawley & Sriskandarajah, 2005).

The media can also influence public opinion through the framing of its news stories. While a news article may not overtly transmit propaganda, a point of view is often expressed through quotes, quote placement, visuals, metaphors, caricatures and catchphrases (Nelson *et al.*, 1997). A choice of a particular frame renders some facts more salient than others, giving them more weight when attitudes are formed.

In the UK, several studies have analyzed the discursive representation of refugees, immigrants and asylum seekers through critical discourse analysis (CDA), corpus analysis or both. Baker and McEnery (2005) compare concordances of *refugee(s)* and *asylum seeker(s)* in articles from British newspapers and The UNHCR Office, which is directly concerned with refugee welfare. The researchers find that refugees tend to be described in terms of their country of origin and current country of residence. Notably, they unearth several common metaphors used to depict refugees, in overarching discourses of victimhood, natural disasters, tragedy, crime and nuisance (Baker & McEnery, 2005).

Gabrielatos and Baker (2008) report on a 10-year data sample of 19 UK newspapers concerning refugees, asylum seekers, immigrants and migrants (RASIM). Analysis reveals that the vast majority of themes commonly associated with RASIM are negative and include references to destinations, numbers, economic problems, residence, repatriation, legality and plight. The researchers conclude that in doing so, the British press creates and sustains what can be described as a moral panic (Hill, 2008) around RASIM (Baker *et al.*, 2008; Gabrielatos & Baker, 2008).

Turning to the US, Santa Ana (2013) analyzes all television network stories reported on the four largest national networks in 2004 to discover what type of Latino news stories are covered and what percentage of these stories concern immigration. He finds that through the story framing, networks portray immigrants and refugees from Cuba, the Dominican Republic and Mexico in a different light: Mexican migrants are depicted as irresponsible parents and criminals, while Cuban migrants are described with admiration and positive regard (Santa Ana, 2013).

Methodology

The data for this chapter come from a larger pool of qualitative data amassed from 2010 to 2013, which includes a newspaper corpus of citizenship discourse in *The New York Times*. Specific to this chapter is an expanded newspaper corpus encompassing issues of citizenship, immigration and refugeehood.

Corpus data and analysis

The media is a popular data source for corpus and thematic analysis because of its position as a powerful institution and prolific producer of discourse. This chapter's discussion of the discursive strategies of news articles comes from a corpus created through a LexisNexis Academic search of the word *citizenship*. All articles and blogs from *The New York Times* were retrieved during the period from April 1 to September 21, 2011, resulting in 270 total articles and over 300,000 words. *The New York Times* was selected as the basis for analysis because of its widespread presence and influence. Stories reported in *The New York Times* not only affect the national discourse, but are also syndicated in local newspapers. The corpus was stored as a Microsoft Word document, and various Excel spreadsheets were created to account for discourse genre, keywords, key people, concordances, collocations and context. While the style of corpus assembly required a smaller sample, the degree of researcher involvement allowed for a closer control of the data.

For this chapter, all articles from this larger corpus that included the words *refugee*, *alien* or *immigrant* were selected for an in-depth analysis. Because *citizenship* was also referenced in each article, this limited the number of total news articles amassed. This had the advantage of creating a manageable corpus size, and ensuring that refugees, aliens and immigrants were discussed in the larger context of naturalization, which is the goal of this chapter. As a result, 27 tokens (from 12 articles) of the word *refugee*, 13 tokens (from 10 articles) of the word *alien* and 298 tokens (from 70 articles) of the word *immigrant* were collected. Excel spreadsheets were created to explicitly focus on the concordances (10-word spans) and collocations for these three words, to reveal the media's tendency to link particular words together. When two or more words co-occur, they are portrayed as natural associations and their presence becomes accepted without critical evaluation.

The benefit of corpus data is that it reveals large-scale trends and provides numerous uses of the words *refugee, alien* and *immigrant*. It lends objectivity and overall scope to qualitative thematic analysis, such as CDA, which is often criticized for its subjective nature (see Mautner [2009] for a more detailed account of the advantages and critiques of combining CDA and corpus analysis). When conjoining these two approaches, the large-scale corpus analysis informs CDA by revealing keywords, clusters, collocations and concordances, which CDA can then investigate from a closer standpoint (Baker *et al*., 2008; Gabrielatos & Baker, 2008; Mautner, 2007, 2009). Thus, in this chapter, two articles from each 'alien' group were selected for a closer analysis of each article's repeated words and overall themes, to ensure that these themes were analyzed in context.[4]

Findings: Positionings in the Media

News articles employ collocations, concordances and naming strategies to chronicle stories about refugees, aliens and immigrants in a certain light. Through a corpus analysis, it is apparent that there are similarities and differences in the depictions of *refugees, aliens* and *immigrants*, with respect to genre, collocations and metaphor.

Refugees

Stories about refugees largely appear in the foreign news genre. There are two tokens in two obituary articles, one of which happens to be the obituary of Osama bin Laden on May 2, 2011. There is one national news article, entitled 'Friends of U.S.: Terrorists in eyes of law', which includes the word *refugee* in the following context: 'immigration officials wrestle with how to handle people previously granted political asylum or refugeehood in this country, but whose past affiliations technically bar them from permanent residency' (Frosch, 2011: A14). In this excerpt, the token *refugee* is discussed in terms of a status to be granted, much like how *citizenship* is often framed as a tangible document that can be conferred and denied (Loring, 2013b). The word *refugee* often collocates with words that depict a refugee's nationality or current country of residency (Baker & McEnery, 2005), as depicted in Table 2.3.

Thus, 12 of 27 tokens of *refugee* (44%) include an immediate reference to a geographic locale. Examples include: 'refugee from Eritrea', 'Haitian refugees' and 'refugees coming into Peshawar, Pakistan'. Also occurring

Table 2.3 *Refugee* collocations

Collocation	No. of tokens
Refugee from [(city of) country]	5
[Ethnicity/nationality] refugee	5
Refugee coming into [country]	2
Refugee camp	2
Refugee status	2

more than once are the collocations 'refugee camp' and 'refugee status', which highlight the geographic trajectory of refugees and describe them in terms of official status.

There are four predominant metaphors employed in refugee discourse: quantification, tragedy, veracity, and crime and nuisance. These metaphors are aligned with others encountered in public news corpora to describe immigrants and refugees (Baker & McEnery, 2005; Gabrielatos & Baker, 2008; Santa Ana, 2002), and the fourth metaphor additionally is an iteration of US government policy discourse.

Quantification is the tendency to talk about immigrants or refugees in terms of numbers. This ranges from numerical figures, to numerical estimations, to vague comments about 'growing numbers' and often reproduces an underlying discourse of apprehension or distress (Baker & McEnery, 2005). In the corpus analyzed for this chapter, the theme of quantification is seen in the following quote: 'His [President Sarkozy of France] opponents, particularly on the right, play to French fears of an influx of refugees from Libya and other North African countries' (Landler, 2011: WK1). The word *influx* not only gives a vague approximation of a large number of refugees, but within the larger phrase 'fears of an influx of refugees' it helps reinforce the association of *refugee* with *alarm*.

The tragedy metaphor is seen in discourse that uses words such as *despair, stricken, dying* and *tragedy* itself. It constructs refugees (as well as other minority groups) as powerless and unfortunate (Baker & McEnery, 2005). Two examples of this theme from *The New York Times* are: 'the plight of Palestinian refugees' (Kershner, 2011: A6) and '[Norway] tends to take some of the poorest victims of conflict as refugees – whether Vietnamese boat people decades ago or Somalis and Eritreans now' (Erlanger, 2011: A8). Both examples also depict the previously mentioned tendency to describe refugees in terms of their country of origin.

The theme of veracity is present in the following quote from an article entitled 'In father's memory, fighting to stay in Britain':

Like governments throughout the Western world, Britain's has come under increasing pressure to increase expulsions, cut immigration and restrict citizenship. At stake for officials is 'managed migration,' a way to maintain an influx of the most desirable settlers and genuine refugees by forcibly excluding the rejected – in an effort to rein in the hostility toward foreigners that is mounting from Australia and the United States to Norway and France. (Bernstein, 2011: A1)

Of note is the collocation *genuine refugee*, which implies that refugees can be evaluated by the veracity of their status. This, along with other expressions such as *illegal asylum seeker* and *bogus immigrant* are 'nonsensical terms', to use the expression of Gabrielatos and Baker (2008: 31), because the term *refugee* isn't conferred unless someone's application has already been successful, thus rendering all refugees genuine.

The fourth commonly seen metaphor, crime and nuisance, is reported to be a less common construction that encourages refugees to be 'seen as a threat to the capitalist way of life by reducing the value of property' (Baker & McEnery, 2005: 208). However, this study locates three examples of this metaphor from the 27 tokens in the corpus (Table 2.4).

The first two examples are indicative of the crime metaphors, in that the concordance span includes words such as *protest* and *terrorists*. The third example, in using the collocation *economic burden*, brings to mind the INA Section 412 discourse of promoting 'economic self-sufficiency' among refugees. This example comes from an article discussing the treatment and attitudes of Haitian refugees and migrants in the Dominican Republic and around the world. Not present in the immediate concordance span are other images of *blame, waning international sympathy, deportations, influx, invasion,* and 'steady flow of people from Haiti who have slipped through the porous border' (a direct quote from the Dominican Republic's immigrant director). Evident in this language is the metaphor of refugees as movement (Baker & McEnery, 2005), what Santa Ana (2002: 68) terms 'immigration as dangerous waters', whereby migrants are dehumanized and likened to a natural disaster. This article also mentions a policy implemented by the International Organization for Migration: paying Haitian refugees 50 dollars and relocation assistance to voluntarily return to Haiti (Archibold, 2011: A1). Implicit in all these examples is the underlying belief that there is a certain time frame in which refugees should be treated with philanthropy and financial assistance, but there is also a point at which generosity is exhausted.

Table 2.4 Crime and nuisance metaphors in *refugee* discourse

'Protests erupted over the refugees' presence, and a number of migrants fled' (Archibold, 2011: A1)
'As a result, an assortment of refugees and asylum-seekers are deemed terrorists or to have aided terrorist groups' (Frosch, 2011: A14)
'But refugees are now an economic burden...' (Archibold, 2011: A1)

Aliens

The term *alien*, appearing in article genres such as arts & leisure, national, editorial and magazine, is a far less prolific descriptor. In 10 articles, it most commonly appears in collocations with *illegal*, collocations with *registration card/number* or as part of the acronym DREAM Act (Development, Relief and Education for Alien Minors Act) (Table 2.5).[5]

The expression *illegal alien* appears in three places, and once in scare quotes to directly connote its polarizing language. There is an additional token, *undesirable alien*, which works as part of the same negative discourse. The other collocations can be subsumed under the theme 'status and documentation'. It appears that when the word *alien* occurs in news discourse, it is mainly used in reference to larger policy language that uses the same expressions. However, policy discourse prefers the term *alien* to *refugee* and *immigrant*, as it uses *alien* as a neutral term to describe someone in the process of applying, but who legally is not yet a refugee or immigrant. The three tokens of *illegal alien* pale in comparison to the widespread use of the collocation *illegal immigrant*, as discussed in the next section.

Immigrants

The word *immigrant* is by far the most popular of the three terms to appear in articles that reference citizenship. Of the 298 tokens, 32% (95) appear in the collocation *illegal immigrant*.[6] Far less prevalent, but a less biased term is *undocumented immigrant*, which appears nine times (3%). Taking a closer look at the article genres, it appears that *illegal immigrant* is the term preferred in national and metropolitan news articles, while *undocumented immigrant* is vastly preferred in editorial articles (Table 2.6).[7]

Foreign genre articles rarely use the collocation *illegal immigrant* and never use *undocumented immigrant*; rather, they are likely to include a reference to the immigrant's geographical domain. This includes examples such as 'immigrant from Eastern Europe' (Roberts, 2011: para 3), 'Asian and Latino immigrants' (Shih, 2011: A27) and 'Jewish immigrant' (Freedman, 2011: A15). Other occasional collocations are *immigrant rights*, as in 'he often marches for immigrant rights' (Rice, 2011: MM20), and *anti-immigrant*, which occurs in phrases such as 'anti-immigrant laws', 'anti-immigrant sentiment' and 'anti-immigrant groups'. The expression 'path(way) to

Table 2.5 *Alien* collocations

Collocation	No. of tokens
Illegal alien	3
Alien registration card/number	2
DREAM Act	2

Table 2.6 *Immigrant* collocations

Collocation	No. of tokens
Illegal immigrant(s)	95
In national genre	56 (59%)
In metropolitan genre	16 (17%)
In editorial genre	13 (14%)
In foreign genre	2 (2%)
In other genre	8 (8%)
Undocumented immigrant(s)	9
In national genre	1 (11%)
In editorial genre	8 (89%)
Immigrant from (country)	7
(Ethnicity/nationality/religion) immigrant	15
Immigrant rights	7
Anti-immigrant	8
Path(way) to citizenship for (illegal) immigrants	8

citizenship for (illegal) immigrants', occurring eight times, demonstrates a common way that (illegal) immigration is often associated with citizenship (Loring, 2013b).

The common metaphors pertaining to *immigrant* are both shared with the refugee themes (quantification and tragedy), and unique to this particular theme (legality and movement).[8] Quantification, as discussed above, is a reference to numbers, usually vague, when discussing refugees, asylees and immigrants. Examples of this metaphor in the immigrant discourse are provided in Table 2.7.

An underlying assumption behind this discourse is that a greater number of immigrants threaten the status quo. It also reduces the immigrant experience to a mere description of numbers, indicating that their quantity is the most important aspect of the story.

The theme of tragedy, while also occurring in refugee discourse, appears to be more common in immigrant discourse (Table 2.8).

Table 2.7 Quantification metaphors in *immigrant* discourse

'with a million or more immigrants coming each year' (DeParle, 2011, A1)
'FAIR was founded on complaints about the immigrants' numbers' (DeParle, 2011: A1)
'stopped hundreds of thousands of immigrants who lack legal status' (Preston, 2011: A10)
'nearly 7 of 10 Britons felt the country had too many immigrants' (Bernstein, 2011: A1)

Table 2.8 Tragedy metaphors in *immigrant* discourse

'At 25, she was poor, pregnant and an illegal immigrant' (Semple, 2011a: A17)
'..., many American-born children of illegal immigrants are still hobbled by serious developmental and educational deficits resulting from their parents' lives in the shadows...' (Semple, 2011a, A17)
'... a country where immigrants had struggled to move ahead' (Saltmarsh, 2011: B12)
'Supporters of the bill argued that it would help lift struggling immigrant families' (Tavernise, 2011: A16)

The first two examples in Table 2.8 additionally associate the tragedy theme with *illegal immigrants*. Common words that imply that immigrants are down on their luck and in unfortunate situations are *poor, struggle, hobbled* and *deficits*.

Legality is a predominant theme in *immigrant* discourse. The many tokens of *illegal immigrant* and *undocumented* are evidence of this focus. Less common phrases such as 'lawful immigrants' (Semple, 2011b: A14) and 'legal status to some illegal immigrants' (Steinhauer, 2011: para 1) are also used to associate immigration with legality. Within this theme, *deportation* is an oft-repeated word to describe one of the legal actions that can affect immigrants' status. Illegal immigrants are usually the ones who are discussed with *deportation*, such as in the following example: '... while Mr. Dawkins's case was unusual, it fit a broader pattern of the government's pursuing seemingly minor passport violations in an effort to deport illegal immigrants' (Nesmith, 2011: A16).

The final metaphor related to immigration is movement. Santa Ana (2002: 72) exemplified this theme in *The Los Angeles Times'* reporting of the California Proposition 187 campaign, in expressions such as 'the inexorable flow', 'a sea of brown faces' and 'awash under a brown tide'. Baker and McEnery (2005) also find this metaphor used in refugee discourse. From the current corpus, this theme was not very common, but did appear occasionally in phrases such as 'Asian and Latino immigrants have arrived in droves'[9] (Shih, 2011: A27) and 'whether immigrants today differ from the waves of Jews and Italians who arrived a century ago' (Roberts, 2011: para 14).

Implications

This chapter has demonstrated that discourse about refugees, aliens and immigrants is dynamic and multifaceted. In INA policy, these three categories of non-citizens are explicitly defined and separately framed. Lacking in immigrant discourse but prevalent in refugee discourse are the repeated references to 'documentation', 'burden of proof' and 'economic self-sufficiency' that describe the application process and desired outcome for refugees.

In media discourse, references to refugees, aliens and immigrants suggest that non-citizens in general are portrayed with metaphors of quantification, tragedy, veracity and legality, crime and nuisance and movement. The prevalence of these images, and collocations such as *illegal immigrant* have consequences as to how readers understand refugees and immigrants.[10] Frequent exposure to discourse that stresses non-citizens' document status, hardships and the effect on the economy results in a tendency to think about non-citizens as a singular group, in an overly broad narrative. Differences within this diverse group, be they geographic, economic, social or political, are ignored or overlooked. Consequently, dehumanizing language can lead to political and social actions that treat immigrants and refugees as a problem. This discourse is cyclic and iterative; the media and people in positions of power both shape the public debate and are shaped by popular public opinion. Thus, these positionings are important to analyze because not only does the media have the power to influence interpretations of citizenship and resettlement, but it also reflects what ideologies are already present.

Notes

(1)   Israel includes the 'Law of Return' for any and all Jews to immigrate and become citizens (Shachar, 2000).
(2)   This has led to current debates in the US about the legal status of 'anchor babies' born to undocumented parents.
(3)   See Loring (2013a,b) for a critical analysis of how the 'ordinary usage' of English is interpreted in the language of the naturalization test.
(4)   These six articles were selected because they included more than one token of the word *refugee*, *alien* or *immigrant* and were centrally related to an immigration news event.
(5)   This act, while passed by the US House of Representatives in 2010, did not pass in the US Senate and never became law. It would have provided a path to citizenship for undocumented immigrants brought to the US as children. In 2012, President Obama signed an executive order called Deferred Action for Childhood Arrivals, which provided undocumented young adults with a temporary means to receive employment authorization and a driver's license.
(6)   One additional token makes use of this collocation in scare quotes, so it has been omitted from this percentage.
(7)   This includes the magazine genre, where articles appeared such as Jose Vargas' (2011) 'coming-out' 'Outlaw' article and the corresponding 'Reply Letters' two weeks later.
(8)   While *movement* was mentioned in the refugee discourse, it was not a part of the immediate concordances.
(9)   The use of *droves* here is also an example of the quantification metaphor.
(10) In April 2013, the Associated Press ceased using the phrase 'illegal immigrant' except in direct quotes. *The New York Times* did not eliminate its use, but recommended using alternative expressions (Haughney, 2013).

References

Archibold, R. (2011) As refugees from Haiti linger, Dominicans' good will fades. *The New York Times*, August 31, p. A1.

Baker, P. and McEnery, T. (2005) A corpus-based approach to discourses of refugees and asylum seekers in UN and newspaper texts. *Journal of Language and Politics* 4 (2), 197–226.

Baker, P., Gabrielatos, C., Khosravinik, M., Krzyzanowski, M., McEnery, T. and Wodak, R. (2008) A useful methodological synergy? Combining critical discourse analysis and corpus linguistics to examine discourses of refugees and asylum seekers in the UK press. *Discourse & Society* 19 (3), 273–306.

Becerra Ramirez, M. (2000) Nationality in Mexico. In T.A. Aleinikoff and D. Klusmeyer (eds) *From Migrants to Citizens: Membership in a Changing World* (pp. 312–341). Washington, DC: Carnegie Endowment for International Peace.

Bell, A. (1991) *The Language of News Media*. Cambridge, MA: Blackwell.

Bernstein, N. (2011) In father's memory, fighting to stay in Britain. *The New York Times*, August 21, p. A1.

Blommaert, J. (2009) Language, asylum, and the national order. *Current Anthropology* 50 (4), 415–441.

Crawley, H. and Sriskandarajah, D. (2005) Preface. In R. Greenslade (ed.) *Seeking Scapegoats: The Coverage of Asylum in the UK Press* (pp. 1–40). London: Institute for Public Policy Research.

DeParle, J. (2011) The anti-immigration crusader. *The New York Times*, April 17, p. A1.

Eades, D. (2009) Testing the claims of asylum seekers: The role of language analysis. *Language Assessment Quarterly* 6 (1), 30–40.

Erlanger, S. (2011) Attack reignites immigration debate in divided Oslo. *The New York Times*, July 26, p. A8.

Freedman, S.G. (2011) Prayer, and bug juice, at a summer camp for Jews of color. *The New York Times*, August 13, p. A15.

Frosch, D. (2011) Friends of U.S., terrorists in eyes of law. *The New York Times*, September 19, p. A14.

Gabrielatos, C. and Baker, P. (2008) Fleeing, sneaking, flooding: A corpus analysis of discursive constructions of refugees and asylum seekers in the UK Press, 1996–2005. *Journal of English Linguistics* 36 (1), 5–38.

Garrett, P. and Bell, A. (1998) Media and discourse: A critical overview. In A. Bell and P. Garrett (eds) *Approaches to Media Discourse* (pp. 1–20). Malden, MA: Blackwell.

Haughney, C. (2013) The Times shifts on 'illegal immigrant' but doesn't ban the use. *The New York Times*, April 23. See http://www.nytimes.com/2013/04/24/business/media/the-times-shifts-on-illegal-immigrant-but-doesnt-ban-the-use.html?_r=0 (accessed 1 May 2013).

Hill, J.H. (2008) *The Everyday Language of White Racism*. Malden, MA: Wiley-Blackwell.

Immigration and Nationality Act, 8 U.S.C. § 101.

Immigration and Nationality Act, 8 U.S.C. § 208.

Immigration and Nationality Act, 8 U.S.C. § 312.

Immigration and Nationality Act, 8 U.S.C. § 313.

Immigration and Nationality Act, 8 U.S.C. § 316.

Immigration and Nationality Act, 8 U.S.C. § 337.

Immigration and Nationality Act, 8 U.S.C. § 412.

Kershner, I. (2011) In the Golan Heights, anxious eyes look east. *The New York Times*, May 22, p. A6.

Klaaren, J. (2000) Post-apartheid citizenship in South Africa. In T.A. Aleinikoff and D. Klusmeyer (eds) *From Migrants to Citizens: Membership in a Changing World* (pp. 221–252). Washington, DC: Carnegie Endowment for International Peace.

Klusmeyer, D. (2000) Introduction. In T.A. Aleinikoff and D. Klusmeyer (eds) *From Migrants to Citizens: Membership in a Changing World* (pp. 1–21). Washington, DC: Carnegie Endowment for International Peace.

Landler, M. (2011) An odd-couple alliance. *The New York Times*, April 10, p. WK1.

Local Integration (n.d.) United Nations High Commissioner for Refugees. See http://www.unhcr.org (accessed 9 February 2014).

Loring, A. (2013a) The meaning of 'citizenship': Tests, policy, and English proficiency. *The CATESOL Journal* 24 (1), 198–219.

Loring, A. (2013b) Language and U.S. citizenship: Meanings, ideologies, and policies. Doctoral dissertation. ProQuest Dissertations and Theses (UMI No. 3596915).

Mautner, G. (2007) Mining large corpora for social information: The case of 'elderly'. *Language in Society* 36 (1), 51–72.

Mautner, G. (2009) Checks and balances: How corpus linguistics can contribute to CDA. In R. Wodak and M. Meyer (eds) *Methods of Critical Discourse Analysis* (pp. 122–143). Thousand Oaks, CA: Sage.

McNamara, T. and Shohamy, E. (2008) Viewpoint: Language tests and human rights. *International Journal of Applied Linguistics* 18 (1), 89–95.

Naturalization Fact Sheet (2013) US Citizenship and Immigration Services. See http://www.uscis.gov/ (accessed 22 May 2014).

Nelson, T.E., Clawson, R.A. and Oxley, Z.M. (1997) Media framing of a civil liberties conflict and its effect on tolerance. *American Political Science Review* 91 (3), 567–583.

Nesmith, S. (2011) Veteran of Iraq War now fights his own deportation. *The New York Times*, June 24, p. A16.

Office of Immigration Statistics (2012) *2011 Yearbook of Immigration Statistics*. See http://www.dhs.gov/ (accessed 10 April 2013).

Piller, I. (2011) *Intercultural Communication: A Critical Introduction*. Edinburgh: Edinburgh University Press.

Preston, J. (2011) A family reunited after a rare return from deportation. *The New York Times*, August 8, p. A10.

Rice, A. (2011) Life on line. *The New York Times*, July 31, p. MM20.

Roberts, S. (2011) Century-old immigration debate has familiar sound. *The New York Times Blogs,* June 14.

Saltmarsh, M. (2011) Bias inquiries clear French coach. *The New York Times*, May 11, p. B12.

Santa Ana, O. (2002) *Brown Tide Rising: Metaphors of Latinos in Contemporary American Public Discourse*. Austin, TX: University of Texas Press.

Santa Ana, O. (2013) *Juan in a Hundred: The Representation of Latinos on Network News*. Austin, TX: University of Texas Press.

Semple, K. (2011a) Illegal immigrants' underground lives hobble their US-born children, study says. *The New York Times*, May 21, p. A17.

Semple, K. (2011b) U.S. warns schools against checking immigration status. *The New York Times*, May 7, p. A14.

Shachar, A. (2000) Citizenship and membership in the Israeli polity. In T.A. Aleinikoff and D. Klusmeyer (eds) *From Migrants to Citizens: Membership in a Changing World* (pp. 386–433). Washington, DC: Carnegie Endowment for International Peace

Shih, G. (2011) San Mateo's Asian and Hispanic voters speak up. *The New York Times*, May 15, p. A27.

Steinhauer, J. (2011) Senate democrats reintroduce Dream Act. *The New York Times Blogs*, May 11.

Tavernise, S. (2011) Immigrant advocates file suit on petition signatures. *The New York Times*, August 2, p. A16.

van Leeuwen, T. and Wodak, R. (1999) Legitimizing immigration control: A discourse-historical analysis. *Discourse Studies* 1 (1), 83–118.

Vargas, J.A. (2011) Outlaw. *The New York Times*, June 26, p. MM22.

3 The Different Meanings of the Word *Refugee*

Bernadette Ludwig

> *'Refugee,' I think it has transform[ed] over the years. [...] [During] normal time[s] 'refugee' [...] was not a positive or appealing [...] word. [...] Liberians themselves have been refugee[s] in the past [...] 20 years. [...] I don't think there's any stereotype attached to that word [...] During [...] normal time[s] it used to be people who are in need and it could [...] even be equated to homelessness. [...] [It] has become a part of a normal diction for Liberian[s], [...] because Liberians have lived that life.*
>
> Mr. Thomas Bono[1]

Introduction and Chapter Overview

Although the word *refugee* is frequently used by policymakers, governments, the media and those labeled as such, there seems to be little consensus on what *refugee* really means (Gabrielatos & Baker, 2008). The 1951 Office of the United Nations High Commissioner for Refugees (UNHCR) Convention relating to the Status of Refugees (hereinafter referred to as '1951 UNHCR Convention') defines a *refugee* as

> someone who, owing to a well-founded fear of being persecuted for reasons of race, religion, nationality, membership of a particular social group or political opinion, is outside the country of his nationality and is unable or, owing to such fear, is unwilling to avail himself of the protection of that country; or who, not having a nationality and being outside the country of his former habitual residence as a result of such events, is unable or, owing to such fear, is unwilling to return to it.

But this international definition was not adopted by US legislation until 1980. Prior to that, *refugees*, according to US immigration law (e.g. Refugee-Escapee Act of 1957), were exclusively defined as those fleeing communist countries or the Middle East; a definition influenced by Cold War politics. Today, there is a different debate among scholars and policymakers, whether people displaced by natural disasters and global warming be considered refugees although they are not covered by the 1951 UNHCR Convention (Williams, 2008). These examples show that the language around *refugee* is not unequivocal but rather contextual, which also becomes clear when speaking to individuals who were displaced because of war in their native country. For example, Ms Zaiway Paye, who fled Liberia in 1999 and lived for five years in refugee camps in Côte d'Ivoire and Ghana until she was resettled under the US Resettlement Program as a refugee in the US, responded to my question whether she considered herself a refugee or not:

> Well, yes and no. Because coming to another country is [being] a refugee. But America make[s] us to feel like we are at home [...]. So sometimes I say, 'Oh I'm a refugee,' and sometimes I say, 'Well [...] [I'm not because] America [...] take[s] care of every citizen, [not just those born here]'.

While most people in the US would argue that Ms Zaiway Paye – at least at some point – was a refugee, opinions whether US citizens can also be refugees are even more controversial; something that became clear when American-born citizens were displaced by Hurricane Katrina.

Hence, in this chapter, I give an overview of how the term *refugee* has been used in the US and about some of the different meanings that are attached to the word *refugee*. In my discussion of the various applications and interpretations of *refugee*, I draw on existing literature and ethnographic data I collected on the Liberian refugee community in New York. I start the chapter with a brief analysis of diverging opinions in the scholarly literature about who refugees are, and whether they are a separate group from immigrants. This discussion was also common among Liberians, making obvious that there is no universal understanding of *refugee*. But *refugee* also has some very concrete meanings. For example, to a lot of Liberians, *refugee* was the equivalent of being selected for the US Resettlement Program that brings about 80,000 refugees, from different parts of the world, annually to the US. While in this case being identified as *refugee* was positive for Liberians because it offered an opportunity to escape the miserable conditions in the refugee camps and hope for a safer and better future, other times, *refugee* for Liberians and presumably others, just meant victimhood and suffering from which one needed to be rescued. As the state of 'being rescued' already indicates, *refugee* to many also means lack of agency and control over where one resides, in other words, being forcefully displaced. While images of victims' suffering and forced displacement generate sympathy and hence help with raising and providing aid to those in need, that provision of aid can quickly be seen as an economic burden on society. This is especially the case when aid, refugee, and race – and in particular being Black – are conflated because this elicits common American stereotypes of Blacks and welfare. Here, the language that is used to describe 'real' refugees or those perceived as such is key, because *refugee* here can become synonymous with negative representations.

Who is a Refugee? Are Immigrants and Refugees the Same?

Scholarly debate

Elsewhere, I have argued for the need to distinguish between legal refugee status and informal refugee label as so often these two definitions are conflated (Ludwig, 2013). In addition, there is no consensus among scholars as to who counts as a refugee. While present-day US legislation clearly differentiates between refugees (who left their native countries because of persecution or fear of persecution) and immigrants (who come to the US to be reunited with family members or for economic reasons), social scientists disagree on how important the refugee–immigrant distinction actually is. Some, like Tepper (1980), argue that refugees are not immigrants, who voluntarily migrate to seek a better life for themselves (and their children). Others disagree and contend that refugees are a particular type of immigrant (Brown, 2011; Kibria, 1993). Gold (1992) states that refugee status is a legal status made by the federal government to determine eligibility for government services. Thus, the differentiation between who is a refugee and who is not hinges on the policies that the US government currently pursues. Portes and Rumbaut (1996: 23) come to a similar conclusion: 'Being a refugee is therefore not a matter of personal choice but of governmental decision based on a combination of legal guidelines and political expediency'. From the standpoint of individual migration motives, however, the first concern of a refugee is to flee an intolerable or life-threatening situation. Whereas immigrants can, and usually do, choose their destination according to employment opportunities and wage levels, refugees cannot. Indeed, for refugees, the concept of destination choice is less relevant and 'push' is the overwhelming force (Zolberg *et al.*, 1989). Hence, immigrants and refugees differ in their migration motives and in their legal status once they arrive in the US.

Hein (1993) sums up these differences by stating that refugees and immigrants are distinct groups because of their relationship with the state. Frequently, government policies in their native countries are the push factors that cause refugees to flee (Zolberg *et al.*, 1989). Once outside their country and selected for refugee resettlement in a third country, the state (of the new home country) plays an active role, and by extension becomes an integral factor in refugees' networks. While most immigrants rely on their networks in finding a place to settle and work, forced migrants in the US do not make these decisions, but rather the state does through its intermediaries, refugee resettlement agencies, better known as voluntary agencies (Volags)

(Patrick, 2004). However, it should be noted that secondary migration, usually motivated by the refugees' desire to be near relatives and friends and better economic and benefits prospects, occurs frequently among refugee communities (Mott, 2009; Portes & Rumbaut, 1996).

There are also multiple other categories of refugees such as internally displaced persons (IDPs), asylees and individuals on temporary protective status (TPS) and deferred enforced departure (DED), and each status is different in its access to legal rights, benefits and services. For example, the legal refugee status in most countries also brings with it several advantages compared to the title of IDP. Refugees, for instance, become subject to the laws of the state in which they are seeking refuge; they should be guaranteed protection under International Refugee Law and are not supposed to be repatriated if their lives or liberty would be at risk (*non-refoulement* principle in international law). IDPs remain under the legal system of their own government, frequently one that they are trying desperately to escape from, which makes their situation worse compared to that of refugees (Entwisle, 2010; Gupte & Mehta, 2007; Kälin, 2000). Whether forced migrants become refugees or IDPs usually depends on where they can flee to, it is not by choice.

Refugees in the US also have advantages over immigrants, because the former are – for a limited time – eligible for a number of government benefits including Refugee Cash Assistance, Medicaid, Supplemental Nutrition Assistance Program (SNAP) and Supplemental Security Income (Singer & Wilson, 2006). And while asylees in the US also qualify for these programs, refugees have access to additional benefits such as obtaining loans for their transportation (from e.g. refugee camps to the US) and furnished apartments set up by Volags before their arrival in the US. Individuals with temporary refugee status such as TPS and DED do not qualify at all for these benefits (Bergeron, 2014; Ludwig, 2013; Menjívar, 1993, 1997; Simmelink, 2011).[2] But studies have shown that access to these government benefits and the programs offered by Volags, which are aimed to assist refugees with their adjustment to the US, have positive effects on the refugees themselves and also on their children (Gold, 1992; Hein, 2006; Kasinitz, 2008; Kibria, 1993; Portes & Rumbaut, 2001; Zhou & Bankston, 1998).

Liberian debate

Just like scholars, Liberians had diverging ideas of who a refugee is. Those I spoke with frequently said that Liberians who had not come via the US Resettlement Program were not refugees. For example, Ms Janjay Waggah, a single mother who fled from Liberia to a refugee camp in Côte d'Ivoire, noted:

> I came on the refugee program, [...] because I came during the war, but some Liberian[s], they came here like immigrants, their parents live[d]

here and [...] filed for their children, and so they are immigrant[s]. They came here as immigrants, and we came as refugees, so not everybody is a refugee, no, only [those that] came on the refugee program.

Her son-in-law who was in the room at the time of the interview interjected, arguing that other Liberians who could no longer return to Liberia may also be considered refugees:

Well, [...] a lot of people came on political asylum, student visa[s], visiting visa[s], and just end[ed] up staying. [...] You will still consider [them] refugee[s] because they all came here against their will because of the status of their country at the time. [...] But those [whose] parents were [US] citizens [and] they sent for them ... they're not refugees.

He was not alone in this interpretation of the term; his interpretation is in line with US immigration law in which refugees and asylees are only differentiated by the country in which they obtained their refugee or asylee status.

Liberians, especially those working in refugee organizations, distinguished between the legal definition of *refugee* and Liberians' *de facto* refugee status. Mr Varney Yarkpolo (VY), a former caseworker, who had left Liberia in 1998, explained:

BL: Who is a refugee?
VY: Those that fled the war, [...] the civil conflict and came to the United States as a refugee, because once you enter as a refugee, you are a refugee.
BL: What about Liberians who were in the US maybe waiting to get asylum or never even filed for it?
VY: Well no, they don't have [that] status. [...] It's not legitimate to say they're refugees, but between you and me, we know they're refugees. Because they fled their country from war and they came here, we know that. But legitimately they're not. Because you see, in order for you to be a refugee you must have status ... but I mean naturally we understand that anyone who fled their country from war, [...] they should be considered a refugee.

Mr Garsuah Janjay is one such example of a person who was not deemed a legal refugee by the US government. In 2000, he came to Kentucky to attend a church conference, during which time he received calls from his family and friends in Liberia telling him that it was not safe to return because Charles Taylor's loyalists accused him of being against the current regime. These calls brought back memories of a previous time when Mr Janjay encountered the rage of Taylor's supporters, and he and his wife were arrested by Taylor's forces. Shortly after he was released, he was arrested again along with his daughter and his mother. 'They took all of us. See, so every time they come for me they grab[bed] everybody in the household [too]'. Remembering his arrests and subsequent torture, Mr Janjay wanted neither to have to experience these cruelties nor put his family at risk again and therefore he decided to stay in the US and file for asylum. It is understandable that he thinks of himself as a refugee even if he was not legally classified that way:

> Actually, I consider myself a refugee. Except [...] the way I came to the United States, I did not come to the United States as a refugee because I wasn't like running away from anything that I perceived to be [of] danger [...]. But when I came to America, then I got hint of the danger ... the pending danger that was there for me, and I had to decide whether to take the risk to go back or whether to remain in the United States.

Others discussed how having legal refugee status can make one's transition to a new country easier and that they were excluded from that privilege. For example, Ms Love Juah had tried to come to the US during the war to join her daughter in Boston, Massachusetts. But since she was an IDP in Liberia, she was not eligible to come under the US Resettlement Program:

> I didn't come over [on a] refugee status, so I don't refer to myself as a refugee. But I went through the war. So I have the same experience, it's just that I didn't have the opportunity to come on that status here at that time.

At other times, Liberians conceded that even those who had originally entered the US as immigrants or on other non-refugee visas could at some point be considered refugees. For example, Mr Samuel Collins arrived in the US in the early 1980s, following his parents who had left Liberia because they were targets of the Liberian regime at that time. He came to the US using a different identity and, along with his brother, obtained legal status through the Immigration Reform and Control Act of 1986 (IRCA).[3] When I asked Mr Collins if he considered himself a refugee, he indicated that he could possibly do so now, but not when he initially arrived:

> No, no. I didn't come as a refugee. I came after the coup, I guess, and probably I would have been called a refugee at the time ... but [...] the war was raging and you were picked up by helicopters [...] or you got on a bus or were forced to exit ... that's what I see [as being a] refugee. We got on [a] Pan Am [flight]. So it wasn't as bad as that. At

the time I guess I wouldn't [have been] categorized as a refugee, but when Taylor became president everybody that came ... they were all refugees. [chuckles]

Liberians who had refugee status or were granted asylum are keenly aware that they are in a privileged position when compared to those with TPS/DED. Mr James Paye, an asylee and social service provider, said:

They are in [a] legal limbo; there's a huge difference to those with [refugee/asylee] status. [...] They don't have access to resources. [...] People on TPS [...] have been in the back seat, [...] they've been under [...] the radar. They're [...] demoralized. They feel powerless to advocate for themselves. They live in a constant fear of deportation. [...] So it's about access to resources and the benefit to change your status from asylum status to [US] citizenship. But if you have DED ... you are stuck there, you can't move forward.

Another Liberian, Mr Garsuah Janjay, concurred. He recounted how he had only entered the US in 2000 but had already obtained his green card – after his asylum application was approved – while his cousin in Minnesota who had been in the US for over 20 years was still on DED and could not bring her family to the US.

The Liberian Refugee Community: Data and Methods

'Little Liberia' in Staten Island, NY

Data for this research were collected over a period of six years of ethnographic research between 2009 and 2015 among the Liberian community in Staten Island's North Shore in New York City. This area around the Park Hill neighborhood has the biggest per capita concentration of Liberians outside of Liberia. This is not surprising, given that Staten Island was the second most common resettlement destination for Liberian refugees of the US Resettlement Program when it resettled about 25,000 Liberians in the US between the mid-1990s and mid-2000s in the entire country (Office of Refugee Resettlement, 2011).[4] Staten Island's North Shore is also home to many other Liberians who have different immigration statuses including TPS/DED, legal permanent residence, asylum and naturalized US citizens, or those who lack legal immigration status. Community estimates put the number of Liberians in Staten Island at 6000.

The vast majority of these Liberians in Staten Island and in other areas in the US came to the US after fleeing Liberia, a country that has a long history of violence between different ethnic and socioeconomic groups. In 1822, Liberia was established as a colony by the American

Colonization Society to 'repatriate' free(d) Black Americans. This group established a society modeled after (Southern) US plantations and denied indigenous ethnic groups many rights, including the right to be citizens (until 1904) and to vote (until 1964) (Ellis, 1999) because the Americo-Liberians[5] regarded them as uncivilized pagans (Gershoni, 1985). In 1980, Samuel Doe, a member of the Krahn ethnic group, seized power in a coup d'état and became the country's first indigenous president. Initially, Doe created a government that included various ethnic groups, including Americo-Liberians, but it became a Krahn hegemony before long. In 1985, Thomas Quiwonkpa, an ethnic Gio and one of Doe's former comrades-in-arms who attempted to oust him, was mutilated and killed by Doe's followers. Doe did not stop there; he retaliated with brutal attacks against the Gio and Mano groups in Nimba County. By exploiting 'ethnic divisions which had been dormant for well over a century' (Levitt, 2005: 201), Doe made it difficult for different ethnic groups to build a united front against his increasingly autocratic regime.[6] In 1989, an uprising began against Doe which ultimately led to the first civil war; the rebellion was under the leadership of Charles Taylor, a Liberian of Americo-Liberian and Gola descent, and mostly involved Gios and Manos who also had the support of governments in some neighboring countries (Levitt, 2005). The war and Doe's reign ended when Taylor took control of the Liberian government in 1996. Hoping to end the violence, and possibly fearing Taylor's wrath in the event of a loss, Liberians elected Taylor as their president. But peace did not come. Like his predecessor, Taylor quickly curtailed the freedom of the political opposition and the press, sending thousands of Liberians into exile once again. Internal conflict combined with Taylor's involvement in the neighboring countries of Sierra Leone and Guinea, eventually led to the second civil war in Liberia from 1999 to 2003 (Levitt, 2005). Both civil wars were brutal events, and included the use of child soldiers, mutilations, torture and sexual violence, caused at least 250,000 fatalities and made almost 50% (1.5 million) of Liberia's population refugees or IDPs (Alao et al., 2000; Ellis, 1999).

Data and methods

I initiated contact through various 'points of entry', that is, diverse members of the community (women, men, community leaders and refugee resettlement workers). This multiple-entry method ensured that I avoided interviewing Liberians involved in only a very limited number of personal networks, which often occurs in traditional snowball sampling (Jones-Correa, 1998). In the end, I was able to recruit a purposive sample (Maxwell, 2004). The data include 55 in-depth interviews conducted in English (each lasting between 1.5 and 2.5 hours) and countless hours of participant observation. Of the 55 interviewed individuals, 52 were Liberians. Among these 52 were 4 Liberians who had worked with Liberian refugee resettlement efforts as caseworkers either for Volags or for the UNHCR. The three non-Liberians – one American, one Senegalese and one Kenyan – were involved with the Liberian community through their employment with a Volag, a local non-governmental organization (NGO) or the UNHCR. The Liberian research participants were from a variety of ethnic groups and educational backgrounds, and ranged in age from 16 to 79. More women (29) than men (26) were interviewed, reflecting the preference given to female Liberian refugees in the US Resettlement Program (Schmidt, 2008).

After reading through the interview transcripts and ethnographic field notes, a framework analysis was employed to analyze the data thematically (Suzuki *et al.*, 1999). According to the method, familiarization was followed by developing a thematic framework, indexing, mapping and interpretation.

Refugee: Resettlement in a Third Country

Many Liberians while in refugee camps in West Africa, like other refugees (Kibreab, 2004; Zetter, 1991, 2007) equated language around the word *refugee* with being resettled in the US. With that in mind, many Liberians wanted to be classified as *refugees* during that time. For example, Ms Love Juah, the IDP who had desperately wanted to join her daughter in the US for safety, said, 'Yeah, if I had an opportunity at that time, I would prefer it [refugee status]. Because I hear they really give you a lot of opportunity and I could have come here'.

Resettlement to a third country, and the US in particular, was by far the preferred option among Liberians in the refugee camps in West Africa (Dick, 2002; Essuman-Johnson, 2011; Omata, 2013; Porter *et al.*, 2008). This preference among Liberians is striking given that resettlement to third countries is an option for only about 1% of the global refugee population (Dwyer, 2010).[7] Desperate to be part of this very select group, Ms Asha Onyango, a native Kenyan, who worked with the UNHCR in the refugee camp in Ghana, recalled how Liberians turned to prayers to be selected for resettlement:

> Even the [Liberian] churches [in the camp] took advantage of this. They will like tell people we're having prayer sessions for you to go to America. Because I remember, even the US had come with the UN to tell people that the situation now in their country has stabilized such that we were stopping or were reducing the resettlement from the camp. But they [people in the camp] did not believe this. So they have prayer sessions to open the way for resettlement. […] They have this perception that they could be resettled to America.

Hence, it becomes clear why being classified as *refugee* was something desirable while in a refugee camp as it led to the chance of being selected for resettlement in the US.

Refugee: Suffering Victims in Need of Rescue

In public discourse, refugees are depicted as individuals who are 'homeless, aimless, and with little more than a handful of clothes in the way of material possessions' (Masquelier, 2006: 735). Put differently, the word *refugee* is often synonymous with victims who are suffering and need help and protection. Subsequently, refugees are also expected to conform to standard images of victimhood and to comply with a set of standards (e.g. speaking a particular language) that government officials have drafted to be used as an assessment tool for individuals claiming refugee/asylum status; and if they fail to live up to these expectations, they are not deemed bona fide refugees but rather they are seen as 'liars' (Blommaert, 2009: 428). Humanitarian agencies have often used images of refugees as victims who are suffering to garner support (DeLuca, 2008; Harrell-Bond, 1985; Moeller, 1999; Musarò, 2011). Gabrielatos and Baker (2008) in their analysis of the discursive construction of refugees, asylum seekers and immigrants, show that newspapers in the UK also had a tendency to depict refugees worthy of compassion and aid, but only when they were far away from the UK, and were very unlikely to enter the country. Malkki (1996: 390) cautions that such images 'for representing refugees and the language of raw human needs [...] have the effect of constructing refugees as a [...] merely biological or demographic presence', and subsequently becoming 'speechless emissaries'.

But refugees themselves have also used these compelling images of vulnerability and victimhood to (continue to) receive support as refugees and improve their situation (Agier, 2011). For example, Brown (2011) documents that Volag staff advised their refugee clients to write *refugee* in bold letters on application forms for government benefits, suggesting that this would increase their chances of receiving services. This is another example where language is used to signal that *refugee* means 'person in need'.

In addition to being seen as a victim, Liberians commented on the fact that refugees were in need of rescue. For example, Ms Desai Kpoe Monbello, an older, single (grand)mother who arrived with several of her children and grandchildren in Staten Island from the refugee camp in Ghana, said:

Refugee mean[s] you run away from your country and [are] being rescued. That [is what] it mean[s]. They rescued us. Refugees need rescue. [...] Refugee that mean[s] to rescue me [...]. Well, it's not [a] bad word, they rescue[d] me, they gave me free food, […] they […] give me [a] house to live in.

She was not alone in emphasizing 'having been rescued'. Ms Janjay Waggah also stressed that when we talked. Ms Janjay repeatedly thanked the US government for 'rescuing' her and her children and she also made it clear that this 'rescue' saved her life:

God save[d] my life through these people [US government]. […] Refugee, to me […] it's […] [when they] air-lift us because of the war from my country to another country. […] When … during the war, and when […] they're rescuing you. […] The American government went and rescue[d] us to bring [us] over as refugees. They gave us that name. But actually I don't know what it means […] I think the meaning is that is what I'm telling you [when in] [….] your country […] war's going on […] and when they air-lift you and bring you into another country, then you are refugee.

Ms Janjay's use of 'being rescued' shows that refugees can and do internalize language around being 'speechless emissaries' (Malkki, 1996: 390) and start to see themselves as victims without agency.

Refugee: Displaced and Without Agency

Refugee is often used when describing people who are wandering around aimlessly and have little or no control over their own destinies and lives. Mr Varney Konneh – conceivably based on his years of being an IDP in Liberia – defined refugees as wanderers, 'I would just call it wanderers, people who [are] just wandering around. […] Sometimes I [would] just say "forgotten people", people who have nowhere [to go], no status. They just become like nobody'. This sentiment was also echoed by Ms Wannie Jacobs who was a refugee in Côte d'Ivoire. She stressed the lack of direction for refugees, 'Refugee, I mean […] it triggers let's say people living in a camp, not having any direction of where to go and not having relatives, struggling […] trying to find […] somewhere peaceful'.

Living in a refugee camp under the auspices of the UNHCR also intensified the feeling that they were at the mercy of others, and that these others – namely international organizations and governments, and also relatives sending remittances – decided their fate (see also Agier, 2011). Mr Wright Talley, a single father of seven, recalled how he felt helpless when he was in the refugee camp in Ghana and depended on others:

It's terrible, [being a] refugee. […] My own experience of the refugee life is very tedious because when I was in [the] refugee camp in

Buduburam, Ghana, I had [a] number of [...] friends and relatives [who were] in the United States of America that I [...] call for help and nobody cares to help you. Probably not because they hate you but sometimes people don't have resources to share with you. [...] When you are in a refugee setting [camp], [...] you've lost your prestige. [...] Why? You've lost your income. And so once you've lost your income your family does not [...] depend on you [...] for anything, others give them things. [...] So at the end of the day, you no longer have dignity [...]. [chuckles] You've lost your pride, you lost your income and your voices are not heard.

Mr Zubah Kpadeh, who arrived in New York from a refugee camp in Côte d'Ivoire as a teenager, had a similar response when he discussed that he and other refugees had little choice and agency and had to accept what others decided for them or gave them:

Refugee[s] don't have too many choices like [the type of] clothes or food [they get]. It's what [ever] they give to refugee[s]. [...] You can't [...] say, 'I don't [like] this, I don't want that ... this is what I want [...].' You got to eat [what they give you]. [...] That's the life of [a] refugee.

Another factor associated with this lack of agency is that individuals become refugees because they are displaced from their homes against their will or because of reasons beyond their control. Mr Dorgbah Weemongar, a Liberian man who found refuge in Ghana before being resettled in the US, talked about how anybody could become a refugee (again):

Anybody can become a refugee. [...] Refugee is relative. [...] It can be [...] internal and external [displacement]. For example if [...] I can't pay [my] rent [and] they kick [me] out [from the Park Hill neighborhood] and I went to go live in West Brighton [another neighborhood in Staten Island's North Shore] to live [...] with [...] a friend or with a cousin [...] I [would be] [...] a refugee in West Brighton (laughs) to my own understanding because I left here for reason[s] beyond my control.

Hence, if one applied this logic that *refugee* denotes people who have been displaced, it becomes clear why the media has referred to US citizens who were forced from their homes due to hurricanes and natural disasters as refugees. This has been well documented about 'Katrina refugees' from New Orleans (e.g. Bernstein, 2005; Gordon, 2009; Masquelier, 2006; Peinado Abarrio, 2012; Sommers *et al.*, 2006) and to a lesser extent about 'Sandy refugees' on the East Coast (Chen, 2012; Conlin, 2012) and 'refugees' from California wildfires (Associated Press, 2008; Egan, 1994).

Refugee: Black, Poor Welfare Recipients

The term *refugee* also has different meanings depending on the time period and on the racial group the term is applied to. For the most part, refugees escaping communism in Eastern Europe, the former Soviet Union and Cuba (prior to the 1980s), who were White and often had higher socioeconomic status, were seen as 'voting with their feet' (Gold, 1992; Kasinitz *et al.*, 2008; Skop, 2001). Although they qualified and received generous welfare benefits, the language used to describe them did not focus on that, but rather on their heroic accomplishments and success stories. The picture is quite different for non-White refugees, and in particular Black refugees from Africa, Haiti and Cuba. Their 'less-than-favorable reception' (Portes & Stepick, 1985: 496) in the US was undoubtedly marked by race. For example, Mariel Cuban refugees who included larger proportions of Black and racially mixed individuals were often labeled as 'scum' and the criminal history of some of the Marielitos was emphasized (Skop, 2001). Similarly, the discriminatory treatment of Haitian asylum seekers has been well-documented (Charles, 2006; Lennox, 1993; Stepick, 1992). Haitians, who are almost exclusively Black, have experienced high stigmatization not only because they have been labeled *economic migrants* and therefore have been seen as an economic burden, but also have been brought in conjunction with infectious diseases such as HIV/AIDS and tuberculosis (Charles, 2006; Coreil *et al.*, 2010; Gabrielatos & Baker, 2008; Ogletree, 2000; Stepick, 1992). Somali refugees have also often been targeted as welfare burdens (Voyer, 2013; Waters, 2013). This conflation is especially prominent in media 'word pairings' such as 'hordes of refugees' and 'illegal (Haitian) asylum seekers' and this matters as individuals do not remember the text verbatim but rather the 'interpretation of the propositions put forward in the text' (Gabrielatos & Baker, 2008: 20). Subsequently, individuals recall, in this case, the negative 'word pairings' which reinforce stereotypes of particular refugees and asylum seekers as economic burdens – without it ever having been explicitly stated (Gabrielatos & Baker, 2008: 22).

The view that Black refugees are a drain on public resources and the local economy is especially distorted since all of these refugees receive significantly less generous resettlement benefits than the earlier waves of Cuban, Eastern European and Southeast Asian refugees.

Many of the Liberian respondents in this study also talked about this conflation of race, refugee and welfare recipients. For example, Mr Samuel Black, who came as a refugee to Staten Island with his siblings and his mother after his father had been killed in Sierra Leone, said, '[Refugee] means foreigner. [A] person coming from Africa that has not much going on'. Other Liberians, including Ms Keisha Kole, a young, single mother who had arrived in the US as a child, reported that her American classmates used 'refugee', 'African (booty scratcher)' and 'monkey' interchangeably as insults for her and other Liberians. In addition to these assaults targeted at their geographic heritage, Liberians were also confronted with accusations of being dependent on welfare, which they resented as Ms Cynthia Sherif, an Americo-Liberian, who fled Liberia via Switzerland and ultimately found refuge with an aunt in Staten Island in 1986, explained:

> [Liberians] were not here for handout[s] but they needed a start. There were people that had 20 family members that came at one time. Food is expensive, medical [care] is expensive, you can't put 20 people at one time on your health [care] coverage and these programs were here just to get people [...] on their feet. [...] Not [...] everybody wants to just stay on public assistance or help from the government, a lot of the people just need[ed] it as a start because they want to do something and this is a place of opportunity and so people want that opportunity. [...] Like they classified us as the African Americans who don't wanna work ... who [...] wanna do nothing.

To be sure, Liberians as refugees and asylees were the recipients of government benefits themselves, but they were quick to point out that for them this was only temporary and hoped by doing so to distance themselves from the widespread stereotype that depicts African Americans as 'lazy welfare dependents/queens' (Hancock, 2004). In addition, in American society, 'receipt of welfare is usually grounds for disrespect—a threat to, rather than a realization of citizenship' (Fraser & Gordon, 1998: 114). The issue of citizenship is also interesting, as it is used differently by foreign-born and native-born Blacks to make claims to receive services from the government.

The Congressional Black Caucus and native-born Blacks affected by Hurricane Katrina rejected the use of the label *refugee* because, as Representative Diane Watson argued, 'refugees calls up to mind people that come from different lands and have to be taken care of' (Pierre & Farhi, 2005: para 7). Rather, Watson and other native-born Blacks stressed that those displaced by Katrina were 'American citizens' and that the US government had a responsibility to help and provide services to its citizens (Brock, 2008; Gemenne, 2010). It was also a reminder that citizenship in the US has always been shaped by race (Charles, 2006). Furthermore, by calling native-born African Americans 'refugees', they were being disenfranchised, othered and denied citizenship (Gavin, 2008), and yet again, as Du Bois (1994 [1903]) already pointed out in *The Souls of Black Folk*, being Black *and* American still seems to be irreconcilable to many. But native-born Blacks are not the only ones who made claims to the government based on citizenship. Liberian refugees in California demanded to be protected and to receive welfare benefits from the US government because their country of birth is no longer doing so and the US 'proactively resettled' (Brown,

2011: 151) them to the US. While Liberians in Staten Island did not make demands on the US government in terms of welfare benefits, they argued, as the earlier statement by Ms. Sherif indicates, that they only needed a helping hand initially so they could stabilize their lives and families and then pursue and achieve the American dream like so many immigrants have done before. Volags have also made the case that refugees are worthy of government benefits because they will, in due time, become contributing members of society (Nawyn, 2011). For Liberian refugees, embracing an immigrant narrative, which after all is a positive trope in the US, allowed them to distance themselves from the stigmatizing language which is used to describe Black refugees.

Conclusion

Refugee is not an obscure word that we hardly encounter, rather it is used quite frequently by the media, policymakers and sometimes even in everyday conversations. However, the definition and the meaning of the word are not always clear. Legally, there is a definite answer to the question who refugees are, those fleeing from persecution or fear of persecution based on race, religion, nationality, membership of a particular social group or political opinion. But as the discussion has shown, everyday language and different contexts bring with it many other ideas and meanings that are attached to the term; presenting a great variation depending on who is using the term and who is being described. For example, to refugees in refugee camps, *refugee* often only stands for their hope and yearning to escape their dire living conditions and to be selected for resettlement in a third country. At the same time, for some of the same individuals, the language around *refugee* is less optimistic, and the term reminds them of suffering. The image of suffering victims in need of rescue is often used by the media to describe refugees who are in these refugee camps far away from Western countries. However, the language quickly changes when these refugees make it to Western countries and then are seen as economic burdens. This is especially the case when Black people are described as refugees; then *refugees* often becomes synonymous with (Black) poor welfare recipients. Hence, it is important to pay attention to the contextual complexities in which *refugee* is used.

Notes

(1)   This name, like all others in this chapter, is a pseudonym chosen by the research participants themselves. All individuals cited in this chapter are Liberian refugees/asylees/immigrants unless noted.

(2)   These statuses, conceived as temporary, but as a rule have lasted much longer, in some case more than 20 years, are given by the US government to nationals of

countries that are deemed unsafe to return to because of ongoing armed conflicts, an environmental disaster or other extraordinary and temporary conditions (Simmelink, 2011).

(3) Under this act, undocumented immigrants who had lived in the US continuously since 1982 were able to regularize their status in the US.

(4) Email conversation with Office of Refugee Resettlement in January 2011

(5) Descendants of Black American settlers.

(6) For a critical analysis of using solely ethnicity to explain wars in Africa and overlooking other factors, see Braathen *et al.* (2000).

(7) The UNHCR pursues three different durable solutions for refugees: (voluntary) repatriation to the home country, integration into the host country or resettlement to a third country with the first being the most popular since the mid-1990s (Chimni, 2004).

References

Agier, M. (2011) *Managing the Undesirables: Refugee Camps and Humanitarian Government.* Cambridge: Polity Press.

Alao, A., MacKinlay, J. and Olonisakin, F. (2000) *Peacekeepers, Politicians, and Warlords: The Liberian Peace Process.* New York: United Nations University Press.

Associated Press (2008) California wildfire turns residents into refugees. *NBC News*, July 10. See http://www.nbcnews.com/id/25581653/ns/weather/t/calif-wildfire-turns-residents-refugees/#.U26zZ1OSOsM (accessed 10 May 2014).

Bergeron, C. (2014) Temporary protected status after 25 years: Addressing the challenge of long-term 'temporary' residents and strengthening a centerpiece of US humanitarian protection. *Journal on Migration and Human Security* 2 (1), 23–43.

Bernstein, N. (2005) Refugee groups reaching out to victims of hurricane. *New York Times*, September 18. See http://tv.nytimes.com/learning/students/pop/articles/bernstein1.html?scp=1&sq=refugees%20from%20politica%20storm%20bernstein&st=cse (accessed 29 October 2011).

Blommaert, J. (2009) Language, asylum, and the national order. *Current Anthropology* 50 (4), 415–441.

Braathen, E., Bøås, M. and Sæther, G. (2000) *Ethnicity Kills? The Politics of War, Peace and Ethnicity in Sub-Saharan Africa.* New York: Palgrave Macmillan.

Brock, A. (2008) Race matters. African Americans on the web following Hurricane Katrina. In F. Sudweek, H. Hrachovec and C. Ess (eds) *Proceedings Cultural Attitudes Towards Communication and Technology* (pp. 91–105). Perth: Murdoch University.

Brown, H.E. (2011) Refugees, rights, and race: How legal status shapes Liberian immigrants' relationship with the state. *Social Problems* 58 (1), 144–163.

Charles, C. (2006) Political refugees or economic immigrants?: A new 'old debate' within the Haitian immigrant communities but with contestations and division. *Journal of American Ethnic History* 25 (2/3), 190–208.

Chen, D.W. (2012) Some city employees lost their offices in the hurricane. *New York Times*, December 13. See http://www.nytimes.com/2012/12/14/nyregion/some-city-employees-lost-their-offices-in-the-hurricane.html (accessed 18 March 2014).

Chimni, B.S. (2004) From resettlement to involuntary repatriation: Towards a critical history of durable solutions to refugee problems. *Refugee Survey Quarterly* 23 (3), 55–73.

Conlin, M. (2012) Sandy refugees say life in tent city feels like prison. *Reuters*, November 10. See http://www.reuters.com/article/2012/11/10/us-storm-sandy-tentcity-idUSBRE8A90BV20121110.

Coreil, J., Mayard, G., Simpson, K.M., Lauzardo, M., Zhu, Y. and Weiss, M. (2010) Structural forces and the production of TB-related stigma among Haitians in two contexts. *Social Science & Medicine* 71 (8), 1409–1417.

DeLuca, L. (2008) Sudanese refugees and new humanitarianism. *Anthropology News* 49 (5), 17–18.

Dick, S. (2002) *Liberians in Ghana: Living without Humanitarian Assistance* (No. Working Paper 57). Geneva: UNHCR. See http://www.unhcr.org/3c8398f24.html (accessed 16 April 2012).

Du Bois, W.E.B. (1994 [1903]) *The Souls of Black Folk*. New York: Dover Publications.

Dwyer, T. (2010) *Refugee Integration in the United States: Challenges & Opportunities*. New York: Church World Service. See http://www.churchworldservice.org/site/DocServer/Refugee_Integration_in_the_United_States.pdf?docID=3923 (accessed 12 August 2012).

Egan, T. (1994) New hazard in fire zones: Houses of urban refugees. *New York Times*, September 16. See http://www.nytimes.com/1994/09/16/us/new-hazard-in-fire-zones-houses-of-urban-refugees.html (accessed 10 May 2014).

Ellis, S. (1999) *The Mask of Anarchy: The Destruction of Liberia and the Religious Dimension of an African Civil War*. New York: New York University Press.

Entwisle, H. (2010) *The End of the Road? A Review of UNHCR's Role in the Return and Reintegration of Internally Displaced Populations*. Geneva: UNHCR. See http://www.unhcr.org/refworld/docid/4d0f55462.html (accessed 15 September 2010).

Essuman-Johnson, A. (2011) When refugees don't go home: The situation of Liberian refugees in Ghana. *Journal of Immigrant & Refugee Studies* 9 (2), 105–126.

Fraser, N. and Gordon, L. (1998) Contract versus charity: Why is there no social citizenship in the United States? In G. Shafir (ed.) *The Citizenship Debates: A Reader* (pp. 113–127). Minneapolis, MN: University of Minnesota Press.

Gabrielatos, C. and Baker, P. (2008) Fleeing, sneaking, flooding: A corpus analysis of discursive constructions of refugees and asylum seekers in the UK press, 1996–2005. *Journal of English Linguistics* 36 (1), 5–38.

Gavin, A. (2008) Reading Katrina: Race, space and an unnatural disaster. *New Political Science* 30 (3), 325–346.

Gemenne, F. (2010) What's in a name: Social vulnerabilities and the refugee controversy in the wake of Hurricane Katrina. In T. Afifi and J. Jäger (eds) *Environment, Forced Migration and Social Vulnerability* (pp. 29–40). Heidelberg: Springer.

Gershoni, Y. (1985) *Black Colonialism: The Americo-Liberian Struggle for the Hinterland*. Boulder, CO: Westview Press.

Gold, S.J. (1992) *Refugee Communities: A Comparative Field Study*. New York: Sage.

Gordon, R. (2009) Katrina, race, refugees, and images of the third world. In J.I. Levitt and M.C. Whitaker (eds) *Hurricane Katrina: America's Unnatural Disaster* (pp. 226–254). Lincoln, NE: University of Nebraska Press.

Gupte, J. and Mehta, L. (2007) Disjunctures in labelling refugees and oustees. In J. Moncrieffe and R. Eyben (eds) *The Power of Labelling: How People are Categorized and Why It Matters* (pp. 64–79). London: Routledge.

Hancock, A.-M. (2004) *The Politics of Disgust: The Public Identity of the Welfare Queen*. New York: New York University Press.

Harrell-Bond, B. (1985) Humanitarianism in a straitjacket. *African Affairs* 84 (334), 3–13.

Hein, J. (1993) Refugees, immigrants, and the state. *Annual Review of Sociology* 19 (1), 43–59.

Hein, J. (2006) *Ethnic Origins: The Adaptation of Cambodian and Hmong Refugees in Four American Cities*. New York: Russell Sage Foundation.

Jones-Correa, M. (1998) Different paths: Gender, immigration and political participation. *International Migration Review* 32 (2), 326–49.

Kälin, W. (2000) *Guiding Principles on Internal Displacement: Annotations* (Vol. 38). Washington, DC: The American Society of International Law. See http://www .brookings.edu/~/media/research/files/reports/2008/5/spring-guiding-principles/ spring_guiding_principles.pdf (accessed 30 March 2012).

Kasinitz, P. (2008) Becoming American, becoming minority, getting ahead: The role of racial and ethnic status in the upward mobility of the children of immigrants. *The Annals of the American Academy of Political and Social Science* 620 (1), 253–269.

Kasinitz, P., Mollenkopf, J.H., Waters, M.C. and Holdaway, J. (2008) *Inheriting the City: The Children of Immigrants Come of Age.* Cambridge, MA: Harvard University Press.

Kibreab, G. (2004) Pulling the wool over the eyes of the strangers: Refugee deceit and trickery in institutionalized settings. *Journal of Refugee Studies* 17 (1), 1–26.

Kibria, N. (1993) *Family Tightrope: The Changing Lives of Vietnamese Americans.* Princeton, NJ: Princeton University Press.

Lennox, M. (1993) Refugees, racism, and reparations: A critique of the United States' Haitian immigration policy. *Stanford Law Review* 45 (3), 687–724.

Levitt, J. (2005) *The Evolution of Deadly Conflict in Liberia: From 'Paternaltarianism' to State Collapse.* Durham, NC: Carolina Academic Press.

Ludwig, B. (2013) 'Wiping the refugee dust from my feet': Advantages and burdens of refugee status and the refugee label. *International Migration.* doi:10.1111/imig.12111.

Malkki, L.H. (1996) Speechless emissaries: Refugees, humanitarianism, and dehistoricization. *Cultural Anthropology* 11 (3), 377–404.

Masquelier, A. (2006) Why Katrina's victims aren't refugees: Musings on a 'dirty' word. *American Anthropologist* 108 (4), 735–743.

Maxwell, J.A. (2004) *Qualitative Research Design: An Interactive Approach* (2nd edn). Thousand Oaks, CA: Sage.

Menjívar, C. (1993) History, economy and politics: Macro and micro level factors in recent Salvadorean migration to the US. *Journal of Refugee Studies* 6, 350–371.

Menjívar, C. (1997) Immigrant kinship networks and the impact of the receiving context: Salvadorans in San Francisco in the early 1990s. *Social Problems* 44 (1), 104–123.

Moeller, S.D. (1999) *Compassion Fatigue: How the Media Sell Disease, Famine, War and Death.* London: Routledge.

Mott, T. (2009) *African Refugee Resettlement in the United States.* El Paso, TX: LFB Scholarly Publishing.

Musarò, P. (2011) Living in emergency: Humanitarian images and the inequality of lives. *New Cultural Frontiers* 2 (October). See http://www.newculturalfrontiers.org/ wp-content/uploads/New_Cultural_Frontiers_2_2_Musaro%CC%80.pdf (accessed 19 March 2012).

Nawyn, S. (2011) 'I have so many successful stories': Framing social citizenship for refugees. *Citizenship Studies* 15 (6–7), 679–693.

Ogletree, C.J.J. (2000) America's schizophrenic immigration policy: Race, class, and reason. *Boston College Law Review* 41 (4), 4.

Omata, N. (2013) Repatriation and integration of Liberian refugees from Ghana: The importance of personal networks in the country of origin. *Journal of Refugee Studies* 26 (2), 265–282.

Patrick, E. (2004) *The US Refugee Resettlement Program.* Washington, DC: Migration Policy Institute. See http://www.migrationinformation.org/feature/display. cfm?ID=229.

Peinado Abarrio, R. (2012) 'Like refugees in their own country': Racial formation in post-Katrina U.S. *Odisea* 13, 113–127.

Pierre, R.E. and Farhi, P. (2005) 'Refugee': A word of trouble. *Washington Post*, September 7. See http://www.washingtonpost.com/wp-dyn/content/article/2005/09/06/AR2005090601896.html.

Porter, G., Hampshire, K., Kyei, P., Adjaloo, M., Rapoo, G. and Kilpatrick, K. (2008) Linkages between livelihood opportunities and refugee–host relations: Learning from the experiences of Liberian camp-based refugees in Ghana. *Journal of Refugee Studies* 21 (2), 230–252.

Portes, A. and Rumbaut, R.G. (1996) *Immigrant America: A Portrait* (2nd edn). Berkeley, CA: University of California Press.

Portes, A. and Rumbaut, R.G. (2001) *Legacies: The Story of the Immigrant Second Generation*. Berkeley, CA: University of California Press.

Portes, A. and Stepick, A. (1985) Unwelcome immigrants: The labor market experiences of 1980 (Mariel) Cuban and Haitian refugees in South Florida. *American Sociological Review* 50 (4), 493–514.

Schmidt, S. (2008) *Liberian Refugees: Cultural Considerations for Social Services Provider*. Washington, DC: Bridging Refugee Youth & Children's Services (BRYCS).

Simmelink, J. (2011) Temporary citizens: U.S. immigration law and Liberian refugees. *Journal of Immigrant & Refugee Studies* 9 (4), 327–344.

Singer, A. and Wilson, J.H. (2006) *From 'There' to 'Here': Refugee Resettlement in Metropolitan America*. Washington, DC: The Brookings Institution.

Skop, E.H. (2001) Race and place in the adaptation of Mariel exiles. *International Migration Review* 35 (2), 449–471.

Sommers, S.R., Apfelbaum, E.P., Dukes, K.N., Toosi, N. and Wang, E.J. (2006) Race and media coverage of Hurricane Katrina: Analysis, implications, and future research questions. *Analyses of Social Issues and Public Policy* 6 (1), 1–17.

Stepick, A. (1992) The refugees nobody wants: Haitians in Miami. In G.J. Grenier and A. Stepick (eds) *Miami Now: Immigration, Ethnicity, and Social Change* (pp. 57–78). Gainesville, FL: University Press of Florida.

Suzuki, L.A., Prendes-Lintel, M., Wertlieb, L. and Stallings, A. (1999) Exploring multicultural issues using qualitative methods. In M. Kopala and L.A. Suzuki (eds) *Using Qualitative Methods in Psychology* (pp. 123–134). Thousand Oaks, CA: Sage.

Tepper, E. (ed.) (1980) *Southeast Asian Exodus: From Tradition to Resettlement. Understanding Refugees from Laos, Kampuchea and Vietnam in Canada*. Ottawa, Canada: The Canadian Asian Studies Association.

Voyer, A.M. (2013) *Strangers and Neighbors: Multiculturalism, Conflict, and Community in America*. New York: Cambridge University Press.

Waters, A.M. (2013) Racial formation and anti-Somali ideologies in Central Ohio. *Bildhaan: An International Journal of Somali Studies* 12 (1), 53–85.

Williams, A. (2008) Turning the tide: Recognizing climate change refugees in international law. *Law & Policy* 30 (4), 502–529.

Zetter, R. (1991) Labelling refugees: Forming and transforming a bureaucratic identity. *Journal of Refugee Studies* 4 (1), 39–62.

Zetter, R. (2007) More labels, fewer refugees: Remaking the refugee label in an era of globalization. *Journal of Refugee Studies* 20 (2), 172 –192.

Zhou, M. and Bankston, C.L. (1998) *Growing Up American: How Vietnamese Children Adapt to Life in the United States*. New York: Russell Sage Foundation.

Zolberg, A., Suhrke, A. and Aguayo, S. (1989) *Escape from Violence: Conflict and the Refugee Crisis in the Developing World*. New York: Oxford University Press.

4 Restraining English Instruction for Refugee Adults in the United States

Diana M.J. Camps

Introduction

Currently, the contradictory nature of discourses in refugee policies, combined with policy mechanisms, undermines efforts to adequately prepare refugees, linguistically and culturally, for life and employment in the US. This chapter intends to show the link among discursive representations of refugees in policies and acquisition planning. A discourse analytic approach sheds light on the interaction of policies at different scales and how they entextualize specific perspectives with regard to second language acquisition of refugees in the US. The analysis focuses on key national and state policies that shape English language programs for newly arrived refugee adults within the current framework of the US Refugee Admissions Program (USRAP). The data demonstrate how two distinct discourses regarding language and economic self-sufficiency in the Refugee Act (1980) are entextualized in other national and state policies. This results in the articulation of a new hybrid discourse which has a significant impact on the framing of English as a second language (ESL) programs for refugee adults and the allocation of federal social service funds. Moreover, I argue that understanding the (re)framing of discourses within refugee policies will help educators and advocates construct counter-discourses of their own.

For decades, the US has played an important role in providing a safe haven for vulnerable populations, admitting more than three million refugees[1] since 1975 (Office of Refugee Resettlement, n.d.). Historically, the US has welcomed more refugees than all other resettlement countries combined and despite a decrease in refugee admissions, the US remains the world's largest resettlement country (Patrick, 2004; US Committee for Refugees and Immigrants, 2009; US Department of State, 2013). In 2012, more than 58,000 refugees arrived in the US from more than 80 countries (Office of Refugee Resettlement, 2013).

Refugee studies across a variety of social disciplines from sociology to anthropology to geography have examined varied aspects of resettlement and integration of refugees in the US (Franz, 2003; Hume & Hardwick, 2005; Ives, 2007; Kenny & Lockwood-Kenny, 2011). Others have addressed challenges with the current approach to resettlement (Brick et al., 2010; Bruno, 2011; Human Rights Institute, 2009; Kerwin, 2011). Recent reports point to a mismatch in goals between the Department of Population, Refugees and Migration's focus on 'resettling the most vulnerable and on bringing in diverse groups of refugees' (Brick et al., 2010: iii) and the Office of Refugee Resettlement's (ORR) primary concern with '[providing] the benefits and services necessary to help refugees and other vulnerable populations become self-sufficient and integrated members of American society' (United States Department of Health and Human Services, 2012: 1). ESL education was one of the services deemed inadequate due to a shortage of service providers and the poor quality of instruction (Human Rights Institute, 2009: 22[2]). Despite facing common struggles in acculturation and language learning, refugees differ from voluntary migrants in that they are often burdened by trauma and loss. ESL education in the early stages of resettlement is markedly different from other adult ESL programs as funding sources and policy texts dictate a specific timeline for English language acquisition and obtaining employment. For refugees, in particular, language skills in the dominant language are considered vital for integration and long-term self-sufficiency (Ager & Strang, 2008; Ives, 2007; Potocky-Tripodi, 2004).

An important factor often neglected as a variable affecting second language acquisition is the impact of language planning on the processes of second language learning (Tollefson, 1981). That is to say that the various cognitive and environmental factors involved in second language acquisition intersect with language planning decisions that shape the environment in which learning occurs. Policies, whether explicit or implicit, frame what is possible within a given educational context. Even when policies do not aim explicitly to affect language behavior in a particular way, they can become a vehicle for language planning when the goals of policies impact contexts in which language acquisition takes place (Spolsky, 2004). In the sense that refugee policies determine the scope of ESL services, these policies may be regarded as forms of language policy.

US Refugee Policies and the Resettlement Framework

Policies affecting refugees in the US play a juggling act between foreign policy objectives, providing humanitarian relief, domestic policy interests and national security concerns. These complex forces link international migration, foreign policy and refugee/immigration policy. The terminology used within the field and in policies is problematic as there is an inherent tension between applying the label *refugee*, thereby granting a certain status in order to provide humanitarian relief and protection, and simultaneously categorizing a large number of people as if they share a common identity. Clearly, the designation of refugee is strictly governed by legal mandates and provides protection to various eligible groups, including refugees, asylees, Cuban and Haitian entrants, trafficking victims, Amerasians and Iraqi and Afghan immigrants (Bruno, 2011).

Historically, refugee policies have been closely linked to federal legislation on immigration and national security. Early on, the manner in which policies in the international arena addressed refugee admissions to the US was often through *ad hoc* pieces of legislation, such as the Displaced Persons Act of 1948. In the years immediately following World War II, this act facilitated the admission of approximately 400,000 refugees, primarily from Western Europe, to the US (Reimers, 2012). In 1951, the Convention Relating to the Status of Refugees (Refugee Convention) established a formal refugee definition and subsequently passed the Immigration and Nationality Act (INA) in 1952 to serve as the basis of immigration law (US Department of Homeland Security, n.d.).

The Refugee Act of 1980, incorporating the United Nations' definition of refugee, amended the INA (1952) and established the current framework for the USRAP. It also established the ORR within the Department of Health and Human Services. Despite a formal framework for resettlement, refugee policies are not constant and are influenced by foreign events and other pressures. World affairs continue to significantly impact migration patterns and refugee policies at home and abroad. As such, the end of the Cold War significantly changed how the USRAP operated worldwide, beginning with the resettlement of increasingly culturally, religiously and linguistically diverse populations (US Department of State, US Department of Homeland Security and US Department of Health and Human Services, 2010). Despite this change in focus toward resettling the most vulnerable populations, the USRAP has remained largely unchanged since its establishment in 1980 (Brick *et al.*, 2010). Whereas refugee arrivals were fairly homogeneous during the early years of the resettlement program, recent arrivals have been highly diverse. At the time of the study, the largest groups of refugees to the US came primarily from Iraq, Iran, Burma, Bhutan, Somalia, Cuba, the Democratic Republic of Congo and Eritrea (Office of Refugee Resettlement, 2012). With a focus on resettling the most vulnerable, large numbers of refugees began arriving from refugee camps where they had often endured for many years, sometimes for decades. Many lacked formal education, native literacy and the basic skills required to participate in the US job market (Lugar, 2010). A more recent example of the influence of world affairs is the US Patriot Act's amendment of the INA in 2001 following the events of September 11. This Act tightened restrictions on the admission of refugees and immigrants in an effort to secure national borders and combat terrorist activities.

Thus, the resettlement process essentially entails a two-pronged approach, one which operates in the international arena for the protection of vulnerable populations and facilitating third country resettlement and the other at the local level with the aim of integrating newly arrived refugees into the host society. At the local level, refugee social service organizations provide a range of comprehensive services, such as cultural orientation, case management and health, education and employment assistance.

The policy analysis that follows investigates policies that impact provisions for ESL education programs. I show how discourses at different scales, national and state, constrain the provision of ESL services in local communities. The notion of scales is useful in describing how relationships of social organization, in this case between institutions and policies, are layered, occurring at different levels or scopes (Blommaert, 2007; Hult, 2010). An analysis of policy documents not only entails an examination of the text itself, but also explores how each text, in turn, interacts with and entextualizes other policies.

(De)constructing Refugee Policy Texts

A critical approach to discourse analysis can be fruitful for analyzing the connections between discourses and society and making explicit underlying power relations and ideologies. Discourses may be described as 'language-in-action' (Hanks, 1996) or be perceived as encompassing 'all forms of meaningful semiotic human activity seen in connection with social, cultural, and historical patterns and developments of use' (Blommaert, 2005: 3). Discourses construct a certain image of the world and are most easily differentiated by features of vocabulary. Vocabulary usage 'lexicalizes' the world in a specific way in that when we speak or write we have a choice in the words we use and how we use them (Fairclough, 2003). Political discourses, in particular, must be understood in context; they are made manifest at a particular time, but have deep connections to history, culture and other discourses. As such, Ball (1994: 10) defined policy as 'both text and action, words and deeds, it is what is enacted as well as what is intended'. Conceptualizations of policy should entail ways of thinking about policy beyond policy as *a thing* or something tangible and include ideas about policies as processes and outcomes. Rather than perceiving policy as a dichotomy of *policy as text* and *policy as discourse*, they should be seen as 'implicit in each other' (Ball, 1994: 15). A policy text, although a document with physical properties, has 'interpretational and representational history' (Ball, 1994: 17); it has been read, interpreted, represented and reinterpreted many times. In addition, its readers, as well as the context in which it is read, embody their own histories. The power in *policy as discourse* lies in the discursive effect of reallocating what Ball (1994: 23) calls 'voice'; to ascertain that only certain voices are heard or construed as meaningful. In other words, when discourses are in opposition or competition, certain discourses may be foregrounded while others are relegated to the background. Furthermore, perceived problems are constructed within the text in a specific manner. This particular perspective, articulated through language, realizes certain discourses in policy texts and frames problems in a certain way. Hence, a problem and its proposed solution are both constructed by the policy itself (Rizvi & Lingard, 2009).

A useful tool for analyzing language policies is entextualization, which refers to the process by which discourses are taken from one context and transferred to a new context, thereby creating a new discourse (Blommaert, 2005). However, in this process, an 'ideology of fixed text' interacts with discourse practices that may extend or alter the *original* text (Blommaert 2005: 201). These 'reformulations' (re)frame the text through other discursive practices and representations; they may be incomplete and open to interpretation. It is this space for interpretation or possible entextualizations inherent in the original text that gives it validity; any attack on its meaning may be framed as a misinterpretation or misrepresentation *not* a fault with the original text, which is seen as neutral.

Policy texts emerge in a variety of political processes and in this sense entextualization in policy documents represents a discursive trace of political debates. The resulting discourses that circulate are considered metadiscourse, or rather discourse about the discourse, reflecting the social reality of how language learners, in this case, refugees, should be perceived. Once again, language ideologies become a salient factor in how discourses in policy texts are entextualized. Thus, text and context must not be treated as mutually exclusive units, but must be seen as closely connected. This may be achieved by drawing on the concept of intertextuality, referring to the notion that each text is situated in relation to other texts and to the structures of language itself. Essentially, the words we use are already imbued with meaning and value, because they have been used countless times before (Bakhtin, 1981; Blommaert, 2005).

For this analysis, I draw on data from a study conducted in Texas in 2012.[3] Table 4.1 provides an overview of the policy texts analyzed. These documents represent key policies shaping English language programs for newly arrived refugee adults.

Additionally, these texts demonstrate how federal law is interpreted in federal and state regulatory documents and their connection to policies for the purposes of procuring providers and directing the provision of services. Figure 4.1 depicts the relationship between texts.[4]

Table 4.1 Policy data sources[a]

[F] Refugee Act, 8 U.S.C. §1521[b] (1980).
[F] Refugee Resettlement Program, 45 CFR pt. 400 (2011).
[S] Texas Health and Human Services Commission, 1 TAC §376 (July 2, 2004) (Refugee Social Services).
[S] Texas Health and Human Services Commission. (2008a). Refugee Social Services Provider Manual (RSSPM).
[S] Texas Health and Human Services Commission. (2008b). Request for Proposals (RFP) for Refugee Social Services (RFP No. 529-08-0181).

[a]Throughout this document, [F] at the beginning of each excerpt denotes a federal policy text and [S] denotes a state policy text.

[b]Title 8 of the US Code (U.S.C.) outlines the role of aliens and nationality and entails the Immigration and Nationality Act (INA) of 1952. The Refugee Act of 1980 (8 U.S.C 1522), which amended Chapter 2 of Title IV of the INA, established a framework for the historic role of the US in refugee resettlement. The Refugee Act (1980) adopted the formal definition of *refugee* established by the Refugee Convention (1951) and created the Office of Refugee Resettlement within the US Department of Health and Human Services. The Refugee Act (1980) amended the INA (1952), which stands alone as a body of law. However, the Act is also contained in the US Code (U.S.C.). The US Code citation is used to refer to the Refugee Act of 1980.

These documents thus reflect different levels within the policymaking process, allowing for the examination of interdiscursive connections within each context, federal or state, as well as the relationship between policies at different scales.

	US Law	US Code	Guiding Document for the Administration & Delivery of RSS Services	Functional Document for the Procurement of RSS Services
Federal	Refugee Act (1980) →	Code of Federal Regulations (2011[a])		
State		Texas Administrative Code (2004) →	Refugee Social Services Provider Manual (2008)	Request for Proposals for Refugee Social Services (2008)

[a]The date reflected in Figure 1 for the CFR (2011) indicates the latest version of text available, but this piece of the CFR was enacted right after the Refugee Act was passed in 1980. Clearly, intertextual connections to other texts would not be possible unless versions of the CFR existed prior to 2011.

Figure 4.1 Correlations between refugee policy texts across scales. Note that the date reflected for the CFR (2011) indicates the latest version of text available, but this piece of the CFR was enacted right after the Refugee Act was passed in 1980. Clearly, intertextual connections to other texts would not be possible unless versions of the CFR existed prior to 2011.

A New Discourse: English for Employment

In this section, I present excerpts from the data to demonstrate how discourses are articulated together to create a new discourse. Moreover, I demonstrate how this new discourse is realized and creates a framework for ESL instruction.

The first excerpt (Table 4.2) shows how the Refugee Act of 1980 frames issues regarding employment and English language training in resettlement. The Refugee Act (1980) makes a clear distinction between providing resources for employment training and placement to foster economic self-sufficiency and providing the opportunity to gain English language skills to facilitate resettlement. Although the need for English language abilities is explicitly recognized, the difference in lexical choices between the first and second statement is worth noting. With regard to employment-related activities, an imperative statement 'make available sufficient resources' is used. However, with regard to learning English, refugees need only be provided with the *opportunity* [emphasis added] to acquire *sufficient* [emphasis added] language training'. The word *sufficient* is indistinct and leaves space for varied interpretations. This space is made possible by the ideology of fixed text in that the belief or assumption that a policy text is neutral grants it a status of authority.

Table 4.2 Authorization for programs for domestic resettlement of and assistance to refugees

[F] Refugee Act (1980) [8 U.S.C. 1522]
(a) Conditions and Considerations.
(1) (A) In providing assistance, the Director shall, to the extent of available appropriations,
(i)   make available sufficient resources for employment training and placement in order to achieve economic self-sufficiency among refugees as quickly as possible,
(ii) provide refugees with the opportunity to acquire sufficient English language training to enable them to become effectively resettled as quickly as possible
(iii) insure that cash assistance is made available to refugees in such a manner as not to discourage their economic self-sufficiency, in accordance with subsection (e)(2), and ...
(B) It is the intent of Congress that in providing refugee assistance under this section-
(i)   employable refugees should be placed on jobs as soon as possible after their arrival in the United States;
(ii) social service funds should be focused on employment-related services, English-as-a-second-language training (in non-work hours where possible), and case-management services; and...

The notion of self-sufficiency is also discursively constructed in the statement 'employable refugees should be placed on jobs as soon as possible after their arrival in the United States' (8 U.S.C 1522 (a)(1)(B)(i)). Use of the word *placed* belies any guise of agency on behalf of refugees for obtaining jobs. Rather, this framing characterizes refugees as having no agency whatsoever and distinctly designates the state as the authoritative agent. As demonstrated with the next excerpt from the Code of Federal Regulations (CFR, 2011), this notion of *agency* is often contested within refugee policies (Table 4.3).

In contrast to the previous excerpt, which essentially portrayed refugees as having no individual agency in the process of obtaining employment, the CFR (2011) states that funds must be used for services that help refugees '*achieve* [emphasis added] economic self-sufficiency'. The use of the word *achieve* is particularly significant because it places primary responsibility on the role of refugees for the attainment of self-sufficiency as opposed to the role of the director (head of the ORR) in funding and administering proposed assistance. Language use in this instance reflects a belief by policymakers that the responsibility for achieving self-sufficiency resides with refugees. Thus, lexical choices, when evaluated within their context of use, go beyond mere referential meaning by also indexing social relationships. The focus on individual responsibility also parallels ideological shifts in adult education, which began in the early 1970s with the common notion of adult literacy learners 'pulling themselves up by the bootstraps' (Sandlin & Clark, 2009: 1025–1026). As a lack of linguistic capital can lead to social inequalities (Bourdieu, 1991), agency becomes an important factor in the language learning process to increase social and cultural capital. To this end, a number of studies have shown the importance of exercising individual agency to negotiate and to resist imposing discourses, as well as to gain access to target communities of practice (Menard-Warwick, 2007; Warriner, 2004, 2007).

Furthermore, the CFR (2011) outlines how the goals of effective resettlement and economic self-sufficiency are to be achieved. The CFR (2011) introduces the term *employability services*, which consist of employment services, employability assessment services, on-the-job training, English language instruction, vocational training, skills recertification, day

Table 4.3 Funding and service priorities for use of funds

[F] 45 CFR §400.146 (2011)
The State must use its social service grants primarily for employability services designed to enable refugees to obtain jobs within one year of becoming enrolled in services in order to achieve economic self-sufficiency as soon as possible.

care for children, transportation, translation and interpreter services, case management services and assistance for obtaining employment authorization documents (45 CFR §400.154). Employability services are 'designed to enable an individual to obtain employment and to improve the employability or work skills of the individual' (45 CFR §400.71). One important distinction from the Refugee Act (1980) is that employment services and English language training are now both deemed employability services among a variety of other services. The definition of employability services creates a hierarchy in which employment is elevated as the primary goal and ESL and other services are positioned as a means of achieving this aim.

The CFR (2011) also specifies that jobs should be obtained within one year and reiterates that self-sufficiency must be achieved as soon as possible. Intertextual connections to the Refugee Act (1980) are evident in the repetition of the words *achieved* and *as soon as possible*. Not only is economic self-sufficiency a primary goal in resettlement, but it should also be attained swiftly.

Framing pedagogical practice

Although the Refugee Act (1980) reflected two distinct discourses of achieving economic self-sufficiency and acquiring sufficient English language training, the following examples show a noticeable shift in how language instruction is framed as an employability service (Tables 4.4 and 4.5).

The focus of ESL is narrowed by placing the emphasis of instruction on what is relevant for employment. Clearly, the Refugee Social Services Provider Manual (RSSPM; Texas Health and Human Services Commission, 2008a) shows intertextual connections by repeating nearly verbatim the text in the Request for Proposals (RFP; Texas Health and Human Services Commission, 2008b: 18). Furthermore, the focus on survival English for *finding and keeping a job* shows little regard for which type of employment – it seems that any job will do – and whether or not language skills are sufficient to facilitate upward mobility and long-term self-sufficiency goals.

Table 4.4 Guidelines for employability services

[F] 45 CFR §400.154 (2011) – Employability Services

A State may provide the following employability services -- ....

(d) English language instruction, with an emphasis on English as it relates to obtaining and retaining a job.

Table 4.5 Emphasis for ESL services

[S] RSSPM §3100 (2008a) – English as a Second Language (ESL) Services

The emphasis for ESL instruction is on survival English for use in finding and keeping a job.

Hence, the notion of ESL as an employability service creates a new hybrid discourse. It is a significant departure from the separate discourses reflected in the Refugee Act (1980) in that rather than treating economic self-sufficiency and language acquisition as separate goals, these discourses articulate together to create a new hybrid discourse. This new discourse reflects the goals associated with achieving economic self-sufficiency and eliminates any references about language learning for reasons other than employment. Therefore, the process of entextualization reduces English language skills to merely a means to an economic end (Ruiz, 1984). Thus, by regarding English language training, both explicitly and implicitly, as primarily the means to an economic objective, the broader implications of second language acquisition in resettlement are ignored. More specifically, English language instruction for refugees is not portrayed as an opportunity to expand an existing linguistic repertoire, but rather as a remedy for a perceived deficiency.

Furthermore, the notion of *survival English* is problematic in that it makes an unquestioned assumption that English is the only or most important language that refugees need for survival in the US. Yet, research has shown that with respect to employment this situation is considerably more complex in today's global economy. Given the high number of migrant workers in entry-level positions, the working language in daily routines may not be the nation's dominant language at all. My work with Bosnian refugees in Chicago in the late 1990s reflected this trend as many employers in the hotel and garment industries relied on the language skills of their supervisors to communicate with workers and provide necessary safety training. Hence, as long as workers and their supervisor shared the same language, the ability to speak English became secondary, at least with respect to entry-level employment.

Also, in recent years, there has been increased attention on the commodification of language and issues of identity (e.g. Heller, 2003; Heller & Duchêne, 2012), and Shrestha (this volume) challenges the underlying assumptions of English language as *skill*. She demonstrates how learning English does not automatically and unequivocally result in meaningful and equitable employment. In fact, Shrestha argues that by learning to speak *good* English, Nepali refugees working as maids, nannies, domestic workers and housekeepers essentially reproduced their labor subordination by becoming silent workers. Nepali women in the New York ESL classes she led described a complex relationship between learning to speak *good* English, not speaking Hindi and obtaining better employment.

Table 4.6 Alternative definition of self-sufficiency

[S] RFP (2008b: 5)

To assist refugees in becoming self-sufficient as soon as possible after their arrival in the US. Self-sufficiency is defined as economic and social and cultural adjustment.

For them, better employment was not perceived as obtaining work in a different field without the demands of manual labor, but rather as working for 'American' (white, middle-class) families within the same labor industry. Speaking *good* English served as a means to express limitations and objections within current working conditions, but not necessarily overcome them. Thus, postmodern realities obfuscate the notion of *survival English* and highlight ongoing tensions between the global, the local and problems of racialization and marginalization within the labor market.

The narrow view of language in resettlement expressed in the CFR (2011) and RSSPM (Texas Health and Human Services Commission, 2008a) is also repeated in the RFP (Texas Health and Human Services Commission, 2008b: 18). However, the RFP attempts to provide a broader definition of self-sufficiency (Table 4.6).

Notably absent from the RFP's (Texas Health and Human Services Commission, 2008b) definition of *self-sufficiency*, however, is any explicit mention of linguistic adjustment. The role of language is at best implied in notions of social and cultural adjustment. Fairclough (2003: 207) states that 'discourses include representations of how things are and have been, as well as imaginaries – representations of how things might or could or should be'. Although the RFP's definition of self-sufficiency reflects a counter-discourse to the dominant interpretation of self-sufficiency, only the notion of economic self-sufficiency is iterated within and across policy texts.

The new discourse created by constructing ESL as an employability service determines the training focus for ESL and frames how services will be provided. The value of English language training is further revealed by how ESL is positioned in relation to other employability services and employment (Table 4.7).

The word *other* clearly repeats the new discourse of ESL as an employability service. Additionally, and perhaps more importantly, the fact that ESL must be offered *concurrently* with other employment-related services implies the relative lower status of English instructional programs

Table 4.7 Scope of refugee social service requirements

[F] 45 CFR §400.156 (2011) – Service requirements

(c) English language instruction funded under this part must be provided in a concurrent, rather than sequential, time period with employment or with other employment-related services.

---

and matters of language proficiency. In other words, if English proficiency were considered a critical part of employability, ESL instruction would precede employment and employment training rather than be offered simultaneously. This brief excerpt raises questions not only about the role of English proficiency in obtaining employment, but also regarding the value of formal instruction.

Restraining ESL Services

The following examples define the guidelines regarding the duration and intensity of English language instruction (Table 4.8).

Note again the blending of discourses and the primary emphasis on English for the purpose of employment, as expressed in the CFR (2011) and Texas Administrative Code (TAC 2004). In addition, the RFP (Texas Health and Human Services Commission, 2008b) places emphasis on the stipulated hours for instruction. The differentiation in style, bold text, serves to highlight the number of instructional hours (80) and the notion that this training should be provided in tandem with other employability services. However, after emphasizing in bold text that at least 80 hours of instruction are required, the RFP (Texas Health and Human Services Commission, 2008b) then states that a minimum of 40 hours is required for intensive ESL (50% attendance is required) prior to testing and counting clients as having completed the course. It is unclear whether the 50% attendance requirement is an explanation for the minimum of 40 hours or whether the RFP means 50% attendance of 40 hours, which is 20 hours. Hence, the RFP leaves plenty of room for further entextualization as evident in the following example from the RSSPM (Texas Health and Human Services Commission, 2008a) (Table 4.9).

Table 4.8 Guidelines for education services

[S] RFP (2008b: 18–19) – English as a Second Language
ESL programs provide English language training to refugees aged 16 or older who are not full time students in elementary or secondary schools. The training focus is on teaching survival English for use in finding and keeping a job. The Mainstream English Language Training (MELT) curriculum, materials and instruction methods are recommended. ESL courses must consist of at **least 80 hours of instruction and should be provided concurrently with** [original emphasis] other employability services. Classes should be offered during non-work hours to meet the needs of employed refugees. Intensive ESL training with shorter course lengths and with the same total hours of instruction can be provided. A minimum of 40 hours is required for this training (50% attendance is required) prior to post-testing and counting a client as a completion.

Table 4.9 Specific requirements for ESL components

[S] RSSPM §3100 (2008a) – English as a Second Language (ESL) Services
Regular ESL classes under contracted services should include a minimum of 80 hours of instruction spreading over 13–27 weeks dependent upon the number of instruction hours per week (no less than three hours per week).
ESL intensive classes may be offered; however, these intensive courses should be restricted to a maximum of 30% of the classes in a contract because these coursed do not address the needs of persons employed full-time....
ESL is a supplemental service that is provided with employment services and will continue after employment. It is not allowed as a substitute for employment or as the goal of employment services.
A client who attended at least 50% of the classes during the course period (40 hours) and took the post-test at the end of the course is considered to have completed regular ESL classes. Contractors are required to post test all clients who have completed 40 hours of ESL instruction within a reasonable time frame but no later than two weeks following the completion of 40 hours....

The RSSPM (Texas Health and Human Services Commission, 2008a) initially repeats the number of hours set forth in the RFP (Texas Health and Human Services Commission, 2008b), which is a minimum of 80 hours. However, in its interpretation of the number of required hours of instruction, the RSSPM (Texas Health and Human Services Commission, 2008a) emphasizes that a client who participates in at least 50% of the classes (40 hours) and takes the post-test is considered to have completed regular ESL classes (§3100). Hence, the RSSPM (Texas Health and Human Services Commission, 2008a) now frames successful ESL completion as 40 instructional hours plus taking a post-test. The word *took* is also a noteworthy lexical choice in that the RSSPM (Texas Health and Human Services Commission, 2008a) includes no explicit measures of achievement for ESL courses. Consequently, the RSSPM (Texas Health and Human Services Commission, 2008a) places primary emphasis on client completion rather than progress.

Additionally, classifying ESL as *supplemental* to employment services also discursively constructs ESL as an adjunct service to employment rather than a service of equal value. Furthermore, the assertion that ESL will continue after employment is an ideal often contradicted by reality. Participants in Ives's (2007) study, for example, reported working long hours for low wages in entry-level positions. Often, these refugees had to work more than one job to meet their family's financial obligations, leaving little time for additional ESL instruction.

Policy Mechanisms

The preceding examples demonstrate how policy texts reflect planning decisions regarding English language instruction for refugee adults. Language policy is the primary means for influencing language behavior and, as evident in the interdiscursive connections between these refugee policies, occurs at different scales of decision-making. However, policy texts are not the only mechanisms that influence the way policies are enacted. Although policies may provide explicit directives that stipulate language behavior, other devices often indirectly affect language practices and thereby become *de facto* policies (Shohamy, 2006). These policy devices become apparent when stated policies explicitly promote a certain goal or action, yet are contradicted by other mechanisms. Two policy devices that interact with policy texts are laws and regulations and program funding.

First, laws and regulations are particularly powerful instruments for affecting language practices because they mandate the way that language behavior should be managed (Shohamy, 2006). As is evident in the policies examined here, regulations garner such power from their ability to impose penalties and sanctions for non-compliance. Refugee clients must comply with strict rules and regulations that govern the provision of financial assistance to avoid sanctions. With drastically reduced time frames of financial assistance to a maximum of eight months, refugees have no choice but to comply with regulations and accept the earliest employment available. This significantly impacts the time that these newcomers have for learning English and getting settled, which contradicts research findings showing the benefit of intensive instruction, especially for low-literacy learners (Center for Applied Linguistics, 2010). Providing financial support to refugees for a longer period of time would allow them to increase their language skills or pursue higher education, thereby better preparing them for long-term success (Connor, 2010).

Secondly, program-funding allocations, which provide a fairly accurate picture of how authoritative values are distributed, may also counteract policy aims. These values are made explicit by how problems are framed within policies. It is not surprising then that the majority of federal funds for refugee social services are designated for employment services as this echoes the dominant discourse of economic self-sufficiency embedded within policy texts. Historically, one of the major obstacles in language-in-education planning has been the disparity between stated policies and allocating the resources necessary for realizing policy goals (Kaplan & Baldauf, 1997). In other words, language planning often fails at the stage of implementation due to lack of resources. Figure 4.2 reflects the allocation of federal funding for refugee priority service areas, based on the results of a statewide survey in the federal fiscal year 2008.

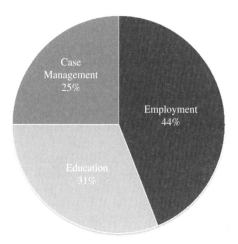

Figure 4.2 Priority service areas for federal funding allocations for refugee social services (Texas Health and Human Services Commission, 2008b: 9)

Despite the fact that ESL is considered an employability service and must be provided concurrently with other employability services, its financial support comes from Refugee Social Services Education Program funds (Texas Health and Human Services Commission, 2008b: 18). Education program funds, constituting 31% of federal provisions, must support not only ESL services, but also general education development (GED), (cultural) orientations, drivers' education and citizenship services (RFP, Texas Health and Human Services Commission, 2008b: 18). This suggests that financial resources for ESL programming are limited due to the number of programs supported through education program funds.

Conclusion

This analysis of refugee policies revealed competing discourses and tensions between policy goals of self-sufficiency and goals of language in resettlement. In the US, national and state refugee policies are interdiscursively linked across scales through the interplay of repeating discourses. These discourses, while reflecting educational planning decisions for refugee adults, also constitute social relationships between refugees, on the one hand, and the state on the other. The new discourse of *English for employment* reflects a reframing of discourses by regarding language skills primarily as an economic objective. The narrow framing of language as an employability factor foregrounds the importance of economic self-sufficiency and reframes English language learning as a tool for getting a job. As a result, a host of other reasons for language learning vital to successful adaptation and resettlement are ignored.

Moreover, the reframing of the relationship between language and self-sufficiency has a significant impact on the structuring of educational programs for refugee adults and shows how policies can become a means for acquisition planning. Some of the examples reflected principles of acquisition planning explicitly, such as requirements for the number of instructional hours. However, closer analysis revealed that such requirements were often contradicted in other parts of a policy or across policies. Rules and regulations counteracted explicit goals in policies, and refugee social service programs were shown to lack adequate and equitable funding for educational services. Thus, to accurately interpret refugee language policy, one must take into account the different factors and mechanisms that operate in conjunction with stated policies to bridge language ideologies and practice. It is not sufficient to examine only the stated or *de jure* policies, but one must also consider how policy mechanisms create *de facto* policies.

Despite conflicting discourses and a pervasive discourse of economic self-sufficiency, an awareness of framing within refugee policies can help educators and advocates be intentional about structuring new discourses that foreground the role of language, not just for employment, but in *all* aspects of resettlement and integration. Accordingly, it is imperative to teach language learners to claim their own voices to resist discourses that impose marginalizing identities and social positions.

Notes

(1) A *refugee*, as defined by the 1951 Convention relating to the Status of Refugees (Refugee Convention), is 'someone who is unable or unwilling to return to their country of origin owing to a well-founded fear of being persecuted for reasons of race, religion, nationality, membership of a particular social group or political opinion' (189 U.N.T.S. 150, 1954).
(2) See also Bruno (2011), International Rescue Commission (2009) and Lugar (2010).
(3) Given my access to resources in Texas at the time of the study, state policies and regulatory documents refer to this particular context. However, the purpose of the study is to demonstrate the interplay of policies and discourses at different scales and the resulting impact on educational programming, which is applicable to other contexts.
(4) Documents are categorized according to scale (federal or state) and according to type (law, code, guiding or functional document).

References

Ager, A. and Strang, A. (2008) Understanding integration: A conceptual framework. *Journal of Refugee Studies* 21 (2), 166–191.
Bakhtin, M.M. (1981) *The Dialogic Imagination: Four Essays* (C. Emerson and M. Holquist trans.). Austin, TX: University of Texas Press.
Ball, S.J. (1994) *Education Reform: A Critical and Post-Structural Approach*. Bristol, PA: Open University Press.

Blommaert, J. (2005) *Discourse: A Critical Introduction*. Cambridge: Cambridge University Press.

Blommaert, J. (2007) Sociolinguistic scales. *Intercultural Pragmatics* 4 (1), 1–19.

Bourdieu, P. (1991) *Language and Symbolic Power*. Cambridge, MA: Harvard University Press.

Brick, K., Cushing-Savvi, A., Elshafie, S., Krill, A., Scanlon, M.M. and Stone, M. (2010) *Refugee Resettlement in the United States: An Examination of Challenges and Proposed Solutions*. See https://sipa.columbia.edu/sites/default/files/IRCFINALREPORT_0.pdf (accessed 7 July 2015).

Bruno, A. (2011) *Report for Congress: U.S. Refugee resettlement assistance*. Washington, DC: Congressional Research Service. See http://www.fas.org/sgp/crs/row/R41570.pdf (accessed 7 July 2015).

Center for Applied Linguistics (2010) *Education for Adult English Language Learners in the United States: Trends, Research, and Promising Practices*. Washington, DC: CAL.

Connor, P. (2010) Explaining the refugee gap: Economic outcomes of refugees versus other immigrants. *Journal of Refugee Studies* 23 (3), 377–397.

Fairclough, N. (2003) *Analysing Discourse: Textual Analysis for Social Research*. New York: Routledge.

Franz, B. (2003) Bosnian refugees and socio-economic realities: Changes in refugee and settlement policies in Austria and the United States. *Journal of Ethnic and Migration Studies* 29 (1), 5–25.

Hanks, W.F. (1996) *Language and Communicative Practice*. Boulder, CO: Westview Press.

Heller, M. (2003) Globalization, the new economy, and the commodification of language and identity. *Journal of Sociolinguistics* 7, 473–492.

Heller, M. and Duchêne, A. (2012) Pride and profit: Changing discourses of language, capital, and nation-state. In A. Duchene and M. Heller (eds) *Language in Late Capitalism: Pride and Profit* (pp. 1–21). New York: Routledge.

Hult, F.M. (2010) Analysis of language policy discourses across the scales of space and time. *International Journal of the Sociology of Language* 202, 7–24.

Human Rights Institute (2009) Refugee crisis in America: Iraqis and their resettlement experience. See http://scholarship.law.georgetown.edu/cgi/viewcontent.cgi?article=1001&context=hri_papers (accessed 7 July 2015).

Hume, S.E. and Hardwick, S.W. (2005) African, Russian, and Ukrainian refugee resettlement in Portland, Oregon. *The Geographical Review* 95 (2), 189–209.

Immigration and Nationality Act (INA) (1952) 8 U.S.C §1101.

Ives, N. (2007) More than a 'good back': Looking for integration in refugee resettlement. *Refuge: Canada's Periodical on Refugees* 24 (2), 54–63.

Kaplan, R.B. and Baldauf, R.B. (1997) *Language Planning: From Practice to Theory*. Bristol: Multilingual Matters.

Kenny, P. and Lockwood-Kenny, K. (2011) A mixed blessing: Karen resettlement to the United States. *Journal of Refugee Studies* 24 (2), 217–238.

Kerwin, D.M. (2011) The Faltering US Refugee Protection System: Legal and Policy Responses to Refugees, Asylum Seekers, and Others in Need of Protection. Washington, DC: Migration Policy Institute. See http://www.migrationpolicy.org/pubs/refugeeprotection-2011.pdf (accessed 7 July 2015).

Lugar, R.G. (2010) Abandoned Upon Arrival: Implications for Refugees and Local Communities Burdened by a U.S. Resettlement System that is Not Working (S. Prt. 111-52). See http://www.gpo.gov/fdsys/pkg/CPRT-111SPRT57483/pdf/CPRT-111SPRT57483.pdf (accessed 7 July 2015).

Menard-Warwick, J. (2007) 'Because she made beds. Every day'. Social positioning, classroom discourse, and language learning. *Applied Linguistics* 29 (2), 267–289.

Office of Refugee Resettlement (n.d.) Quick Facts. See http://www.acf.hhs.gov/programs/orr/quick-fact (accessed 7 July 2015).

Office of Refugee Resettlement (2012) Fiscal Year 2010 Refugee Arrivals [data file]. See http://www.acf.hhs.gov/programs/orr/resource/fiscal-year-2010-refugee-arrivals (accessed 7 July 2015).

Office of Refugee Resettlement (2013) Fiscal Year 2012 Refugee Arrivals [data file]. See http://www.acf.hhs.gov/programs/orr/resource/fiscal-year-2012-refugee-arrivals (accessed 7 July 2015).

Patrick, E. (2004) The US Refugee Resettlement Program. See http://www.migration information.org/feature/display.cfm?ID=229#2 (accessed 7 July 2015).

Potocky-Tripodi, M. (2004) The role of social capital in immigrant and refugee economic adaptation. *Journal of Social Service Research* 31 (1), 59–91.

Refugee Act, 8 U.S.C. §1521 (1980).

Refugee Resettlement Program, 45 C.F.R pt. 400 (2011) See http://www.access.gpo.gov/nara/cfr/waisidx_09/45cfr400_09.html (accessed 7 July 2015).

Reimers, D.M. (2012) Refugee policies: Refugees and the Cold War. In *Encyclopedia of the new American nation*. See http://www.americanforeignrelations.com/O-W/Refugee-Policies-Refugees-and-the-cold-war.html (accessed 7 July 2015).

Rizvi, F. and Lingard, B. (2009) *Globalizing Educational Policy*. New York: Routledge/Taylor & Francis E-Library.

Ruiz, R. (1984) Orientations in language planning. *NABE Journal* 8 (2), 15–34.

Sandlin, J.A. and Clark, M.C. (2009) From opportunity to responsibility: Political master narratives, social policy, and success stories in adult literacy education. *Teachers College Record* 111 (4), 999–1029.

Shohamy, E. (2006) *Language Policy: Hidden Agendas and New Approaches*. New York: Routledge.

Spolsky, B. (2004) *Language Policy*. Cambridge: Cambridge University Press.

Texas Health and Human Services Commission (July 2, 2004) 1 TAC §376 (Refugee Social Services). See http://texreg.sos.state.tx.us/public/readtac$ext.ViewTAC?tac_view=4&ti=1&pt=15&ch=376 (accessed 7 July 2015).

Texas Health and Human Services Commission (2008a) Refugee Social Services Provider Manual. See http://www.dads.state.tx.us/handbooks/rss/3000/3000.htm#sec3100 (accessed 7 July 2015).

Texas Health and Human Services Commission (2008b) *Request for Proposals for Refugee Social Services*. (RFP No. 529-08-0181). See http://www.hhsc.state.tx.us/contract/529080181/RFP529-08-0181.pdf (accessed 7 July 2015).

Tollefson, J. (1981) The role of language planning in second language acquisition. *Language Learning* 31 (2), 337–348.

US Committee for Refugees and Immigrants (2009) World Refugee Survey. See http://www.refugees.org/resources/uscri_reports/archived-world-refugee-surveys/ (accessed 7 July 2015).

US Department of Health and Human Services (DHHS) Administration of Children and Families, Office of Refugee Resettlement (2012) Report to Congress FY 2008. See http://www.acf.hhs.gov/sites/default/files/orr/annual_orr_report_to_congress_2008.pdf (accessed 7 July 2015).

US Department of Homeland Security (n.d.) Immigration and Nationality Act. See http://www.uscis.gov/portal/site/uscis/menuitem.eb1d4c2a3e5b9ac89243c6a7543 f6d1a/?vgnextoid=f3829c7755cb9010VgnVCM10000045f3d6a1RCRD&vgnextch annel=f3829c7755cb9010VgnVCM10000045f3d6a1RCRD (accessed 7 July 2015).

US Department of State, Bureau of Population, Refugees, and Migration (PRM) (2013) Refugee resettlement in the United States fact sheet. See http://www.state.gov/j/prm/releases/factsheets/2013/210135.htm (accessed 7 July 2015).

US Department of State, US Department of Homeland Security and US Department of Health and Human Services (2010) Proposed refugee admissions for fiscal year 2011: Report to the Congress. See http://www.state.gov/documents/organization/181380.pdf (accessed 7 July 2015).

Warriner, D. (2004) 'The days now is very hard for my family': The negotiation and construction of gendered work identities among newly arrived women refugees. *Journal of Language, Identity, and Education* 3 (4), 279–294.

Warriner, D. (2007) 'It's just the nature of the beast': Re-imagining the literacies of schooling in adult ESL education. *Linguistics and Education* 18, 305–324.

Part 2

Resettlement Practices and Effects on Education

5 Building a Participatory Program for Iraqi Refugee Women and Families: Negotiating Policies and Pedagogies

Emily M. Feuerherm

Introduction

This chapter examines the development of a local English as a second language (ESL) program for Iraqi refugees, focusing on the use of community-based participatory action research (PAR) as a means for developing culturally sensitive program policies and pedagogies. Current research on refugee education has focused on the need for culturally sensitive pedagogies in the classroom (Watkins *et al.*, 2012) as well as school and program policies that account for the various and diverse needs and backgrounds of refugees (Cranitch, 2010; Due & Riggs, 2009; Kanno & Varghese, 2010). Program development is essentially the localized expression of educational policy development: the methods, structure and curriculum are influenced by macro-policies, but the localized nature of the program is influenced by the identities of the participants (i.e. administrators', teachers' and students' identities). In this way, program development is a localized exploration into the creation and mechanics of policy development. As such, a critical exploration of a local language learning program for refugees can offer insights beyond the local and highlight larger ideologies about refugees, education and language.

In adult education, Watkins *et al.* (2012) highlight the difficulties faced by Karen refugee women in traditional Western classroom environments and suggest that a one-size-fits-all approach to language teaching is not optimal. They suggest that the effects of students' culture, gender, motivations and context be taken into consideration when reviewing established classroom practices. Although their suggestions for altering pedagogical practices to be more culturally sensitive are useful, they do not show the process or the effects of altering the pedagogical practices. Similarly, Stevenson and Willott (2007) argue that tailored resources for refugee high school students are needed because the existing resources are not adequate, and yet they do not discuss how this might be accomplished. Cranitch (2010), however, examines a special literacy program developed specifically for Sudanese refugees, and shows that such programs can be successful in preparing students for high school. However, this is a pilot program, and so it is limited in scope and does not show reflexive program development. This chapter will demonstrate such reflexive processes and the effects of programmatic, pedagogical and other changes to the program as they were made.

Mainstream ESL curricula developed by experts outside of the community of learners tend to make dramatic assumptions about the population of learners and their needs. As Tollefson (1989) shows, a mainstream ESL curriculum developed for Indochinese refugees inculcated the attitude toward self-sufficiency and only prepared students to work in entry-level jobs. In opposition to mainstream approaches to curriculum development, participatory approaches have at their core a system of program building that is created with the participation of the students. This chapter will outline a community-based English language program for Iraqi refugees where a participatory orientation to curriculum development was instituted. Through focus groups, interviews and ethnographic data, pedagogical recommendations are made for local community-based programs working with refugees who want to expand their participation.

Juxtaposing Traditional and Participatory Curricula

Participatory approaches to education were first championed by Freire (1968) and have been used especially for adult learners. Wallerstein and Auerbach are two researchers who have connected participatory approaches directly to the teaching of adult ESL (Auerbach, 2002; Auerbach et al., 1996; Wallerstein, 1983). The participatory approaches to curriculum design have at their core a system of program building that is created with the participation of the students. Problem-posing is a method often used in participatory approaches because it allows for the validation of the students' identities, engages them by acknowledging the skills and experiences they bring to the classroom, and presents their position as mutable and changing. This approach stands in stark opposition to the deficit paradigm of curriculum design, where students are vessels that must be filled with knowledge; a paradigm that places the curriculum designer and teacher in a position of power over the student.

Additionally, educational programs and policies for refugees that have been created without the influence of students during program creation have been shown to position students in subservient stations. For example, Tollefson (1989) reviews the competency-based curriculum endorsed by the Center for Applied Linguistics (CAL) in the pre-immigration education centers for Indochinese refugees in the 1980s. According to CAL, cited in Tollefson (1989: 63), 'a competency-based curriculum is a performance-outline of language tasks that lead to a demonstrated mastery of the language associated with specific skills that are necessary for individuals to function proficiently in the society in which they live'. Although competency-based curricula are relevant to adult situations found in daily life, they are not constructed based upon strengths that students already have with the intention of building upon those qualities or skills. Tollefson shows that the development of this curriculum was guided by a series of assumptions about refugees and life in the US, but did not seek input from the refugees themselves. According to Tollefson, the curriculum reflected fears that American resources and values would be jeopardized by the influx of refugees, and that curriculum builders viewed refugees as lazy, dependent, lawbreaking, racist, subservient, backward and skill-less. This curriculum's lack of critical engagement with the positioning of refugees in the US created subservient subjects and served to maintain socioeconomic inequalities as refugees arrived in the US.

In opposition to the mainstream model of curriculum development stands the participatory model, which highlights collaboration between the teacher and students to produce a context-specific curriculum. Freire's (1968) *Pedagogy of the Oppressed* critically recognizes and values the local knowledge of students and situates the teacher in a dialogic position with students, where each learns from the other and power is shared between teacher and student. Freire's orientation to education is the basis upon which Wallerstein's (1983) ESL curriculum was designed, as well as Auerbach's (1992) Family Literacy Project. Both of these researchers advocate constant listening and observing the community while keeping an open and constant dialogue with students about lessons' relevance to their lives. They argue that program policies must be created and agreed upon by the participants, meaning that participants' identities can influence policies, such as the use of the first language (L1) in the classroom. In another participatory ESL program for Somali refugee women, Fridland and Dalle (2002: 37) show that seeking students' input empowered them through 'a sense of ownership of knowledge'.

Refugees, upon resettlement in the US, will have to negotiate identities assigned to them, such as English language learner, in an ideologically linguistic homogeneous nation. Because of this status, they may lack the symbolic capital necessary to attain the employment they had envisioned when granted refugee status in the US. Their resettlement may also represent a drastic change in socioeconomic status (Leudar *et al.*, 2008). Other core identity issues such as ethnicity/nationality, religion and gender may be contested in the new space. Delgado-Gaitan (1994) addresses many of these issues of identity in her study of Russian refugees resettled in Northern California. She shows how notions of family relations and employment were renegotiated throughout the acculturation period, and describes the refugees' reliance upon the religious community. Because Iraqi refugees have already been abused by their own government (and the US government?), a program that problem poses (Wallerstein, 1983) and empowers through participation (Dooley & Thangaperumal, 2011) would be the most effective means of establishing a fair and successful program as well as equitable research.

The Research Site and Methods

This chapter presents the development of a community-based participatory program for Iraqi refugees in the greater Sacramento area, called the Refugee Health and Employment Attainment Program (RHEAP). The program was created in collaboration with a local refugee resettlement agency, the Sacramento Immigrant Resource Center (SIRC),[1] and has been running since June 2010. I began working with SIRC in April 2008 as a volunteer tutor for a family of human trafficking victims. Based on the success of this program and in an effort to address SIRC's growing concerns for the Iraqi refugees who were struggling to find employment, they asked me later that year to create a vocational ESL (VESL) course for their clients. The course began in June 2010, after multiple interviews with SIRC staff and refugees about the needs of Iraqi refugees, as well as approval from SIRC and the institutional review board (IRB) to collect data for the current research.

Data include field notes, interviews, lesson plans, activities and questionnaires, which have been gathered and kept since the beginning of the course and document the development of RHEAP. My positionality in this research is that of participant-observer, RHEAP founder, ESL program director, teacher, curriculum developer and tutoring coordinator. I am truly invested in the program and the research component is, for me, a means to constantly improve and reflect upon the efficacy of the program.

Although this chapter will not outline a one-size-fits-all curriculum for refugees, it will outline the process by which one program developed a participatory curriculum. Because participatory research is cyclical and iterative in nature (Wallerstein *et al.*, 2005), so too must a curriculum using these approaches be. This chapter provides a connection between theories of PAR and the development of a participatory program. Furthermore, what is outlined here may provide other practitioners insight into the benefits and challenges of a participatory curriculum, to determine whether the approach is appropriate for their projects. In the following section, I will compare the creation of RHEAP to the principles of PAR and show to what extent RHEAP is participatory and in which ways that goal was not reached.

The Story of RHEAP

This section is organized chronologically, with particular themes at each stage highlighted. First, the needs analyses that were conducted before the program officially started underscore the importance of cultural sensitivity when working with under-represented members of society. This section is followed by a description of the first two instantiations of the Refugee Employment Attainment Program (REAP) where the process of policy and program creation is explored. This section highlights the evaluative process of program development and the resulting changes that were made based on participants' needs and experiences. The final section connects grant funding and curriculum design by outlining the changes that occurred to REAP upon receipt of a grant. The grant is a community development grant from Church World Service, a parent organization of SIRC, which initiated the addition of a health component and changed REAP to RHEAP.

Cultural sensitivity: Enacting PAR principles in program planning

When defining a problem using PAR, the researcher should rely on the community for the problem to be presented rather than establishing a research agenda without community involvement (Cornwall & Jewkes, 1995). The development of RHEAP began in October 2009 when staff at the SIRC asked me to create a program for Iraqi refugees who were struggling to find employment.

The first step in creating the program was to interview the staff at SIRC to find out what they saw as the needs that prompted the request for a specialized course. When discussing needs analysis, the importance of the local context, the backgrounds of the learners and an emic perspective of the larger society is necessary, particularly for an English for specific purposes curriculum (Belcher, 2006). For this reason, I formally interviewed the staff member who first suggested the program, Joe, and the volunteer coordinator, Rachel, under whom I had been volunteering and who would be helping me to get the program off the ground. I also conducted informal interviews with caseworkers for the resettlement program and their interns.

From these interviews, it was established that the needs of the Iraqi refugees, as seen from those who worked with them directly, were influenced by a few very particular factors: first, that there was identity conflict between the non-profit agency in Sacramento that SIRC partnered with to help refugees find and apply for jobs and the refugees. In an interview with Joe, he said:

> There seems to be a miscommunication between some of the service providers for employment and the refugees … it seems that most of the employment service providers, there is a clash of cultures definitely between the people from the former Soviet Union who are usually the ones that operate those organizations and people from the Middle East. The level of service from some of the people around those employment organizations, a lot of the Middle Eastern people don't feel like they're doing anything. They feel like they're just wasting their time. And that's another issue why the effectiveness of those programs don't work because they're not explaining this is how it's supposed to work in America in a culturally appropriate way. In a way that understands that they have their own culture, you know, and they need to have someone who understands that and doesn't just say things like, someone at the employment agency said that 'oh, you know, Iraqis are so difficult' but that's not the approach. (Interview with Joe, SIRC)

Joe highlights the need for cultural sensitivity and states that his goal for the program is to provide instruction about what is required to get a job in the US. Later in the interview, he states that many Iraqis come to the US with advanced degrees having worked as engineers, professors, government officials and interpreters in Iraq and believe that they should be able to find an equivalent job with good wages and benefits upon arrival in the US. The problem, however, is that their qualifications are not recognized by employers and they must have some entry-level work experience in the US before being eligible for higher-paying employment. This assumption was confirmed in a subsequent interview with a refugee woman, Samara, who said that she had been a professor in Iraq, and was looking for any job to support her family. However, after stating that any job would be agreeable to her, she said that because of her age and experience, she really needed an office job and would not take a job at Subway or Walmart – two employers that the employment agency often sent SIRC clients. Thus, there were also *de facto* policy conflicts regarding employment: the employment agency was operating under the policy that requires refugees to become employed soon after arrival to establish self-sufficiency (discussed more in Chapters 4 and 9, this volume) and thus encourages refugees to take the first job offered; and the employment policy that erases immigrants' employment experience in their home countries, particularly their education and professional certificates – which leaves them feeling that they should have access to higher-paid jobs. These macro-policies later influenced the emergent programmatic policies of RHEAP, particularly the policy that required a focus on vocational ESL.

In addition to the need for culturally sensitive vocational ESL instruction, Joe stated that many of the Iraqi refugees who were coming through SIRC spoke English quite well already, as they had been working as interpreters for the US military in Iraq during the invasion and occupation. In fact, it was this association with the US that placed many of the refugees in compromising positions in their home countries, causing them to become a target in their own country. For many of them, this situation resulted in their refugee resettlement in the US. However, despite their knowledge of the English language, they did not necessarily have the cultural competence, particularly regarding US employment culture, to be able to find a job on their own. The situation had become so dire in a few select cases, that some of the refugees were threatened with homelessness. As Joe said in his interview about the needs of the Iraqis:

> The important thing is not assuming that they understand how it works. One of the things that I've noticed is that a lot of the Iraqis speak really good English, we just assume that they're doing fine because they speak good English, but that's not true. (Interview with Joe, SIRC)

Here, it is clear that cultural sensitivity is necessary not only in the instructional methods, but also in recognizing what is expected in the target culture. In the educational programs for southeast Asian refugees that were used in the 1980s, cultural competence in the workplace was the focus (Tollefson, 1989). These programs were an attempt to teach cultural competence for employment to refugees before their arrival in the US. However, these programs were created without the participation of the refugees and topics of instruction were chosen by officials based on ideologies that refugees were lazy and needed to be taught self-sufficiency (Tollefson, 1989). Participatory program development can bridge the gap between focusing on the needs of the students and on empowering students to become active participants in the larger community.

Another important factor in the needs analysis that was discussed by another SIRC staff member, Rachel, was that in each state, refugees are offered different benefits after the federal benefits are exhausted. Furthermore, each resettlement agency offers different programs and benefits than others (outside of the basic requirements), since all of them are non-governmental organizations. This inconsistency is met with frustration by the refugees, since it can appear that some refugees are getting better (or worse) treatment. This has resulted in many cases of secondary resettlement, where a refugee will leave the agency and location that he or she was resettled in, to join friends or family in another location, and this secondary resettlement reflects poorly on the original resettlement agency. These macro-policies affected the development of RHEAP because the program was established as an effort by SIRC to curb secondary resettlement.

In order to get the program off the ground, Rachel and I invited other interested staff to a focus group where we pitched our ideas and got feedback regarding the design. At this point, the main concern was that there would be no money for the program, and that students might find it difficult to attend if transportation was not offered. The key concerns raised by the focus group had to do with finances; in particular, that there was no extra money that could be earmarked for a program like this. Nevertheless, they agreed that the program should be created, even though the program was not funded at this point.[2]

The next step was interviewing potential students in order to conduct a more thorough needs analysis that incorporated firsthand accounts of the needs of Iraqi refugees. A few difficulties arose in trying to do this. First, I do not speak Arabic and SIRC could not spare a translator, so I was limited to those refugees who spoke English already. Second, because of privacy regulations, SIRC was hesitant to grant me direct access to their clients and my potential students at first, despite the IRB. Initially, they set up meetings with their clients, and when this proved arduous regarding scheduling and communication, they provided me with phone numbers for clients directly. However, many of the refugees were hesitant to be interviewed, many of the phone numbers did not work or there was no answer, so I was only able to conduct formal interviews with five people in three interviews.

The results of these interviews indicated that the topics and skills these refugees were interested in were continuing education or recertification in their field, speaking and listening skills, the social life of Americans, and finding a job (or finding a better job). This part of the creation of the program adhered to the principles of PAR in that the problem was identified by the community and not the researcher. The needs analysis was conducted by the researcher, but in the context of participatory curriculum development. Auerbach (1992: 13) says that the educator should develop the curriculum only after coming in contact with the students and that it should 'be built on the particular conditions, concerns, and contributions of specific groups of participants at a particular point in time'. As such, this initial step was aligned with participatory curriculum development. However, Auerbach also suggests that the materials should come from the students and not just the teacher. Although the materials for REAP were created by the teacher and the assistant teachers, not the students, the materials and curriculum were developed in response to the needs expressed by the students. Materials were not directly produced by the students (in the form of text, picture or photo), but whenever they brought up concerns (e.g. where to shop for food most cheaply) or questions (e.g. how do I start a childcare business), we would address these concerns and/or create materials to do so. Because of this, curriculum development was not directly participatory, but indirectly so.

Program development

The first curriculum was constructed based on the available resources and needs analyses conducted with staff at SIRC and with the clients. The course was a 10-week course beginning July 6, 2010 and ending September 7, for two hours once per week. This schedule was chosen because the two teachers who would be running the program, myself and a master of arts in teaching English to speakers of other languages (MATESOL) graduate, were on a quarter-based system and this schedule would align with other university responsibilities. The Iraqis who had been interviewed voiced no concerns about the timing or duration of the course during the interviews, so although they had the opportunity to influence this situation, it was not utilized. The course was supplemented by an external tutoring program, adapted from the one with which I had volunteered. Volunteers from the community met students outside of the class and tutored one-on-one for approximately two hours once per week. At this point in the program, there was no 'H' for *health* in RHEAP, it was simply the REAP. The focus of the course was employment, as evidenced by the weekly topics:

(1) Intro and exam.
(2) Finding a job: Where and how to read ads.
(3) Resume workshop and applications (for different fields).
(4) Resume workshop cont. and the letter of interest.
(5) Interviews.
(6) Interviews cont. and following up (thank you letters, etc.).
(7) Employment norms (laws, expectations, conflicts).
(8) Promotions.
(9) Higher education (applications, etc.).
(10) Wrap up and exam.

This list of topics, taken from the syllabus, shows that the focus was on the process of finding a job, with one meeting dedicated to higher education. However, a caveat on the syllabus stated that 'this schedule may change, and it does not reflect the additional variety of topics on American culture and survival English that will be covered in this class'. It was planned that emergent issues regarding American life and culture, as well as additional survival English skills would be covered, but these would be based on questions brought to class. For this, a question box was made, where students could anonymously ask questions. Also, students were provided with a journal where they were expected to keep a log of their progress and include any other experiences or questions that they would like to discuss in class and were asked at the beginning and end of the lesson what, if anything, they had questions about. The journal was also meant to be a method for engaging students in the research process, and was presented as such, in order to strengthen the participatory aspect of the research project.

Only two students came to the first meeting of this first session, but the second meeting had seven students. Each student was given a written exam on the first day, which focused on finding employment. The exam was designed to determine which aspects of the job search were most unfamiliar to the students, so that the curriculum could be designed to focus on the needs of the individual students. Additionally, the plan was to give the exam at the beginning and end of the course to measure improvement. However, students had a wide range of English skills, and students helped each other despite admonitions to try to answer the questions themselves. Thus, the test was unsuccessful in both goals: discovering needs/prior knowledge and measuring improvement.

Table 5.1 is a summary table of the first session of REAP, its structure and curriculum, followed by the purpose for each construction and the results. In addition to the structure and topics, Table 5.1 shows that the original plan had flaws that disinclined some students from continuing with the program (seven in total came, but only two stayed). After the course, I interviewed the students to find out what they liked and what worked well in the class. The two students agreed that the instruction on writing resumes and applying for jobs was useful, but added that the idioms and slang vocabulary that were covered was equally useful. They were disappointed that there were not more students because they valued learning from others' experiences and mistakes. They stated that the only reason why some people did not come is because they were already working, and the fact that Ramadan was concurrent with the class made it very difficult for people to attend.

Based on this interview, I kept the structure for the second session mostly the same, but removed the question box and journal as not one student wrote a journal entry during the 10 weeks. However, when the second session ended much like the first – with only two students regularly attending and two teachers to work with them – I conducted an informal focus group with teachers, students, tutors and staff at SIRC. The results of the focus group led to a number of changes, particularly regarding the length and structure of the course. Furthermore, one of the students, Muhammad, wanted to participate in the course not as a student, but in some other capacity. Table 5.2 compares the changes made to the second phase of REAP with the original phase.

As Table 5.2 shows, there were many changes to the structure of REAP between the first and second phases of the program. The number

Table 5.1 Summary of the first session of REAP

	Purpose	Result
10-week course, two hours each evening	To fit the teachers' schedule	Too long of a commitment
Separate meeting with tutor	To provide additional, individualized support	Difficulty scheduling and following through with the meeting
Written exam	To gauge students' needs and progress	Students translated for each other and shared answers, some students were unable to answer any of the questions while some answered all satisfactorily
Question box	To allow students an opportunity to discuss problems or questions with anonymity	Never used voluntarily, when requested to submit something, all said 'no questions'
Journal to be kept by students	To have students participate directly in the research, practice English, and keep track of job interests and applications	No one wrote in his or her journal
Curriculum focus on finding a job	Students had other interests or more specific ones, such as where to buy food cheaply, or how to start a day care	Many of the planned topics were abandoned in favor of pursuing more specific interests
Participation	The most students who came was seven, though one day no one came. One couple came every week but one	Because there were also two teachers (upper and lower level), the situation was often one-on-one
Food	People like to gather for food, but we were constrained financially, and the course was during Ramadan when many students were fasting	Received donation bagels from Noah's Bagels, and I supplied condiments and drinks; however, these were not very popular and often went untouched
Location	Russian community center because it was free and close to where most of the refugees were being resettled	The room was not structured as a classroom and many people had a difficult time finding it
Summary of class	One couple attended most of the classes	Employment-based curriculum used in the first half of the session, the second half was conversational skills and culture lessons

Table 5.2 Comparison of Phases 1 and 2 of REAP

	First phase of REAP (June 6–December 14 2010) 2 sessions	Second phase of REAP (January 11–October 18 2011) 6 sessions
Length of course	One two-hour class per week for 10 weeks	One three-hour class per week for 5 weeks
Tutoring	At a separate time and location from the course	During the final hour of the course, in the same location as the course
Student tracking/exams	Written exam for needs analysis and progress	No exam, tracking students' attendance, evaluation forms at the end of each session for both students and tutors
Participation	Two students finishing each session, two trained ESL instructors	Average of five students finishing each session, two trained ESL instructors and one refugee instructor for the beginning level, one volunteer for childcare of one to four children
Demography	Students were an Iraqi couple in the first session, then two single Iraqi men	Students were mostly single Iraqi men, though some Iraqi women, couples and children participated as well as a few human trafficking victims
Curriculum focus	Beginning with employment, then direct focus on students' interests and needs	Focus on employment at the advanced level, survival English with basic employment skills at the intermediate level and basic vocabulary at the lowest level
Food	Bagels and drinks	Bagels, drinks and potluck-style food brought by Muhammad and tutors
Other	Question box and journal	Prizes for students with perfect attendance, an intern from SIRC to help manage the program and volunteers, addition of field trips to a career center and social events such as barbeques, picnics and a museum trip

of volunteer teachers and tutors as well as students grew. Also, no classes were offered during Ramadan, so there was more than a month's break in the summer.

Participatory research and program development require that the program be regularly re-evaluated to ensure that it is aligned with the needs and goals of all participants. As Wallerstein *et al.* (2005) point out,

> Those of us who are trained researchers based in universities, health and social service agencies, and other institutions may read about the importance of partnerships yet may neglect to engage in ongoing self-reflection about the inevitable challenges and dilemmas we face in initiating, nurturing, and maintaining partnerships (Wallerstein *et al.*, 2005: 31)

Changes in REAP were an effort to continue to engage in the process of reflection on the participatory nature of the program and re-evaluate the program's goals and methods. For example, having the ESL class and the tutoring component separate was a flawed policy and based on reflections with volunteers and students, this policy was changed to have both components occur at the same time. As Elmeroth (2003) shows, refugees often find themselves isolated from the community in which they are resettled, leading to their marginalization. She shows that greater contact with the community, and target language speakers, increases motivation to learn the majority language and diminishes the experiences of isolation and marginalization. Thus, the tutoring component was an important component, and needed the structural support of REAP classes to be effective. Additionally, at this time, REAP's goals were changed to more explicitly attend to the needs of beginning students by engaging a member of the community in teaching ESL using the native language, thus increasing the participatory nature of the program.

The curriculum was participatory at this stage of the process because materials for the beginning level were being created by Muhammad, a member of the community who was engaged in the day-to-day production of the program. He was a great help in recruiting new students and he always made three or four Iraqi dishes for students, teachers and tutors to share. He also functioned as an interpreter when there were announcements. He taught the beginning level bilingually and had between zero and three students each week. If he did not have any students, he would observe another level or help with childcare. He was a boon to the participatory nature of the program and helped explain the needs of the refugees to the non-Arabic speaking teachers and tutors. He also invited me to Iraqi events so that I could recruit students and experience Iraqi culture.

The program's success was another site of subtle negotiation because although I had planned on tracking progress through the use of written exams, these proved culturally inappropriate for the course. As Nykial-Herbert (2010: 7) shows in her study of Iraqi refugee children, cooperation and help between students 'manifested itself as copying from a classmate, or doing part of the work for someone else… [which] meant that school-work had an intrinsic value, and its proper completion was a source of pride'. Using a written exam to show individual progress in REAP was unsuccessful because the test was constructed to evaluate an individual's progress, and presumed that the work would be strictly the individual's own work. However, Iraqi cultural norms of helping those who are not as proficient made the exam a whole-class event where copying and doing another's work were acceptable, despite the gentle reprimands of the teachers. Thus, although the exam was not a method for tracking success, participation became the more important determination of success. Similarly, Menard-Warwick (2002) shows that institutional goals may be counter to the community's goals, and that participation is increased when the target community is engaged on their terms. Fridland and Dalle (2002) also demonstrate that for an ESL program for Somali refugee women, success was based on the active participation of the refugees, not through direct testing. The fact that between the first and second instantiation of REAP, participation increased and the program was made more participatory, shows that program success is directly tied to policies of convenience, instructional levels, and culturally appropriate approaches to instruction and evaluation.

Balancing grantor's and students' needs in a participatory program

Although the second instantiation of REAP was more successful than the first, there still seemed to be a need that was not being met. In May 2011, the staff at SIRC asked me what could be done to make the program grow. Women were clearly the minority in the classes, and finding a way to encourage them to attend would be one method for boosting numbers and attending to a demographic that had far lower attendance. On June 1, 2011, a focus group with four Iraqi women (more had been invited, but only four came), the deputy director of SIRC, one of the REAP teachers, the SIRC intern who managed the REAP volunteers, and I met in the conference room at SIRC. We asked what we could do to interest more Iraqi women in the program: e.g. what topics should we address, what schedule would be optimal, whether classes should be separated by gender, what goals they had and how we could help them achieve these goals. Of the four Iraqi women, one was the wife of the founder of a society for Iraqis in the Sacramento region, and thus a leader in her community. One of the women had been a biologist in Iraq, one a pharmacist and one was a housewife who wanted to go to nursing school.

When asked, all the Iraqi women who attended the focus group said that it would not be necessary to have a separate women's class because in Iraq education was mixed-sex. They all agreed that information about finding a job, getting recertified and going back to college was important to them. Of course, the sampling of clients who participated was once again those who were already fluent in English and had been well educated in Iraq. Despite this, they all mentioned that they wanted to improve their English, and when asked, none said that they were interested in learning about health issues. Health was brought up because of another PAR project being conducted collaboratively between the University of California Davis Medical Center (UCDMC) and SIRC's Iraqi refugee clients where the medical needs of Iraqi refugees were being researched.

In order to get funding for the program through a community development grant from the Office of Refugee Resettlement, it was necessary not only to show what the needs of the refugees were, but also to demonstrate how the program would meet needs that were not already a goal of another federally funded institution. Up until this time, REAP had an employment focus which was supposed to be met by the federally funded employment agencies while the English needs were met by the adult schools. Showing that Iraqi refugees had specific ESL and employment needs in this community would not be enough to be awarded a grant. However, community-based programs and participatory research require a clear knowledge and assessment of the resources of all participants (Israel et al., 2005), and one of those resources brought to the table by SIRC were connections to health research regarding Iraqi refugees. SIRC was collaborating on another program with the UCDMC, and because of their connections in the health industry and knowledge of the needs of Iraqi refugees, it was concluded that this was a means for the program to get funding (despite the women's claim that this topic did not interest them).

The grant application included a health component to REAP, making it RHEAP. The plan was to add health education, especially aimed at women and children, while maintaining an employment and English focus. Upon being awarded the grant, SIRC called for applications for a part-time paid position as a program manager who would be in charge of recruitment, record-keeping, overseeing interns and other clerical duties as needed. An Iraqi refugee woman, Mary, was hired for her strong connection to the Iraqi community because it was believed that she would be able to recruit more women to the course. Additionally, her mother-in-law had been a famous nutritionist in Iraq, with a television show and multiple publications. She agreed to lecture on a variety of health topics in Arabic at every class. Thus, the changes from REAP to RHEAP were participatory because members from the refugee community were engaged in its production. Having a program that is jointly owned by the students is empowering and makes the program more successful, as evidenced in Fridland and Dalle's (2002) article on a participatory ESL program for Somali refugee women.

Table 5.3 summarizes the main changes between REAP and RHEAP. One of the most evident differences between REAP and RHEAP is the change in demography. Whereas students of REAP were mostly men, the great majority of RHEAP students are women and families. One reason for this change is that the resettlement agencies had an almost year-long hiatus of new Iraqi refugees to resettle because of funding cuts and more stringent background checks for Iraqi refugees coming into the US. Because of an eight-month cap on federal welfare support for refugees without dependents, the single men who were arriving needed immediate support in finding employment. By the time RHEAP started again, these refugees had been in the US for a year or more, had found jobs and did not have the time to attend. Refugees with dependents can continue receiving welfare support for five years, at which time continued support requires passing the citizenship test. In addition, recruitment for REAP was conducted by SIRC and Muhammad, a single Iraqi refugee man, whereas recruitment for RHEAP is conducted by the program manager, a married Iraqi refugee woman with three children. Her social network in the Iraqi community thus differs from Muhammad's because of her identity as a married Iraqi Muslim woman, which has likewise influenced the demography of the students. Thus, the macro-policies of refugee resettlement and the identities of the participants heavily influenced the policy building and curriculum development of RHEAP.

Program evaluation also changed from REAP to RHEAP because of the needs of the grantor. Although the evaluation procedures used in REAP had made it evident that evaluation practices common in the US (e.g. written exams) were inappropriate for determining the progress of this program, using only participation as a measure of success was not acceptable for the grantor. For this reason, two new evaluations were created: one ESL speaking exam administered individually by tutors to the students, and one health exam written in Arabic. The ESL exam administered by the tutors allowed for a negotiation of cultural evaluation norms between the American tutors and the Iraqi students. Students and tutors were told that the evaluations would be used to measure progress, and that they should not ask for translations. Despite this, many of the students asked their peers to translate the questions, and some asked to take the evaluation home so they could practice answering. In this case, although the evaluation procedure was not entirely sensitive to the cultural differences, it allowed for a negotiation of cultural differences between the student and their tutor. Furthermore, as Wigglesworth (2011) shows regarding exams in Australia, texts need to reflect students' real and imagined worlds in order to be fair. For this reason, questions on the ESL evaluation were based on stories and

Table 5.3 Comparison of REAP and RHEAP

	REAP second phase (January 11–October 18, 2011)	RHEAP (January 31, 2012 to present)
Length of course	One three-hour meeting per week for 5 weeks	One three and a quarter hour meeting per week for 6 weeks
Organization of course	5–6.30pm ESL class 6.30–7pm food and conversation 7–8pm tutoring	5–6pm ESL class 6–6.45 health class in Arabic 6.45–7.15 dinner 7.15–8.15 tutoring
Childcare	Childcare offered	Children's program for healthy living plus homework help for older children
Student tracking/exams	No exam, tracking students' attendance Evaluation forms at the end of each session for both students and tutors	Health exam in Arabic and speaking English exam given by the tutors at beginning and end of each session
Participation	Average of five students finishing each session, two trained ESL instructors and one refugee instructor for the beginning level, one volunteer for childcare of one to four children	Average of 9 students finishing each session with a maximum of 27 students, 3 trained ESL instructors, 1 refugee instructor for the health component, 2–3 interns/volunteers for children's program with 8–15 children, 3–6 Iraqi refugee teenage volunteers and 1 Iraqi refugee program manager
Demography	Students were mostly single Iraqi men, though some Iraqi women, couples and children participated as well as a few human trafficking victims	Students are mostly Iraqi refugee women of varying ages (the oldest is 75), though one single Iraqi man attends, and multiple couples, the youngest child is 3 years old, only one family that comes is not Iraqi (they are from Syria)
Curriculum focus	Focus on employment at the advanced level, survival English with basic employment skills at the intermediate level and basic vocabulary at the lowest level	Advanced: Employment and conversational English Intermediate: Survival English, employment and health Beginning: Survival English and health vocabulary
Food	Bagels, drinks and potluck-style food brought by Muhammad and tutors	Iraqi women cook a healthy meal after discussing their menu with the nutritionist, always including whole grains, vegetables, fresh fruit, some meat and yoghurt drinks. They are reimbursed for all costs of food. Tutors bring a healthy dish to share, potluck style

situations I had heard the refugees engage in, such as being in a car accident and dealing with their children being bullied in school.

The health evaluation was written by the Iraqi nutritionist who lectured at each meeting. In the first version of the exam, each question was solely focused on the individual's habits, such as 'Do you smoke?' 'Do you get enough exercise?' and 'Do you get regular check-ups at the doctor?' This evaluation did not include knowledge demonstration, such as the causes of heart disease and diabetes or the symptoms of post-traumatic stress disorder (PTSD). Because I was concerned that we would not see the kind of habit changes that would show progress for our funder, I added knowledge demonstration questions to the exam based on the nutritionist's original questions. For example, after a habit question such as 'Do you smoke?', I added the question 'What are the health effects of smoking?', and I had the questions translated into Arabic. This evaluation was written and administered in Arabic, so that linguistic knowledge would not impede content knowledge. Interestingly, habit changes have occurred, so my fears were clearly based on my own assumptions about evaluations. In addition, the program's findings have been strengthened by the participation of the community through the creation of the health evaluation.

Once again, as community ownership of the program increased, so did participation in the program (Fridland & Dalle, 2002). Norton Peirce (1995) has argued that investment at the individual level is important in understanding language learning and its connections to power and identity. This can also be said for language programs: the community's investment in the program is tied up with individual and collective power (real and imagined), and the (ever-changing) identities of the participants. Just as participants (and their identities) change, so too must the program. Recently, the refugees in the program asked for citizenship classes in addition to the language, employment and health components, and because participatory programs must continue to change and adapt with their students, this component has been added.

Discussion

Throughout the development of RHEAP, participation was fostered and a dialogic relationship between the curriculum developer and the program participants was encouraged. The greater the extent to which the refugees took ownership of the program, the greater the participation in and success of the program. As Finn (2010) points out, when working with adult ESL learners who have experienced trauma, such as that which refugees have suffered, building a sense of community is pivotal to successful language learning and to the development of a successful program. In order to accomplish this, the strengths, resources and assets of the Iraqi refugee community were built upon by incorporating members of the community in student recruitment, food preparation, Arabic–English translation, management of the program and teaching English and health topics. For those refugees who were engaged in the teaching and development of the program, they gained experiences that could be translated into the workforce and they became key members in the Iraqi refugee community whose skills and knowledge are still sought by new arrivals. This empowers the individuals and community while nurturing new and important social bonds. Although traditional programs developed and administered through non-participatory means may provide an important service, they are not effective at addressing underlying social inequalities.

Participation in the research process and dissemination were at first challenging (students were not interested in keeping journals as a means of engaging in the research process), but recent collaboration between Mary and I have resulted in presentations of RHEAP to Church World Service and a local meeting of the rotary club as well as a workshop with local high school teachers. We are currently working together on researching the attitudes of Iraqi refugees in relation to the naturalization test and US citizenship. Mary is conducting interviews in Arabic and translating them, and I am writing our findings in a chapter in Loring and Ramanathan's upcoming volume *Language, Immigration and Naturalization: Legal and Linguistic Issues* (2016). Thus, participation in the research process is allowing Iraqi refugee voices to be heard in new ways through research.

The end product of RHEAP is not necessarily a copiable program that can be administered in other locations. The local context has been inextricable from the curriculum in that the curriculum depends upon the demography of the students, teachers, tutors and interns. It is, however, theoretically and provocatively generalizable (Fine, 2008) in that lessons about employment, health, survival, social oppression and forms of resistance may extend beyond the confines of this localized site, and may provoke a reimagining of current situations. Curricula developed in a participatory manner, such as Auerbach *et al.*'s (1996: 158) guidebook, show that 'participatory curriculum development is a powerful model for adult learners'. Furthermore, PAR allows researchers and program/curriculum developers to move away from a modernist worldview based on a positivist philosophy (Bradbury & Reason, 2003) in order to embrace multiple sources of knowledge from multiple voices. The fact that RHEAP has continued to grow over the past two years indicates that the program and its policies have been improving through these PAR practices.

Acknowledgments

I am deeply grateful to all those who contributed to RHEAP and the writing of this chapter. Special thanks to my partners at the resettlement agency, especially Robyn, David B., David D. and Debra, without whose support and belief in the vision of RHEAP, this program would never have been realized. My deepest gratitude to all of the refugees for inspiring me and teaching me so much about my community. Very special thanks to Muhammed, whose early support of REAP helped to grow the program, and to Mary, whose tireless efforts and commitment to her community showed through RHEAP's most significant growth. Thanks as well to all the community partners and volunteers who donated their time, energy and other resources to RHEAP, especially Elizabeth for taking over as director. And finally, thank you to Julia Menard-Warwick, Lenora Timm, Vaidehi Ramanathan and an anonymous reviewer for all the guidance and feedback at various stages of the writing.

Notes

(1) SIRC and all other individuals' names are pseudonyms.
(2) It was also at this meeting that SIRC agreed to allow me to use the program as the site for my research, and signed the IRB.

References

Auerbach, E. (1992) *Making Meaning Making Change: Participatory Curriculum Development for Adult ESL Literacy.* McHenry, IL: Center for Applied Linguistics and Delta Systems, Inc.
Auerbach, E. (ed.) (2002) *Community Partnerships.* Alexandria, VA: TESOL Publishing.
Auerbach, E., Barahona, B., Midy, J., Vaquierano, F., Zambrano, A. and Arnaud, J. (1996) *Adult ESL/Literacy: From the Community to the Community: A Guidebook for Participatory Literacy Training.* Mahwah, NJ: Lawrence Erlbaum Associates.
Belcher, D. (2006) What ESP is and can be: An introduction. In D. Belcher (ed.) *English for Specific Purposes in Theory and Action* (pp. 1–20). Ann Arbor, MI: University of Michigan Press, ELT.
Bradbury, H. and Reason, P. (2003) Issues and choice points for improving the quality of action research. In M. Minkler and N. Wallerstein (eds) *Community-Based Participatory Research for Health* (pp. 201–220). San Francisco, CA: Jossey-Bass.
Cornwall, A. and Jewkes, R. (1995) What is participatory research? *Social Science and Medicine* 41, 1667–1676.
Cranitch, M. (2010) Developing language and literacy skills to support refugee students in the transition from primary to secondary school. *Australian Journal of Language & Literacy* 33 (3), 255–267.
Delgado-Gaitan, C. (1994) Russian refugee families: Accommodating aspirations through education. *Anthropology & Education Quarterly* 25 (2), 137–155.
Dooley, K.T. and Thangaperumal, P. (2011) Pedagogy and participation: Literacy education for low-literate refugee students of African origin in a western school system. *Language and Education* 25 (5), 385–397.
Due, C. and Riggs, D. (2009) Moving beyond English as a requirement to 'fit in': Considering refugee and migrant education in South Australia. *Refuge* 26 (2), 55–64.
Elmeroth, E. (2003) From refugee camp to solitary confinement: Illiterate adults learn Swedish as a second language. *Scandinavian Journal of Educational Research* 47 (4), 431–449.
Finn, H.B. (2010) Overcoming barriers: Adult refugee trauma survivors in a learning community. *TESOL Quarterly* 44 (3), 586–596.

Freire, P. (1968) *Pedagogy of the Oppressed* (trans. M. Bergman Ramos). New York: The Seabury Press.

Fridland, G. and Dalle, T. (2002) Start with what they know; build with what they have: Survival skills for refugee women. In E. Auerbach (ed.) *Community Partnerships* (pp. 27–40). Alexandria, VA: TESOL Publishing.

Israel, B.A., Eng, E., Schulz, A.J. and Parker, E.A. (2005) Introduction to methods in community-based participatory research for health. In B.A. Israel, E. Eng, A.J. Schulz and E.A. Parker (eds) *Methods in Community-Based Participatory Research for Health* (pp. 3–26). San Francisco, CA: Jossey-Bass.

Kanno, Y. and Varghese, M.M. (2010) Immigrant and refugee ESL students' challenges to accessing four-year college education: From language policy to educational policy. *Journal of Language, Identity, and Education* 9 (5), 310–328.

Leudar, I., Hayes, J., Nekvapil, J. and Turner, J. (2008) Hostility themes in the media, community and refugee narratives. *Discourse & Society* 19 (2), 187–221.

Loring, A. and Ramanathan, V. (2016) *Language, Immigration and Naturalization: Legal and Linguistic Issues*. Bristol: Multilingnal Matters.

Menard-Warwick, J. (2002) 'Even I would like to be bilingual': Parents learning English in their children's school. In E. Auerbach (ed.) *Community Partnerships in ESL* (pp. 13–25). Alexandria, VA: TESOL Publishing.

Norton Pierce, B. (1995) Social identity, investment and language learning. *TESOL Quarterly* 29 (1), 9–31.

Nykiel-Herbert, B. (2010) Iraqi refugee students: From a collection of aliens to a community of learners. *Multicultural Education* 17 (3), 2–14.

Stevenson, J. and Willott, J. (2007) The aspiration and access to higher education of teenage refugees in the UK. *Compare: A Journal of Comparative Education* 37 (5), 671–687.

Tollefson, J. (1989) *Alien Winds: The Reeducation of America's Indochinese Refugees*. New York: Praeger.

Wallerstein, N. (1983) *Language and Culture in Conflict: Problem-Posing in the ESL Classroom*. Menlo Park, CA: Addison-Wesley.

Wallerstein, N., Duran, B., Minkler, M. and Foley, K. (2005) Developing and maintaining partnerships with communities. In B.A. Israel, E. Eng, A.J. Schulz and E.A. Parker (eds) *Methods in Community-Based Participatory Research for Health* (pp. 31–51). San Francisco, CA: Jossey-Bass.

Watkins, P.G., Razee, H. and Richters, J. (2012) 'I'm telling you...the language barrier is the most, the biggest challenge': Barriers to education among Karen refugee women in Australia. *Australian Journal of Education* 56 (2), 126–141.

Wigglesworth, G. (2011) Indigenous languages, bilingual education and English in Australia. In C. Norrby and J. Hajek (eds) *Uniformity and Diversity in Language Policy* (pp. 151–156). Bristol: Multilingual Matters.

6 Learning English, Speaking Hindi: The Paradox of (Language) Integration Among Nepalis in the United States

Tina Shrestha

Introduction

Every Sunday in a crowded, single-storey, windowless space with an unfinished basement and offices separated manually by built-in walls in a two-storey house in Woodside, Queens, 150–200 Nepali migrants, refugees and asylum seekers, primarily women, fill Adhikaar's[1] English as a second language (ESL) classrooms with their hushed conversations punctuated by sudden laughter and excruciating silence. In a brightly lit, open space, front of the main entrance, 15 women take their seats around two long wooden tables while others sit in the outer circle, sometimes joining the classroom conversation but often simply sitting next to their friends and relatives that they have not seen in weeks, sometimes months. Depending on the weekly topic and lesson plan, discussions in the classroom turn into an amusing series of anecdotes that ESL participants share from their workplace, and other times they evoke emotionally laden tales of hardship and suffering connected to lived experiences of integration into US society.

'Really, are there that many Nepalis in New York City? Have you gathered data that is representative of them?' I was often asked such questions by colleagues, friends and scholars in New York City, curious about my work with Nepalis, questions I usually tried to evade. Those familiar with the country's history and contemporary sociopolitical conditions have inquired, 'How is it that the end of the civil war[2] resulted in more Nepalis seeking political asylum and refuge in the US?' To some degree the answer lies in the question itself: Nepalis are becoming asylum seekers upon their entry into the US after escaping a decade-long (1996–2006) civil war in Nepal.

The protracted civil war and political instability in Nepal[3] caused decisive and irreversible infrastructural and human damage. The spread of the Maoist movement from rural areas to hill areas made the capital of

Kathmandu valley increasingly porous and interconnected with the rest of the country. Constant movement, rather than settlement or integration, became the norm for Nepalis. The emergent social and political spaces in the construction of a 'new' Nepali society – framed within the globalized language of national development, economic policies, ethnic identity politics and human rights – increasingly made possible new forms of sociality and facilitated an outmigration of Nepalis to the Middle East, Australia, the UK and the US. It is within this much longer, convoluted and contested history of political development, and the continued outmigration of Nepalis, that I situate the emergent integration practices of Nepalis as refugees and migrants in the US. Also, in writing this chapter, rather than trying to rationalize either the in/visibility or the representativeness of Nepalis' 'refugee' experiences, I depict people's interpretations of their everyday lives as migrants and refugees entangled with their labor and language integration in the US.

Over the course of two years (2009–2011), I spent many hours at Adhikaar with Nepali ESL teachers, participants, volunteers, community leaders, organizers and activists. The majority (90%) of people who come through Adhikaar are women in their late-thirties to mid-fifties. They comprise various ethnic and caste groups and diverse linguistic and regional backgrounds (Kathmandu, Pokhara, Solukhumbu, Mustang, Helumbu, India and Tibet). The numbers of years these women have lived in the US vary significantly from 6 months to 10 years. On the basis of interviews with and narratives collected from Nepali migrants, I bring together in this chapter two important elements in contemporary US migration, labor and the language integration process: (a) I document specific ways in which emergent migrant workers' coarticulate work experiences and learning English (re)create, if inadvertently, a mode of sociality; and consequently (b) their socioculturally mediated forms of responses to sustaining what they describe as 'better' employment, paradoxically contributing to their continued language racialization and labor subordination.

In a recent review essay, Dick (2011: 230) proposes that the literature on language and contemporary migration (to the US) focuses on the centrality of two interconnected processes: She writes 'the construction of English as a US national language' and 'the production of covert racializing discourses that (re)create "White public space" dominant' rendering 'racialized actors as entirely unacceptable in the US polity or at least as unacceptable' only in certain arenas not without 'monitor[ing] and sanction[ing] the use of "nonstandard" forms in spaces constituted as "public"'. Indeed, scholars have demonstrated that languages other than English are part of the 'public spaces' (Haviland, 2003; Reynolds & Orellana, 2009) in the US and any intervention concerning 'language problems' (Cameron, 1997; Leibowitz, 1984; Lippi-Green, 1997; Reyhner, 1992; Zentella, 1997b) consistently exacerbate and produce, rather than obliterate, social inequality and racialization. In this chapter, I try to elucidate this interconnection implicitly and not via the conventional division of labor. That is to say, I do not take my interlocutors' knowledge as a 'subjective' understanding of learning English or resisting its dominant usage in their attempt to migrant community formation[4] and use my analysis to reveal the 'objective' (read: factual) ways in which hegemonic ideologies underlying English language[5] acquisition produce and structure migrant lives and communities. Instead, I describe how working-class Nepali migrants understand, interpret and subsequently make meaning out of the hegemonic ideology concerning the *need* to learn, practice and speak English because, and not in spite, of the heightened awareness of their marginalized socioeconomic position as a linguistically and ethnically diverse people working primarily for South Asian and Caucasian employers. In particular, I trace grievances that domestic workers invariably coarticulated with their 'problem' with English that gradually revealed a complicated and deeply contradictory reality: Nepali migrants' declared a 'need' to access English and disengage from Hindi language despite readily accessible employment in the domestic labor industry upon migration.

A larger question, one beyond the scope of my argument here but implicated throughout, concerns the expectations of Nepali migrants to speak Hindi, not unconnected with the designation and reification of 'South Asians' in the US that invoke a static, homogeneous and Indian-centric social formation despite the prevalence of 'multiple nations and homelands' in South Asia (Viswewaran, 1997) and people with distinct migration patterns and histories.[6] This chapter seeks to open up similar discussions concerning 'South Asian' migrants' racial formations in the US through the analytical lens of language and racialization, primarily employed by scholars of contemporary US immigration, and particularly Latino studies (De Genova & Ramos-Zayas, 2003; Perez, 2003). Attention to Nepali migrant workers' subjective responses to speaking Hindi at work, and (un)successful strategies in speaking 'good' English, for instance, allow an incisive critique that combines structural conditions with racialized integration in the US and everyday language practices upon which the broader formation of the 'South Asian' community and migrant labor economy thrive. This study seeks to open up the space for advancing research on recently arrived migrants from South Asia, whose heterogeneous lives and work experiences in the US depend on and simultaneously exceed current interpretations of South Asian migrant communities. In particular, I trace how Nepalis as workers participate in their continued labor subordination through languages – speaking Hindi to retain employment and simultaneously learning English to negotiate better employment – extending the 'need' to access English beyond the realm of language and identity politics to implicate language itself as a *problem* and a possible, if temporary, *solution*, providing the conditions of possibility of their continued labor subordination in the US.

To be clear, I do not read English-speaking 'ability' itself, in terms of linguistic aptitude or skill,[7] as a potential source of social transformation or a uniform experience of upward mobility for its learners and speakers. Rather, I describe and analyze the specific ways that Nepali workers interpret and explain – and the particular mode of relating that information – their 'need' to access English that do not reveal a dominant, straightforward narrative of migrants 'integrating' into US society, negotiating and navigating the labor industry. In this sense, my engagement with the burgeoning literature on language and contemporary labor migration to the US, employing the analytical lens of racialization, arises out of an apparent paradox: scholars continue to severely criticize, and rightly so, the rhetoric that promotes 'lack of *skill* in English as an index of "backwardness" and "irrationality"' (Bauman & Briggs, 2003; Heller, 1999, quoted in Dick, 2011: 231, emphasis mine) among non-English-speaking, working-class migrants, yet the underlying supposition that the acquisition of English should be indexed as a 'skill' has gone largely unchallenged, if and when acknowledged in ethnographic works (De Genova [2005] and Urciuoli [1996] are noteworthy exceptions), and the subsequent indexing of 'work' performed by non-English-speaking migrant workers as 'unskilled'.

I expand on this insight on the pervasiveness of everyday racialization and language acquisition through my own ethnographic engagement and analysis of Adhikaar's ESL classroom conversations with and among Hindi-speaking Nepalis. Following Goldstein (2008), who has demonstrated the value of the ethnographic method in facilitating multilingual classrooms and negotiating diverse linguistic identities that allow student-participants to redirect silences in classroom settings, I emphasize moments of silence as sites for both sustaining productive discussion and regenerating conversations otherwise left unexplored. In particular, I document how the Nepali workers' declared *need* to speak 'good' English, often articulated after a momentary silence and always in relation to their *desire* not to continue speaking Hindi, ran counter to the actual conditions to obtaining and securing employment as live-in or live-out maids, nannies and housekeepers in New York City. The pattern I followed regarding the emphasis on speaking 'good' English regardless of the actual 'need' to obtain employment and the subsequent failure to escape racialization draw on studies (De Genova, 2002; Ramos-Zayas, 2011; Urciuoli, 2008) that critique the dominant paradigm that concludes that migrants' 'inability' to speak English prevents their visibility and active participation in the labor market, making them more vulnerable to labor exploitation. Following De Genova, I argue that it is through speaking 'good' English that Nepali migrants participate in their own effective labor subordination and, paradoxically, produce the conditions of possibility of their continued racialization.

Speaking 'Good' English, Finding Better Jobs

During my first few sessions as an ESL instructor at Adhikaar, I quickly became aware of just how essential learning English was for Nepali New Yorkers. The concerns related to learning and speaking English were interconnected with ESL participants' everyday work practices and experiences of integrating into US society. It compelled me to reconsider the dominant assumptions and narrative about speaking 'good' English to obtain employment in the US. The more I learned, the more confused I became. In-depth conversations with ESL participants later revealed that acquiring English was intricately connected with their desire not to speak Hindi. It was also related to finding better jobs. However, it was not until after almost six months into facilitating English classes that I learned that better jobs did not necessarily translate into acquiring work in a different industry, say in an office setting, where intense manual labor would not be required. For many, it simply meant getting better pay and manageable work hours at their current jobs as housekeepers, maids and nannies. For others, it meant having a better, interchangeably used as more understanding and sympathetic, if not always associated with white American, employer to deal with everyday. But all of them unanimously agreed that a live-out job was still better than a live-in job because you did not feel trapped in someone else's house or become involved, unwittingly, in their lives. It is within these constraints, differently defined and elaborated by individual migrant workers and the anecdotes they shared from work, that the meaning of better was explained to me with vivid descriptions and in painstaking detail.

First day as an ESL instructor

Since Adhikaar had limited resources, I joined a pool of volunteers who had been teaching English on weekends for almost a year. The class I was instructed to facilitate was one that an ESL volunteer had left in the middle of the nine-week ESL session. I was there as a substitute. As soon as I entered the classroom, I was taken aback by the warm welcome – the mixture of curious look and genuine suspicion – that I received from the ESL participants. I politely took the empty seat by the door in that crowded room.

Another volunteer was already facilitating the class. The topic they were discussing that day involved placing calls, and answering and taking messages in English. They were doing role-plays and participants were going around practicing making and answering calls. The volunteer was playing the role of a caller and each ESL participant took a turn responding to whatever question she was asked by the caller. The participants were asked to practice and simultaneously memorize the following phrases and questions related to a telephone conversation:

'Could you please speak very slowly? I cannot understand what you are saying'.

'Could you please spell your name and number for me'.

'Could you please repeat what you said?'

I sat in the classroom and observed them; I was both fascinated and perplexed by this telephone exercise. The ESL participants were receiving instruction and information not only on what to say but also *how* to indicate their 'limited' English-speaking ability to the caller on the other end. As I was trying to make sense of this exercise, I was asked to take over the class by the executive director of the organization. Having had no previous experience facilitating an English class and in that particular context of instructing adult Nepalis, I approached the class with extreme caution and moderate enthusiasm.

I continued with the telephone conversation exercise they were doing. I introduced ways for them to remember details from a telephone conversation. I found myself lecturing on the usefulness of taking notes when answering calls and taking messages for someone else. I went as far as to instruct the ESL participants to make a list, in order of importance, every time they had to answer calls and take messages. I wrote the following words on a blackboard:

Name:
Number:
Message:
Day/time of the call:

When I turned around there were blank stares on people's faces accompanied by an uncomfortable silence. The perplexed faces and half-smiles intimidated me at first. Trying not to be outdone by my nervousness, I quickly changed the topic with what I thought was simply a rhetorical question to generate conversation: why do you *want* to learn English?

I noticed guarded looks being replaced by bright eyes, tensed faces gradually loosening up and transforming into communicative gestures, and hands flying everywhere. In a flurry of Nepali the classroom became alive.

'We *need to* talk on the phone and take messages for our bosses!' one of them exclaimed.

'We *have to* tell their kids to eat, to do homework, and to go to sleep on time', another added.

'We *cannot do* grocery if we do not know the names of the vegetables and fruits that our bosses want us to buy from organic stores', someone from the back shouted.

'We *have to* learn all the names of the cleaning supplies to do our work everyday'.

'We *need to* take the train and change buses to go to work in Long Island, New Jersey, or Connecticut'.

I was struck by these answers. Not a single response had to do with personal reasons (other than for work purposes) to learn and practice English. English for its own sake was not an issue raised by my eager participants. Rather, they collectively voiced the necessity to learn English to make their work – everyday lives – somewhat manageable. On a very basic level, their responses revealed to me my own presumption, one based on a limited and somewhat naïve outlook (often arising out of a privileged social position occupied by 'native' and/or near-native English speakers), about the very framing of the question.

In an attempt to continue the conversation, I mentioned that I understood everything they had just said. I asked them to clarify and expand on what they specifically meant by talking on the phone and taking messages for their bosses. The ESL participants then went on to relate to me that although they spoke 'some' English, they did not speak 'good' English and, as a consequence, were hesitant and even anxious to answer calls at work, take messages and relay them to their employers. Take, for example, the following anecdote shared by Sanju[8] didi,[9] a 48-year-old, Hyolmo Sherpa woman from Helambu region, located 72 km northeast of Kathmandu, who had been working as a live-in housekeeper in Long Island for the last nine years:

> Once a person, who identified herself as Vera, had called for her employer. Because Vera sounded like *Bheda* [sheep in Nepali] Sanju didi thought it would not be difficult for her to remember the name. When the employer came home that night, she could not recall the name of the caller. She knew it sounded like an animal in Nepali but could not remember the animal that the name reminded her of. She ended up telling her employer that *Bakhra* [goat in Nepali] had called while she was out!

All of us broke into laughter when she finished her story. But Sanju didi suddenly became silent and everyone joined her in her silence. It was a comfortable silence – one with which my participants seemed familiar – that made me feel uncomfortable and, at once, a complete outsider. Although I could have interrupted the awkward silence by asking a follow-up question, I decided not to. For it was awkward only for me and not for my ESL participants.

It was one of the early moments during fieldwork that I learned not only to observe the power of collective voice but also to acknowledge the significance of a shared silence among the participants. Sanju didi's anecdote is then emblematic of the stories that the ESL participants recounted to me for several weeks: the difficulty of answering phone calls at work. This difficulty, they emphasized, had to do with their 'limited' understanding of English and a justification for their need to speak 'good' English. These stories, narrated to me with a mixture of light-heartedness and anxiety, while generating a dynamic classroom atmosphere, revealed to me a fairly complicated worldview, and a productive one, to engage with and simultaneously sustain a meaningful conversation with my interlocutors. Once I was able to follow the logic of their answers, the supposed (intended) meaning of my question – 'why do you *want* to learn English?' – had to be revisited and reframed. I became acutely aware that the question was not why (or why not) Nepali migrant workers *wanted to* but why they felt that they *needed to* speak 'good' English and, most importantly, why and how English had come to be seen as something to be *wanted*. At the same time, this concern, seemingly self-evident, was not conveyed to me explicitly.

In that first class session, I learned that there was something just as important as, and even contradictory to, their collective claim about needing to speak 'good' English that needed to be observed closely: the question of silence. Indeed, moments of grave and awkward silences, which sometimes entered the ESL classroom unannounced and oftentimes deliberate, ended up transforming both the classroom space and the direction of our conversation. Unraveling such moments to better illuminate the intricate relationship between workers' individual experience and collective belonging is the task of the next section. Rather than isolate silence, which periodically interrupted our ESL conversation, as a literal act – an *absence* of speech – I consider it in this context as a *presence* entangled with and beyond speaking 'good' English.

In what follows, I trace the gradual transformation of the ESL classroom into a productive ethnographic space not only through continuous dialogue and intense engagement but also through mediation of momentary, abrupt silences. Here, I acknowledge silence as an important and even necessary collective action, performed by the workers, which eventually helped me follow their rationale and understand their unique concern related to speaking 'good' English – not wanting to speak Hindi and, by extension, not working for Indian families; and obtaining 'better' jobs, which translated as working for 'Americans', synonymously seen as white, middle-class families in the same labor industry.

'Just learn Hindi, you will get jobs in the US!'

For the next several weeks, I continued to empathetically listen to numerous work-related scenarios similar to the one recounted by Sanju didi the first day of our class. By now, I had become quite familiar with the issue of speaking 'good' English. However, I kept wondering how these anecdotes, often narrated with a mixture of cynical laughter and distress, were relevant to the workplace responsibilities that they had listed on the first day of class.

A few weeks later, a related discussion ensued in one of the class sessions where I asked about whether they needed to speak 'good' English or know English at all to keep doing what they were doing as live-in/ live-out maids, domestic workers and housekeepers. The ESL participants merely stared at me. I could not tell if they were truly confused by my inquiry or annoyed that I should ask such a question after having facilitated English class for nearly seven weeks. I elaborated the question. I explained that I only had the English language *skill* to communicate and facilitate their class, and furthermore they were the ones with everyday work experience and skills to make the class useful. Then I added a contradictory remark without giving much thought to it: *You know, if you practice English everyday, it will get better over time.*

They simply nodded and some even put on a forced smile. Nobody responded for a long time.

'Tapainko kaam ta sajilo cha ni, English padaune ho. Tara hamro ta dherai gahro cha ghaar ko kaam' ['You have an easy job of teaching us English. Ours is domestic work!'] Mina didi declared. She was a 38-year-old migrant woman from Thongche, Manang region, located northwest of Kathmandu Valley, who used to be a teacher in her village. She came to the US three years ago, and had been working as a live-in nanny in a South Asian household in New Jersey.

Everyone became silent. I was dumbfounded and embarrassed by this pointed but quite accurate, if unexpected, remark. Although not necessarily directed as an accusation, it forced me to stop talking and start reflecting on my role as an ESL facilitator and an ethnographer. It made me extremely self-conscious to continue our ESL conversation. I started speaking in Nepali, instead, in hopes of reversing the situation that had resulted in an awkward silence.

As I was speaking, Tenzin, a 32-year-old Tibetan-Nepali, who was born and grew up in Tibet and worked in Nepal and India before coming to New York four years ago, interrupted me. 'Can you please not speak Nepali? I do not understand what you are saying!' she said firmly. She looked serious.

I was taken aback and utterly lost. I thought the ESL participants were all 'Nepalis' since the organization provided services to Nepalis and Nepali-speaking communities in New York City.

'What language do you speak then?' I inquired with hesitation. It was one of those moments, where, instead of questioning my own linguistic ability to facilitate the class and/or knowledge to meet the participants' needs, I was putting the burden of answering on her. I was ensuring the direction of our ESL conversation. But this time, I was also taking my responsibility, or my job, of teaching English seriously, as Mina didi had rightly pointed out. 'I am from Tibet. I speak Tibetan and Hindi', Tenzin said.

Meanwhile, I caught students from my previous ESL sessions exchange silent glances. Then Sanju didi came to my rescue: *'Bahini, haami ta Sherpa ho ni, tapain po Nepali. Haamilai Nepali ramro aundaina'* ['Sister, you see we are Hyolmo Sherpas and not Nepali like you. We cannot even speak Nepali properly'] We did not go to school at home'.

I was even more confused by Sanju didi's comment about not being 'Nepali'. But before I could ask for an explanation, she changed the subject. Or rather, she redirected our ESL conversation to my earlier inquiry: 'You are right. Even though we do not speak good English, we have experience and what you just said skills...yes, we have that. We know how to cook for them, clean their bathrooms, and take care of their kids' ('their' meaning the employers). There was a hint of uncertainty in her voice. '... but they [employers] know this already', she continued, 'You know my boss always tells me that I will not be able to leave her family. She tells me that even if I find another family, I will not be happy. I just don't talk afterward'. All of us asked Sanju didi if her boss was correct.

She laughed sarcastically. 'Of course it's not true', she said. 'It will not be difficult to leave that job...if I get paid more money somewhere else, why will I stay?' In an elevated voice she added, 'Does she think I am stupid?!' Suddenly, her tone became solemn. 'That's why I am taking English class every weekend. I have a live-in job now. Before I get fired I want to find a live-out job for the same money or more'. She said it in one breath and became quiet. In a split second, her smile vanished. The enthusiasm and light-heartedness with which she began her story was now causing her discomfort.

Just when I thought I was starting to have some control over the direction of the classroom discussion, the other four Hyolmo Sherpas – all Sanju didi's relatives – said something to her in Hyolmo. This time, Mina didi, Tenzin, three of the new participants from the Upper Mustang, northwestern region of Nepal and I were completely lost. Although we did not know what the others were saying to her, it became clear from Sanju didi's reaction that they were trying to console her. But console her of what, I wondered. I was no longer steering our classroom conversation.

'Could you all please speak English because some of us do not understand your language and this is English class', I requested, trying to lighten up the classroom environment, and once again, to redirect our conversation to the ESL topic for the day.

No one responded to me. Everyone was busy talking to Sanju didi in Hyolmo. Just when I thought we had successfully diverted the piercing silence generated by Mina didi's remark, in response to my initial statement, it became evident to me that it was only being dislocated temporarily. A more solemn classroom atmosphere was now replacing the silence. The ESL classroom was gradually transforming into a space for the participants to share their stories and grievances from work.

Then, one of the Hyolmo participants, Pelki didi, Sanju didi's sister-in-law, also from Helambu region in Nepal, offered us an interpretation, only to follow up with a rhetorical question: 'We are telling Sanju didi that at least she is not asked by her American boss to speak Hindi to the kids she looks after. Now you tell us, Tina Miss, how can we practice English when our *sahu* [boss] always tells us to speak Hindi at home...I mean, at work?'

I tried to respond to her question rather clumsily: 'So you do not understand Hindi?' By now I had stopped being obsessively self-conscious of what I was asking. I simply wanted to join the conversation and find out what was causing distress among the Hyolmo Sherpa participants.

'Oh you have a very good job then, why you complain?' the Mustange participants told Sanju didi, completely ignoring my question.

'Maybe your boss is right then! You will not be happy if you leave that job', Tenzin added, almost dismissive of Sanju didi's emotional state.

I was shocked by Tenzin's inappropriate or rather insensitive response to Sanju didi. At the same time, I was getting frustrated, being the only one completely lost and left outside of what seemed to be an intense and engaging conversation taking place among ESL participants. At that moment, my job as an ESL facilitator seemed both insufficient and less useful to facilitating any conversation, let alone meaningful exchanges. I became more interested in learning about this peculiar connection between domestic work and speaking Hindi.

Again, Pelki didi offered to become my interpreter although everyone was already speaking English! 'You see, Tina *bahini*', she took a deep breath and thought for a minute. Then continued, 'So even with all the work experience we have, our bosses do not trust us. We go to an interview and they always ask if we speak English. And we just tell them we speak Hindi. That is why we work for Indian *sahujis*'.

Sanju didi, after composing herself, corrected Pelki didi, 'Yes, but if you don't say you speak Hindi, then you won't get any work'.

'That is why I want to speak good English. I do not want to speak Hindi anymore', Pelki didi emphasized, interrupting Sanju didi. And everyone in the room nodded in agreement.

Mina didi, who was now quietly observing everyone's reaction, including mine, offered to further enlighten me. Perhaps it was evident from my facial expression that although I was following the various explanations and reasons given for learning English, I was finding it difficult to make the connection between learning English, not speaking Hindi and getting a job. She kindly elaborated for me: 'We all understand Hindi. That is why we come here...to speak English. Our Indian *sahujis* in the US don't want their children to forget their language, so they want their children to speak Hindi at home. And that is why we speak Hindi at work. Where is the time to practice English, Miss?'

'You see, after living in the US and working for all these years, we speak Hindi very well!' Tenzin said sarcastically. Her comment generated laughter from everyone.

'You know, Tina *bahini*, we tell our families back home that their Hindi will improve after they come to the US', Pelki didi teasingly added.

'We tell them "Just learn Hindi, you will get jobs in the US!"' Mina didi exclaimed.

And so another ESL session ended in laughter, leaving me amused, somewhat lost and longing.

The production of silent migrant workers

The workers' collective grievances and contradictory statement of not wanting to speak Hindi, working for white, middle-class, 'American' families, unanimously perceived as better jobs offer underlying reasons, if inadequate explanations, for learning English. However, employing such a reading as an analytical end is to overlook an extensive and thorough literature critiquing the dominant, parochial and rather unimaginative narrative advocating the 'need' of non-English-speaking migrants to learn English upon their arrival in the US.[10] It is also to completely miss the analytic quality of a rather convoluted process of contemporary racialization through language and labor subordination.

Concerning the seemingly harmless issue of speaking Hindi as live-in and live-out domestic workers, my interlocutors pointed out to me the inverse relationship between speaking 'good' English and not wanting to speak Hindi. The inherent contradiction surrounding their desire not to speak Hindi and the palpable fear of unemployment affirmed just the contrary of Mina didi's cynical pronouncement: while they advise their family members living in Nepal or India to learn Hindi, the workers themselves disliked having to speak Hindi, despite the likelihood of obtaining and retaining employment, and looked forward to learning English. Indeed, many of them had even come to see certain grievances and frustrations as business as usual, if not unreasonable, so long as they were not asked to speak Hindi by their employers. The Mustange participants' dismissive comment to Sanju didi – '*Oh you have a very good job then, why you complain?*' – is indicative of such cynicism. Sanju didi also implicitly confirmed this reality when she added to Pelki didi's explanation on how they often admit to their potential bosses that they speak Hindi during job interviews: '*Yes, but if you don't say you speak Hindi, then you won't get any work*'.

Migrant workers' intense ambivalence toward speaking Hindi is inseparable from their declared 'need' to learn English: an evidence of their utter dependence on the labor market that the workers know that employers, potential and current, invariably benefit from their continued subordination. In Sanju didi's view, and all those who had previously worked or were working for South Asian families, declaring one's knowledge of Hindi language offered a realistic and readily accessible solution to obtaining employment. Tenzin and Pelki didi's added remarks that their Hindi improved after living in the US reflect a rather convoluted sociopolitical reality of Nepali migrants. The engagement surrounding having to speak too much Hindi and not enough English, as Nepali workers described, were both work-related concerns. According to the workers, the better alternative to not speaking Hindi, and by extension not working for South Asian families, translated into the reality of working in the same industry for Americans, synonymously understood as white families, where speaking 'good' English would be required of migrant workers. Sanju didi's articulation of this blatant irony elicited Tenzin's equally poignant and sarcastic remark, made with both annoyance and apprehension: *'Maybe your boss is right then! You will not be happy if you leave that job'.* Tenzin's admonition signals a recognition, and not a difference in opinion, of a bleak possibility arising out of a shared social position as migrant workers. Further, her pointed and cynical remark paradoxically gave coherence to Sanju didi's earlier assertion that employers are often aware of workers' perpetual anxiety surrounding unemployment despite their skills and actual work experiences as domestic workers from which potential employers, invariably, benefit: *'...but they know this already'.* In pointing out this fact, Sanju didi was actually engaging with other workers and me in the classroom and simply (re)affirming the silence surrounding the common knowledge: the unequal power relationship that exists between employers, South Asians or Caucasians and domestic workers. Her pronouncement, which others in the classroom also attested to, merely established the well-known fact: it is seldom about the knowledge that employers do or do not possess that make them unable to relate to workers' subjective experiences. Rather, it is the generally agreed silence around the pervasive complicity of migrant workers in the social reproduction of their own marginality.

Migrant workers are wary of more than being asked to speak Hindi and speaking 'good' English. They also fear that walking out on their current jobs will only make them more vulnerable to unemployment in the future. 'Do you know our American boss asks all kinds of questions during an interview...as if they are hiring you for office work?' One of the Mustange participants, who had arrived from Nepal six months previously, took me aside one afternoon after class and shared a recent incident. She continued, 'You know my cousin left her job after working for an Indian family for seven years. She speaks good English, but when we both went for the same job interview, I got hired and not her. When I asked my boss why my cousin, who had more work experience and spoke better English, was not hired, my boss told me that she did not have a bright and pleasant face like me and seemed more reserved. Can you believe that? Are they hiring us to clean their houses and take care of their children or look pretty? How can you look happy after having spent all your life cleaning bathrooms in America anyway?' She later learned that her boss had contacted her cousin's former employer for a recommendation. The details of the conversation were never revealed to me, but the story itself offers an unsettling paradox: there is no single logic behind obtaining, what workers interpreted as, better employment, yet it did not deter workers from learning English. Further, workers already employed by Caucasian families, like Sanju didi and a Mustange participant, were the ones adamant about speaking 'good' English.

Inasmuch as workers' desire not to speak Hindi is inversely related to the reality of obtaining readily accessible employment notwithstanding, their declared 'need' to speak 'good' English for securing employment also suggests a reverse logic. For speaking 'good' English, which has very little to do with resolving immediate employment problems in the first place, as the above anecdote and ESL participants' conversation illuminate, ultimately provides neither job security nor an escape from racialization through language. On the contrary, workers participate in their effective labor subordination and continued racialization by speaking English. Take, for instance, Sanju didi's account of her silent response to her employer's rather obtuse comment. Still the poignant retelling of the incident and Sanju didi's question – *'Does she think I am stupid?!'* – directed at her absent boss, and not to us, exemplifies, on a very basic level, the dilemma of having obtained, what other workers considered, a better job. In posing that question and revealing her employer's absurd logic, Sanju didi was implicitly avowing what a community organizer and an interlocutor/colleague once said to me in passing: *'Bahini,* in this country, people think you are stupid if you do not speak good English. Better to remain silent'.

One of the real reasons for discomfort, as exemplified by Sanju didi's emotional outburst and Tenzin's seemingly tactless response, was facing constant humiliation at work. Workers' 'limited' English language ability, as they insisted, was fatal since it constantly exposed them to being misunderstood at work, or worse, being *understood* as stupid. In light of this serious matter that workers' explained to me, Sanju didi's proclamation – *'Does she think I am stupid!'* – takes on a new meaning, a life of its own and a potentially powerful self-realization. Embedded in her pronouncement, which other participants attested to by silently witnessing and later sharing her silence, is the possibility of two-sided interpretations: (a) workers are always looking for better options (i.e. better pay, work hours, etc.) no matter the constraints of what 'better' may translate into as far as obtaining employment in the same industry goes; and (b) employers who assume and verbalize that workers, as live-in maids, would continue to stay in their homes even if they had better options and improved social-economic conditions, say getting a better paid or a live-out job elsewhere, must be stupid.

As such, it is particularly revealing to consider an alternative reading of Sanju didi's statement, juxtaposed with the everyday shared silence among participants, beyond participants' acknowledgment of their similarly situated conditions of marginality. Implicit in her sarcastic laughter and silence is the painfully obvious response to her own rhetorical question – '*I am not stupid*' – and further, the inverse of her proclamation – '*Is she [her boss] stupid to think that I would stay if I got a better job?*' This is a probable interpretation, one that is hopeful. Still another, equally plausible and important interpretation of her response as silence is simply that – silence. No word could have possibly transcended the gulf that already existed between her *silenced* encounter with her employer. Hence, Sanju didi's decisive statement: '*I just don't talk afterward*'.

It is the ordinariness of Sanju didi's silenced experience at work, which other participants could immediately relate to even if not everyone agreed, that is not outside but within the condition of possibility of becoming silent. Her reenactment of the grave silence provided an important ground for other participants to share their work experiences and grievances. In expressing disappointment in her employer, followed by cynical laughter and silence, there was no need to speak further. Read as such, silence is a rule, and not an exception, in situations like the one Sanju didi described and other workers heeded in agreement. In narrating the episode of her abrupt interaction at work, Sanju didi was reenacting her *everyday* silenced experience for other workers and me. It is within this context of silence that I want to reread Sanju didi's *chosen* silent response: there is nothing left to say to someone whose absurd rationale prevents him or her from even considering the possibility of another's point of view. Interpreted this way, silence then becomes a deliberate *choice* of disengagement. It is not being unable but refusing to engage in a conversation. This refusal of engagement further makes not knowing or speaking English – whether to defend one's position or to simply participate in a verbal battle – completely irrelevant.

The irony, of course, is that the language in which workers considered themselves unskilled was the basis to relate their complaints about work in the context of the ESL classroom. The initial anxiety that the workers voiced regarding their need to speak English, so as not to speak Hindi and to obtain better jobs, did not suddenly disappear with the renewed classroom engagement about the specificities of their working conditions. Instead, it only allowed participants to articulate the point with which they were all too familiar: intense self-realization that grievances and complaints from work were seldom about the actual *work* they performed or even about having to speak Hindi. In sum, it was workers' keen awareness of the incessant 'problem' with English language itself, revealing a still greater irony: speaking 'good' English should become the very medium through which they express, and not necessarily overcome, the limitations provided by the language at work. As Brian Morgan (2004) has compellingly shown that certain teaching modals can allow language learners to seriously address their feelings of ambivalence and to link them with the macro-structural constraints of society, so the ESL classroom offered a similar space and opportunity for Nepali migrant workers to acknowledge their (perceived) problems with languages as deeply enmeshed in everyday work-related issues.

Conclusion: Working the Language

How can one make sense of the production of the 'need' to speak English in the context of the broader sociopolitical consequences of racialization and migrant labor subordination? I have primarily focused on workers' subjective responses to their desire not to speak Hindi despite readily accessible employment in the domestic labor market and their speaking 'good' English that contributed, ironically, to the workers' effective labor subordination and continued racialization. In this paradoxical relationship, migrant workers, who occupy socially marginalized positions in US society and are perceived to lack English language 'skills', depend on racialized and exploitative labor practices and simultaneously experience racialization through language. In connecting the everyday experiences of racialization through labor and language, the workers' interpretations of their lives and working conditions are congruent with scholars' call to reframe contemporary migration to the US as inseparable from labor exploitation (Burroway, 1976; Harris, 1995). Drawing on their individual and collective experiences, Nepali workers eloquently articulated the opposing effects of speaking 'good' English and the limitations afforded by speaking Hindi. This pattern signals a structural context where migrant racialization is contingent on their frustration with the *excess* of Hindi language and simultaneously the perpetual 'need' for, and not a complete 'lack' of, English language.

Labor subordination and racialization through language both inform workers' views and opinions of accessing English (De Genova, 2002) and further shape their work experiences in terms of linguistic 'need'. From the vantage point offered by his field site and ethnographic engagement with Mexican migrant workers as a workplace-based ESL instructor, Nicholas De Genova (2005) argues, essentially, that to understand the effects of racialization one must understand the highly exploitative and precarious manual labor that non-English-speaking Mexican migrant workers are exposed to everyday in Chicago. He offers an important differentiation: the particularities of Mexican migrant workers' experiences of racialization that he examines unfold in the workers' everyday interactions with the workplace management personnel who consistently regard their supposed labor 'ineffectivity' as a condition to and a consequence of their 'inability' to communicate in English. This language 'inability' or 'problem', De Genova suggests, is predicated on creating a need for workplace-based ESL classes for Mexican workers. The requirement for workers to speak English is far from being innocent. It contributes, De Genova (2005: 35) writes, to the 'generally dehumanizing [experience], displac[ing] the full extent of communication and creative expression possible in the workers' first language [Spanish]'. De Genova (2005: 38) thus argues, 'the production of language is itself a form of production, a production of language that could not be separated from the language of production: the language of "making production" (meeting the production quota), the language of factory, the language of exploitation and labor subordination, the language of oppression'. He further explains that this is related to workers' predicament of learning the language – English – which provides the conditions of possibility for the 'racialization of their [workers'] own language [Spanish] as a palpable feature of the discrimination against them' (De Genova, 2005: 45). De Genova's (2005: 52) engagement with Mexican migrant workers as an ESL instructor leads him to conclude that the workers needed 'to speak English in their confrontations with power – in the United States, English is the language of power'. Or, as one of his interlocutors' succinctly put it: 'para defenderse, to defend yourself' (De Genova, 2005: 52). These contradictions and concerns notwithstanding, De Genova's work among Mexican migrant workers in Chicago illuminates the pervasiveness of the everyday practices of racialization *through* language and labor subordination.

Extending De Genova's insight and engagement, I have argued here that Nepali migrant workers not only acknowledge but also anticipate their continued participation in racialized labor as mediated by linguistic subordination, whether in terms of their declared need to speak English or their desire not to speak Hindi, unsettling the lucid opposition between language and labor subordination. If in speaking Hindi, Nepali workers become a visible mass of labor supply to South Asian households, in speaking English they become a silent and desirable mass of laborers. In explaining how racialized migrant labor is already linguistically mediated, I have drawn attention to the ways in which migrants' collective complaints are both *due to* and *about* work where speaking English, primarily, is a work-related issue. That is to say, the specific ways in which Nepali workers make sense of and express their work 'problems' and 'concerns' are invariably about language subordination integral to the broader process of 'maintaining and renewing' migrant labor (Burroway, 1976). Whether labor subordination is about overt conditions of racialization that focus on language practices or whether processes of racialization are directly addressed and linked to the very conditions of migrant labor subordination, workers' everyday experiences and views of racialized labor and language are constitutive. Nepali migrants both position themselves and are socially positioned within the US as 'low-skilled' workers, whose subjective responses emanating from work result from the reproduction of their marginality.

For Nepali workers see English as a work-related issue, informing their decisions to continue speaking 'good' English while fully knowing their participation in their own continued marginalization through subordinate labor inclusion. In their continued acceptance of their marginalized reality, many workers strive to limit their experiences of humiliation by refusing to speak Hindi and becoming reluctant participants in English language classes. Their logic to continue learning English is, perhaps, inaccessible to, if not beyond the imagination of monolingual speakers, while their participation in the racialized labor economy in the US is a clear testament of the broader sociocultural assumptions of, or rather what counts as, speaking 'good' English.

Acknowledgments

I am grateful to the Institute for the Social Sciences at Cornell University and Adhikaar in New York City for their generous support of the research. I am indebted to my student-participants, community organizers and members of the Nepali migrant community in Queens for their generosity and patience, and sharing with me their everyday experiences. I would also like to thank Nicholas De Genova, Christie Shrestha, Reighan Gillam, Bernardo Brown, Emily Feuerherm and Vaidehi Ramanathan for their helpful comments on previous drafts of this chapter.

Notes

(1) As a resource center for Nepali migrants, asylum seekers and refugees, Adhikaar works with and provides direct services, including English language classes, leadership and employment training, annual health fare and legal and medical translation and interpretation services. In addition to offering services and programs, it conducts advocacy work, organizing and mobilizing people around immigration, worker's rights and labor-related issues and concerns.

(2) What began as rural uprisings against the Nepali state in the Western districts (Rolpa and Rukum) of Nepal in 1996, the Maoist guerrilla war quickly spread throughout the country and resulted in a nationwide civil war claiming thousands of lives (see Thapa & Sijapati [2004], Thapa [2003] and Hutt [2004] for a comprehensive study of the political and social history of the growth of the Maoist armed conflict).

(3) The Nepali civil war reached its peak of brutality in 2001–2002, coinciding with the aftermath of the September 2001 events, which brought Nepal into the limelight of international media. The events leading up to numerous ceasefires in 2002, 2003 and 2006 and the establishment of the interim government in 2007 brought the United Nations (UN)-supported peace accords and in particular, the United Nations Missions in Nepal (UNMIN), to draft a new constitution. In collaboration with several local and international non-governmental organizations (NGOs), including the International Crisis Group (ICG), Nepal had its parliamentary constituent assembly election in 2008. The peace process

facilitated the Maoist Party's entry into the Nepali government through a democratic electoral process. The victory of the Maoist Party in the constituent assembly election and their entry into mainstream politics initiated debates over social justice and human rights juxtaposed with continued economic stagnation and questions of political violence. The continued power struggle between the Nepali Army and the Maoists led to the withdrawal of the Maoist Party from the government in May 2009, leading to more political uncertainty. In August 2011, the Nepali state found its 'future' in the hands of the Maoist Party under the leadership of Dr Baburam Bhattarai from the Unified Communist Party of Nepal – Maoist Party.

(4) Studies that compel a re-evaluation of core assumptions surrounding linguistic practices among racialized migrant communities are in their nascent stage. Scholars specifically document the materialization of everyday discourse and practices among migrants, who are assumed targets of both 'access' to and 'need' for English language, and away from the so-called 'white public' spaces (Hill, 1998). Increasingly, studies (Ramos-Zayas, 2003, 2010; Reyes, 2009; Shanker, 2008) emphasize causes and consequences of language socialization (Ochs, 1990) and racialized identity formations among 1.5- and second-generation migrant youth that have made popular the social construction of 'migrant youth' as a research subject. This approach centers on discourse analysis and, in particular, code-switching (Chun, 2009; Woolard, 2004) and bilingualism (Heller, 2007; Urciuoli, 1991; Zentella, 1997b) that highlight youth participation in or resistance to their everyday socialization into 'standard English' inseparable from their attempts (or failure) to evade racialization.

(5) Studies that emphasize the interconnection between language ideologies in the US and the racialization process have allowed scholars to (re)consider the dominant narrative that espouses, unproblematically, speaking English as evidence for the greater 'integration' of people into US society (Chun, 2009; Cintron, 1997; Mendoza-Denton, 2008), revealing the realities of linguistic hierarchies (Berk-Seligson, 1990; Heller, 2010; Valdes, 1997; Valdes & Angelelli, 2003).

(6) Scholars studying the ethnic and racial formations of South Asians in the US and 'South Asian' identity as a political construct employ a wide range of analytical categories, including ethnicity (Koshy, 1998; Rudrappa, 2004); religion (Kurien, 2001); class (Das Gupta, 2006; Prashad, 2000; Visweswaran, 1993); gender and sexuality (George, 2005; Puar, 1994); questions of home and belonging (Khandelwal, 1995; Radhakrishnan, 2003; Shukla, 2003; Srikanth & Shankar, 1998); and, most recently, youth subculture (Maira, 2002; Shankar, 2008; Sharma, 2004).

(7) Discourse about 'skills' and in particular 'communication skills' and 'life skills', according to Bonnie Urciuoli (2008), encompass a broader debate on neoliberalism and self-making technologies marking the contemporary global workforce since the post-Fordist period in the US.

(8) All names in this chapter are pseudonyms.

(9) *Didi* means older sister in Nepali. Addressing people, new acquaintances, usually a person older than you in kin terms is a sign of respect. The reverse is true, as well; referring to a younger person in kin terms is both a sign of respect and an endearment. I was everyone's *bahini*, or younger sister, at the organization where I volunteered, interpreted and facilitated English classes.

(10) The literature critiquing the 'English-only movement' (Gonzalez & Melis, 2000), for instance, is particularly salient and quite extensive. Several important texts that summarize the significance of hegemonic ideologies underlying the movement include liberal democracy (Woolard, 1990), language 'purity' (Woolard, 2004; Woolard & Schieffelin, 1994), standardizing and naturalizing 'monoglot'

(Milroy & Milroy, 1999; Silverstein, 1996) and 'American Whiteness' (Roediger, 1991) – all contributing to what Dick (2011) has called 'US linguistic nationalism'.

References

Bourdieu, P. (1991) *Language and Symbolic Power.* Cambridge, MA: Harvard University Press.

Briggs, C.L. and Bauman, R. (1992) Genre, intertextuality, and social power. *Journal of Linguistic Anthropology* 2, 131–172.

Burroway, M. (1976) The functions and reproduction of migrant labor: Comparative material from southern Africa and the United States. *American Journal of Sociology* 81 (5), 105–187.

Cameron, C.D.R. (1997) How the Garcia cousins lost their accents: Understanding the language of Title VII decisions approving English-only rules as the product of racial dualism, Latino invisibility, and legal indeterminacy. *California Law Review* 85, 1347–1393.

De Genova, N. (2002) The everyday civil war: Migrant working men, within and against capital. *Ethnography* 7 (2), 243–267.

De Genova, N. (2005) *Working the Boundaries: Race, Space, and 'Illegality' in Mexican Chicago.* Durham, NC: Duke University Press.

De Genova, N. and Ramos-Zayas, A. (2003) *Latino Crossings: Mexicans, Puerto Ricans, and the Politics of Race and Citizenship.* New York: Routledge.

Dick, H.P. and Wirtz, K. (2011) Introduction: Racializing discourses. Special issue. *Journal of Linguistic Anthropology* 21 (S1), 1–9.

Goldsmith, T. (2004) Performed ethnography for critical language teacher education. In B. Norton and K. Toohey (eds) *Critical Pedagogies and Language Learning* (pp. 311–326). Cambridge: Cambridge University Press.

Gonzalez, R. and Melis, I. (eds) (2000) *Language Ideologies: Critical Perspectives on the Official English Movement.* Mahwah, NJ: National Council of Teachers of English.

Grewal, I. (2005) *Transnational America: Feminisms, Diasporas, Neoliberalisms.* Durham, NC: Duke University Press.

Harris, N. (1995) *The New Untouchables: Immigration and the New World Worker.* New York: I.B. Tauris.

Haviland, J.B. (2003) Ideologies of language: Some reflections on language and U.S. law. *American Anthropologist* 105 (4), 764–775.

Heller, M. (2007) *Bilingualism: A Social Approach.* New York: Palgrave Macmillan.

Heller, M. (2010) The commodification of language. *Annual Review of Anthropology* 39, 101–114.

Hill, J.H. (1998) Language, race, and white public space. *American Anthropologist* 100, 680–689.

Khandelwal, M. (2002) *Becoming American, Being Indian: An Immigrant Community in New York City.* Ithaca, NY: Cornell University Press.

Koshy, S. (1998) Category crisis: South Asian Americans and the questions of race and ethnicity. *Diaspora* 7 (3), 285–320.

Kurien, P. (2001) Religion, ethnicity and politics: Hindu and Muslim Indian immigrants in the United States. *Ethnic & Racial Studies* 24 (2), 263–293.

Lippi-Green, R. (1997) *English with an Accent: Language, Ideology and Discrimination in the United States.* London: Routledge.

Maira, S. (2002) *Desis in the House: Indian American Youth Culture in New York City.* Philadelphia, PA: Temple University Press.

Mendoza-Denton, N. (2008) *Homegirls: Language and Cultural Practice among Latina Youth Gangs.* Malden, MA: Blackwell.

Milroy, J, and Milroy, L. (1999) *Authority in Language: Investigating Standard English*. New York: Routledge.

Morgan, B. (2004) Modals and memories: A grammar lesson on the Quebec referendum on sovereignty. In B. Norton and K. Toohey (eds) *Critical Pedagogies and Language Learning* (pp. 158–178). Cambridge: Cambridge University Press.

Ochs, E. (1990) Indexicality and socialization. In J.W. Stigler, R.A. Shweder and G. Herdt (eds) *Cultural Psychology: Essays on Comparative Human Development* (pp. 287–308). Cambridge: Cambridge University Press.

Omi, M. and Winant, H. (1994) *Racial Formations in the United States*. New York: Routledge.

Perez, G. (2003) 'Puertorriquenas Rencorosas y Mejicanas Sufridas': Gendered ethnic identity formation in Chicago's Latino communities. *The Journal of Latin American Anthropology* 8 (2), 96–125.

Prashad, V. (2000) *The Karma of Brown Folk*. Minneapolis, MN: University of Minnesota Press.

Puar, J. (1994) Writing my way 'home'. *Socialist Review* 24 (4), 75–107.

Radhakrishnan, R. (1996) *Diasporic Mediations: Between Home and Location*. Minneapolis, MN: University of Minnesota Press.

Ramos-Zayas, A.Y. (2011) Learning affect, embodying race: Youth, blackness, and neoliberal emotions in Latino Newark. *Transforming Anthropology* 19 (2), 86–104.

Reyes, A. and Lo, A. (eds) (2009) *Beyond Yellow English: Toward a Linguistic Anthropology of Asian Pacific America*. New York: Oxford University Press.

Reyhner, J. (1992) Policies toward American Indian languages: A historical sketch. In J. Crawford (ed.) *Language Loyalties: A Source Book on the Official English Controversy* (pp. 41–47). Chicago, IL: University of Chicago Press.

Reynolds, J.F. and Orellana, M.F. (2009) New immigrant youth interpreting in white public space. *American Anthropologist* 111 (2), 211–223.

Roediger, D. (1991) *The Wages of Whiteness: Race and the Making of the American Working Class*. New York: Verso.

Rudrappa, S. (2004) *Ethnic Routes to Becoming American: Indian Immigrants and the Cultures of Citizenship*. New Brunswick, NJ: Rutgers University Press.

Salzinger, L. (1991) A maid by any other name: The transformation of 'dirty work' by Central American immigrants. In M. Burawoy, A. Burton, A.A. Ferguson, K.J. Fox, J. Gamson, N. Gartrell, L. Hurst, C. Kurzman, L. Salzinger, J. Schiffman and S. Ui (eds) *Ethnography Unbound: Power and Resistance in the Modern Metropolis* (pp. 139–160). Berkeley, CA: University of California Press.

Sandhu, S. (2004) Instant karma: The commercialization of Asian Indian culture. In J. Lee and M. Zhou (eds) *Asian American Youth: Culture, Identity, and Ethnicity* (pp. 131–142). New York: Routledge.

Shanker, S. (2008) Speaking like a model minority: 'FOB' styles, gender, and racial meanings among Desi teens in Silicon Valley. *Journal of Linguistic Anthropology* 18 (2), 268–289.

Shukla, S. (2003) *India Abroad: Diasporic Cultures of Postwar America and England*. Princeton, NJ: Princeton University Press.

Silverstein, M. (1976) The whens and wheres – as well as hows – of ethnolinguistic recognition. *Public Culture* 15 (3), 531–557.

Silverstein, M. (1996) Monoglot 'standard' in America: Standardization and metaphors of linguistic hegemony. In D. Brenneis and R.K.S. Macaulay (eds) *The Matrix of Language: Contemporary Linguistic Anthropology* (pp. 284–306). Boulder, CO: Westview Press.

Silverstein, P.A. (2005) Immigrant racialization and the new savage slot: Race, migration and immigration in the New Europe. *Annual Review of Anthropology* 34, 363–384.

Srikanth, R. and Shankar, L.D. (1998) *A Part, Yet Apart: South Asians in Asian America*. Philadelphia, PA: Temple University Press.

Urciuoli, B. (1991) The political topography of Spanish and English: The view from a Puerto Rican neighborhood. *American Ethnologist* 18 (2), 295–310.

Urciuoli, B. (1996) *Exposing Prejudice: Puerto Rican Experiences of Language, Race, and Class*. Boulder, CO: Westview Press.

Urciuoli, B. (2008) Skills and selves in the new workplace. *American Ethnologist* 35 (2), 211–228.

Valdes, G. (1997) Bilinguals and bilingualism: Language policy in an anti-immigrant age. *International Journal of the Sociology of Language* 127, 25–52.

Valdes, G. and Angelelli, C. (2003) Interpreters, interpreting and the study of bilingualism. *Annual Review of Applied Linguistics* 23, 58–78.

Visweswaran, K. (1997) Diaspora by design: Flexible citizenship and South Asians in the U.S. racial formation. *Diaspora* 6 (1), 5–29.

Williams, R. (1977) *Marxism and Literature*. Oxford: Oxford University Press.

Woolard, K.A. (2004) Codeswitching. In A. Duranti (ed.) *A Companion to Linguistic Anthropology* (pp. 73–94). Malden, MA: Blackwell.

Woolard, K.A. and Schieffelin, B.B. (1994) Language ideology. *Annual Review of Anthropology* 23, 55–82.

Zentella, A.C. (1997a) The hispanophobia of the official English movement in the US. *International Journal of the Sociology of Language* 127, 71–86.

Zentella, A.C. (1997b) *Growing up Bilingual: Puerto Rican Children in New York*. Malden, MA: Blackwell.

7 A 'Slippery Slope' Toward 'Too Much Support'? Ethical Quandaries Among College Faculty/Staff Working with Refugee-Background Students

Shawna Shapiro

Introduction

Over the past several decades, the population of immigrant and refugee students in US higher education has risen rapidly. These students currently make up approximately 10% of undergraduates nationwide (Kanno & Harklau, 2012) and comprise a much higher percentage in certain settings, such as community colleges (e.g. Kibler *et al.*, 2011). The vast majority of these students speak a language other than English at home, and have been classified as English language learners (ELLs) in K-12 schools (Kanno & Harklau, 2012). One key finding in the scholarly literature on ELLs in higher education is that many have gaps in their academic preparation and thus rely heavily on academic support from faculty/staff (e.g. Kanno & Harklau, 2012; Rodriguez & Cruz, 2009). Refugee-background[1] (RB) students in particular often have additional struggles stemming from limited or interrupted access to formal schooling prior to resettlement (DeCapua & Marshall, 2010), as well as from psychosocial issues that are the result of traumatic experiences (McBrien, 2005). Hence, while ELLs in general are often constructed as academically 'needy', ELLs with refugee backgrounds are believed to require an even greater range of supports – sometimes beyond what schools feel prepared to offer (Hannah, 1999; McBrien, 2005). Because most educational research does not distinguish between refugees and other immigrant groups, it tends to overlook the ways that involuntary migration and refugee relocation shape the experiences of RB students in US schools. Furthermore, the labels for national, ethnic and linguistic identification that are often applied to ELLs may not capture the complex identity configurations of those with refugee backgrounds. Hence, questions of educational access, equity and identity are particularly relevant to RB students.[2] Rarely in the literature on this subpopulation, or on ELLs in general, is the concept of 'academic support' problematized. The dominant assumption seems to be that *more* support is always *better* for students. However, recent studies of RB students in higher education (e.g. Hirano, 2011; Vásquez, 2007) have begun to raise the question: Is there such a thing as *too much support*? Or, perhaps more accurately, could the strategies that faculty/staff employ in the name of 'support' at times become a detriment to students' long-term success, or to the mission of the institution? While these questions appear infrequently in the scholarly literature, they likely have a familiar ring for practitioners involved in the day-to-day work of supporting 'underprepared' students, including those who came to the US through refugee resettlement.

In this chapter, I show how concerns about 'too much support' for RB students are informed by ideological tensions that have existed for decades in US higher education, as well as by deficit discourses around 'refugees' in general (Keddie, 2012; Kumsa, 2006; Shapiro, 2014). I introduce three ideological constructs – excellence, equity and agency – that shape conceptions of academic support in higher education. I then highlight areas of scholarly literature in which concerns about excessive or inappropriate support are most prominent. In the remainder of the chapter, I present findings from personal interviews with faculty and staff at a small state college in New England. I identify points of divergence in participants' perceptions of what it means to be supportive to RB students, and suggest implications of these findings for institutional dialogue and scholarly research.

Theoretical Framework

In order to understand the tensions that underlie concerns about 'too much support', one must consider three ideals that undergird the mission of US higher education: academic excellence, institutional equity and student agency. *Excellence*, defined by Bowen *et al.* (2005: 39) as 'high achievement in meeting core objectives', is the ideal with the longest history. Indicators of excellence tend to be hierarchical and exclusionary (Bowen *et al.*, 2005; Fox, 1999). Students who do not fit a desired profile may not be admitted, courses that are not seen as rigorous might not receive credit toward graduation and faculty who cannot demonstrate professional excellence may not be offered tenure or given a contract renewal. These and other policies are designed to ensure that post-secondary education is indeed 'higher' education. This historical linking of excellence with exclusion stems largely from the fact that the central mission for higher education was, until recently, to cultivate the intellectual and moral development of the *elite* class – not to promote social mobility for the non-elite (Bowen *et al.*, 2005; Fox, 1999). It was not until the mid-20th century that higher education came to be seen as a vehicle for achieving another ideal – equity.

Bowen *et al.* (2005: 30) link *equity* to an ideology of 'democratic meritocracy' by which 'merit, accomplishment, and potential' – rather than class background – are the criteria determining access to post-secondary education. One piece of legislation that marked the expansion of access to higher education is the Servicemen's Readjustment Act of 1944, known today as the 'GI bill', which provided the financial means for millions of Americans to attend college. Although originally conceived of as an economic intervention, rather than as educational policy, this bill helped to spark other initiatives focused on expanding educational opportunity (Bowen *et al.*, 2005). Increased diversity in the socioeconomic and educational backgrounds of US college students gave rise to a debate about whether and how excellence and equity could coexist – a debate which continues to mark 'the most fiercely contested terrain' in US higher education. (Bowen *et al.*, 2005: 30; see also Bastedo & Gumport, 2003).

One way that institutions attempt to resolve the perceived tension between excellence and equity is by providing academic support resources, such as remedial classes and tutoring services, for students deemed 'underprepared'. While such resources might appear to promote equity, critics have suggested that they serve an equally important function of preserving the institutional 'status quo' (i.e. standards of excellence) by allowing faculty to 'outsource' the burden of support and accommodation (Rose, 1985; Soliday, 2002). In evaluating whether students are well served by the academic support mechanisms at their institutions, scholars must consider a third ideal – *agency*. If an institution's approach threatens students' sense of belonging or decreases their likelihood of achieving their educational goals, that approach might be thought of as inequitable. Agency is particularly important in considerations of RB students, because such students are often constructed discursively as needy and/or victimized, rather than as resilient and capable (Keddie, 2012; Roy & Roxas, 2011). As a result of these deficit-oriented discourses, many schools fail to 'recognize or assess well [students'] skills and forms of agency and self-reliance' (Rodriguez & Cruz, 2009: 2397–2398; see also MacDonald, 2013).

In sum, tensions between excellence, equity and agency give rise to many of the thorniest issues in US higher education, including the question: are we providing appropriate and effective support to RB students? A member of the faculty/staff who does not provide sufficient support may be accused of compromising the institution's commitment to *equity*, while one who offers 'too much' support might undermine standards of *excellence*. Both might be thought of as threatening student *agency* – either by withholding what students need to be successful, or by preventing students from becoming more self-sufficient. In other words, both lack of support *and* excessive or inappropriate support can be seen as compromising the core values of US higher education.

Literature Review

Having laid out the ideological tensions that underlie concerns about 'too much support' in higher education, I now consider the question: Where have these concerns been raised in the scholarly literature?[5] Studies of undergraduates transitioning into four-year institutions often raise concerns about the expectations for support among incoming students, with faculty/staff claiming that students were accustomed to 'hand-holding' in high school or community college (e.g. Mechur Karp, 2012; Townsend & Wilson, 2006). Similar concerns are often mentioned in regard to students who are academically underprepared and/or have documented learning disabilities, and faculty often struggle with issues of fairness in making accommodations for these groups (Pitts *et al.*, 1999; Zhang *et al.*, 2010). Tensions about fairness are also prominent in regard to grading, as faculty tend to vary widely in the criteria by which they evaluate assignments, as well as what they take into account in assigning an overall course grade (Adams, 2005; Johnson, 2003; Rachal, 1984).

Assessment is a particularly salient issue in discussions of second language (L2) writers. Faculty may recognize that the work of L2 writers is likely to include instances of nonstandard language use – what some scholars call a 'written accent' (e.g. Harris & Silva, 1993) – but may not know how to acknowledge this in their grading practice (e.g. Andrade, 2006; Roberts & Cimasko, 2008; Song & Caruso, 1996). L2 writers are frequently referred to the writing center for language-related concerns, but may be dissatisfied with the lack of directive feedback from tutors, who are often trained to avoid 'editing' or 'proofreading' student work (Harris & Silva, 1993). Hence, faculty and staff who are attempting to promote agency in L2 writers by avoiding explicit attention to language conventions may, in fact, disempower those students by preventing access to what Delpit (1988) calls the 'codes of power'.

Case studies of RB students

While research on RB students in college settings is quite limited, the extant literature raises a number of concerns about academic support. In her study of seven RB students in their first year at a liberal arts institution, Hirano (2011: 258) found that while the 'supportive environment' of the institution was crucial to students' success, the 'uncritical' use of some support resources may have compromised students' growth and agency (abstract). Some students recounted visiting the writing center numerous times for a single assignment, for example, doing very little revision work on their own. Faculty participants admitted that they graded the work of RB students less stringently, but students may not have been aware of this practice. While most students were very appreciative of the support they received, two suggested that they might have at times gotten 'too much help' from faculty and staff (Hirano, 2011: 200, 207–208).

An earlier study by Vásquez (2007) examined the effect of divergent grading expectations on Festina, an RB student originally from Bosnia. Festina received high grades from instructors in her (non-credit) English as a second language (ESL) classes, but very low grades in her (for credit) mainstream courses later on. Vásquez (2007: 345) found that the ESL instructors had rewarded Festina for 'good student' behaviors such as attendance, participation and receptivity to feedback, but that these behaviors were 'insufficient to ensure her academic success' in mainstream courses. This finding echoes studies in secondary school settings, which find that teachers tend to weigh effort and behavior – rather than academic achievement – heavily in their evaluation of RB students (McBrien, 2005; Roy & Roxas, 2011).

Some scholars have found that RB college students may be resistant to academic support that is designed in particular for L2 writers. Ortmeier-Hooper (2008) presents the case of Sergej, an RB student originally from Serbia, who informed his professors that English was not his first language, hoping they would be 'more forgiving' in their grading. Otherwise, Sergej was highly resistant to suggestions for ESL or writing support. Ortmeier-Hooper suggests that Sergej's history with refugee resettlement may have contributed to his resistance to institutional mechanisms that 'marked' him as different from his US-born peers – including the label 'ESL', which has been criticized by RB students in other studies as well (e.g. Bigelow, 2010; MacDonald, 2013).

These studies suggest that what practitioners do in the name of 'equity' can at times be perceived by students as unhelpful or even discriminatory. In other words, pedagogical beliefs and practices around academic support are part of a 'hidden curriculum' that promotes certain values and expectations for RB students (Auerbach & Burgess, 1985; Curry, 2001). In the remainder of this analysis, I explore how faculty and staff at one institution wrestled with questions about appropriateness and effectiveness of academic support, and show how these questions were informed by assumptions about the needs of RB students and the mission of higher education.

Background and Methods

Institutional context and researcher involvement

This study is centered on 'New England State College'[4] (NESC), a public institution located in a rural part of New England. NESC has just under 2000 students, approximately two-thirds of whom are from in-state. A majority of NESC students are from low-income families, according to federal Pell Grant data. NESC's webpage highlights that the student population includes many 'nontraditional' students, and describes the campus as 'friendly' and 'inclusive', with faculty committed to giving students the 'support they need to succeed'. NESC's curriculum aims to prepare graduates for 'careers and civic engagement', as well as to promote a 'love of learning'. The college's degree requirements reflect these priorities, with a heavy focus on applied/professional skills, but with general education requirements for all undergraduates.

The number of RB students at NESC is small – fewer than 20 each year, according to participants. However, these students have been the focus of a number of campus-wide discussions, and some faculty/staff have been asked to devote additional time to support this population in recent years. One of these individuals, Pat, was a tenured professor in the English department, who had recently returned from a sabbatical project looking at the experiences of RB students in K-12 schools around the state. Pat's goal was to understand more fully the academic backgrounds of RB students entering NESC. Pat and I were introduced via email by a mutual acquaintance who was aware of our overlapping research interests. Pat invited me to visit NESC to interview colleagues and students, in order to help evaluate the effectiveness of NESC's support system for RB students. She felt that participants might be willing to speak more openly with a researcher who was not employed by the college. Pat consulted with me on recruitment letters and interview protocols, but she was not directly involved in the interview process and did not have access to recordings or notes from individual interviews.

Faculty/staff interviews centered on three themes:

(1) Perceptions: e.g. What have you observed about RB students[5] at NESC? What have you heard in conversations with colleagues about these students?
(2) Support: e.g. What forms of support have you found to be effective for RB students? Do you have any concerns about the type of support available and/or suggestions for ways that NESC might better support these students?
(3) Success: How well do you think NESC is serving the needs of its RB students? How would you evaluate the overall educational outcomes for these students?

Participants, data collection and data analysis

Participants were recruited via an invitation letter. Eight faculty/staff agreed to participate (see Table 7.1 for details). Interviews were structured loosely around the above themes and questions. Each interview lasted approximately one hour, and was audio-recorded with the written consent

Table 7.1 Participants[a]

Name	Title	Length of time at NESC (years)	Nature of interaction with refugee-background (RB) students
Henry	Assistant professor of sociology	5	Has two to three RB students in his introduction to sociology course each semester.
Jakala	Math tutor	5	Frequently tutors RB students in math. Consults occasionally with faculty/staff on issues related to RB students.
Janet	Director of academic support services	10	Supervises tutors and other staff who work with RB students. Consults frequently with faculty. Meets occasionally with students.
Joy	Academic advisor, writing tutor and (former) adjunct instructor of English	7	Tutors and advises RB students. Taught English courses in the past.
Kate	Professor of biology	20	Has occasional RB students in her biology courses. Worked extensively with one particular RB student.
Rebecca	Director of advising and career center	10	Oversees academic advisors. Consults frequently with faculty. Meets occasionally with students. Served in the past as advisor for RB students.
Sandra	Coordinator of learning center (including writing center)	1	Supervises tutors. Consults frequently with faculty. Meets occasionally with students. Teaches occasional courses in anthropology (her disciplinary expertise).

[a]One other participant in this study, Steve, was an adjunct professor of English who had taught a special section of his English course for ELL students. His comments informed my overall understanding of RB students at NESC, but he did not address any of the issues that are central to this analysis, and is therefore not included in the table.

of the participant.In the first phase of data analysis, I created topical outlines of each interview, in order to develop a summary for Pat's purposes. I then transcribed and coded the data, with the aim of documenting the prevalent institutional lore about NESC, its RB students and effective or ineffective forms of academic support. I identified individuals who embodied the assumptions and the tensions prevalent in the discourse at NESC. I drew on the conceptual framework of excellence, equity and agency to highlight points of consensus and divergence among participants.

Findings

Institutional lore about NESC

Before discussing the prevalent lore about RB students at NESC, it is important to consider how participants perceived the institution, since this perception informs their sense of mission and their beliefs about academic support. As was discussed earlier, NESC advertises itself as having a friendly climate, a student-centered philosophy and a career-oriented curriculum. The values of equity and agency are therefore central to the college's public image. These values were also reflected in faculty/staff interviews: Joy described the campus as 'really welcoming and small and supportive'. Janet said, 'You couldn't find a faculty that care more about students'. She went on to say that although college has a 'very needy' student population, the work is worthwhile, because 'you know you've had a piece in helping students succeed'. Other participants also acknowledged that the campus overall has a 'high-need' population. Sandra works in the TRIO program, which serves students who are from low-income households, are first-generation college students and/or have documented learning disabilities. She said that 75% of NESC's students would qualify for TRIO services, if they all applied. Sandra pointed this out in part to emphasize that RB students were not necessarily *more* needy or deserving than other NESC students. Participants seemed particularly attuned to students' financial difficulties, including the fact that most take out student loans to finance their education. As a result, gainful employment was seen as a primary goal for NESC graduates, as a steady income would allow students to repay their loans.

In essence, the values of excellence and equity were closely linked at NESC, because a college degree was seen as a path to social mobility. This linking of equity and excellence informs the way that faculty/staff at NESC understand student *agency* as well. Participants defined success by asking the question: are our graduates prepared to achieve their personal and professional goals? When the answer to this question was uncertain, this raised concerns about whether students had received appropriate and effective academic support, as will be discussed later on.

Institutional lore about RB students

Below are the most prevalent commonplaces about academic support for RB students at NESC, according to participants:

(1) Many RB students graduate from high school without the academic and/or linguistic proficiencies needed for college-level work – especially in math and English.[6]
(2) Many RB students have educational and/or professional goals that are not in line with their academic and linguistic capabilities.
(3) Many RB students rely heavily on academic support from faculty/staff in order to be successful at NESC.
(4) Some RB students are more proactive than others in making use of academic supports available to them, and those students are usually more academically successful.
(5) Some faculty are more sympathetic to RB students than others. Certain departments (e.g. business) tend to have more of these faculty than other departments (e.g. biology).

Several questions emerge from this narrative of RB students at NESC: first, if many such students are not prepared for college-level work yet have lofty aspirations, should faculty/staff be held accountable if those students do not achieve their goals? Does this suggest, moreover, that NESC's definition of 'success' for RB students should be reconsidered? Finally, in light of these concerns, what does it mean for faculty and staff to be 'supportive' to RB students? In the section that follows, I highlight divergence in faculty/staff participants' responses to these questions, as reflected in their pedagogical beliefs and practices.

Two faculty perspectives: Henry and Kate

Henry had been teaching sociology for five years at NESC at the time of our interview. Pat had mentioned Henry as a colleague who was extremely supportive to RB students. A number of these students had successfully completed Henry's introduction to sociology course, and advisors had begun to recommend that course for all incoming RB students. When asked what he did to support these students, Henry emphasized foremost that his goal as a teacher was reflection and application of learning – not simply the accumulation of content knowledge. Hence, when Pat requested that he allow open-book tests and quizzes for RB students, he complied, because, he said 'I don't feel like most of the time I'm strictly testing memorization anyway... it's more of just for understanding'.[7]

In keeping with this pedagogical rationale, Henry gave all students a choice between a research paper and a 'sociological memoir' for their final project. Most RB students chose the latter option, and Henry had been very pleased with their essays, describing them as 'truly remarkable' and occasionally 'dazzling'. When asked about the quality of the writing, Henry said that most RB students did a 'great job', but admitted that 'no doubt they have a little help' from support staff. This did not seem to trouble him, because his focus was on students' connections to content – not the development of writing skills. When asked whether he had any concerns about upholding academic standards, Henry said, 'It's not a huge hang-up of mine, quite honestly. I'm much more interested in helping them to understand sociology and to further help them assimilate into American culture than I am holding them to some artificial standard'. As will be discussed later on, Henry's approach would be interpreted by some participants as supportive, but by others as ineffective or even unfair.

Kate had been a faculty member in the biology department at NESC for 20 years at the time of the study. She 'rarely' had RB students in her classes, but there was one recent student that she 'felt very strongly about', and for this reason, she had accepted the invitation to be interviewed. Most of my conversation with Kate was focused on this one student, Abdullah, who had chosen to major in biology – widely seen as one of NESC's most difficult programs of study – despite receiving low grades in introductory courses. According to Kate, Abdullah had received Cs or below in nearly all of his biology courses, but had been allowed to continue on as a major. Kate did not meet Abdullah until his junior year, when he took her microbiology course. Early that semester, Kate became 'very concerned' about him: 'I couldn't understand how this student got to this point as a major', she said, citing difficulties with understanding course material, following lab instructions and writing lab reports. After talking with colleagues, Kate concluded that Abdullah had been 'getting grades based on effort and not on academics'. Kate was bothered that Abdullah did not approach her to discuss his performance in her course, but she admitted that she 'didn't take any action either'. Abdullah was able to pass the course with a 'borderline' D grade, although he told her that he had expected to receive a C.

The next semester, Abdullah asked to continue working with Kate on an independent senior project. Kate told him that she was 'not comfortable' having him work on her own research, which involved pathogens that had to be handled carefully. Kate was aware, however, that Abdullah wanted to pursue a career in health sciences, and that more research experience 'would help him get a job'. She therefore helped to arrange an alternative, whereby Abdullah worked on another faculty member's project, but Kate supervised his writing. Kate saw significant improvement in both the content and style of Abdullah's work that semester. While she had not finished reading his final report at the time of our interview, she had taken an initial glance and was 'impressed'.

Reflecting on the experience, Kate concluded that 'we [the biology department] did him a disservice' by not offering 'early intervention'. Kate did have questions about how much the department should have done for Abdullah, however, since 'when one gets a job, you're not going to have one-on-one [support]'.

A 'strong divide' among faculty?

While both Henry and Kate seemed to care deeply about the success of RB students, their pedagogical choices diverged, particularly around assessment. Kate felt that it was important to ask for the same outcomes from every student, while Henry seemed comfortable giving students a variety of options for demonstrating their learning. These two faculty exemplify what some staff participants characterized as a philosophical 'divide' regarding support for RB students. As Joy explained, some faculty are 'really willing to go out of their way' and others are 'much more hard line'. Rebecca said that 'flexibility' was a key difference between the two: 'Some are extremely willing to accommodate', she said, 'and some of them are stone-cold, no way, nothing's gonna be done differently'. Both of these participants admitted that assessment was a particularly thorny issue for faculty on the more 'accommodating' side of the spectrum. Joy said faculty sometimes asked her for grading advice, saying, 'I can't really grade this using the rubric for the other students, but I want to give him credit for how much work he's put in'. Joy believed that effort and growth should be taken into account, but did worry about students who passed a course but '[hadn't] really mastered the material'. Sandra, who taught occasional courses in anthropology, said she felt there was an 'ethical dimension' to grading: She said she tried to ask herself, 'How can I be fair? How can I nurture this [student], but also not pass someone on so it's injurious to them in the future?'

Indeed, other participants claimed that some of the pedagogical decisions made by more accommodating faculty were detrimental to students in the long run. Jakala said that many faculty lowered their expectations for RB students, simply because they were 'very sympathetic to [their] story'. 'It's compassionate', he pointed out, 'but...the long-term effect of that, it's actually very negative'. Jakala claimed that some RB students accused him of being 'less sympathetic' because he held them to high standards of achievement – an approach he characterized as 'tough love'.[8] Janet held a similar view, claiming that 'social promotion' was a problem in many departments, because faculty think, '[RB students] have had terrible lives. Horrible things have happened to them – you know? How can we hold them back?'

Jakala and Janet mentioned several students who they felt had been ill-served by these more 'sympathetic' faculty. Janet said that one RB student in the business department (a department Rebecca described wryly as 'very – uh – supportive') had cheated on exams and plagiarized on assignments numerous times – including in her final semester – but had never been subjected to disciplinary action. One of the business professors had suggested that 'perhaps it's a cultural difference – that she didn't see cheating as a horrible thing'. Janet found this a dubious excuse, and was angry that the department had referred the student to her office each time an incident occurred, rather than addressing it themselves: 'They always wanted us to do the hard work', she said. Jakala mentioned another RB student whom he had encouraged to take calculus, after he saw how well she was doing in her algebra class. The student was nervous about taking the course, but he told her, 'You can do it!' and promised that he would be available to tutor her. The student later informed Jakala that her advisor had steered her toward a lower-level course instead. This was extremely frustrating to Jakala: 'If nothing else', he said, 'just challenge them! This girl could even be a motivation to the other Africans!' Jakala felt, like Janet, that faculty decisions were often motivated by selfishness, rather than concern for the student. He claimed that many faculty and staff lowered their expectations in part because they 'don't want to have the pain of failing these kids in the class'.

There was one recent graduate, William, whose case was referenced by several participants as particularly worrisome. William had struggled a great deal in many of his classes as a business major, and seemed unlikely to be able to finish his degree. One professor in the department chose to intervene and 'allowed [William] to do sort of special things to finish', as Janet put it. William completed multiple independent studies with that professor, as a substitution for some of the more challenging upper-level business courses. Faculty in the department had also helped William to raise funds for a nonprofit organization he was starting, focused on providing clean water to a village in Sudan. Many hoped that upon graduating, William would find a well-paying job that would allow him to use his business degree and to continue his humanitarian efforts. After graduation, however, William struggled to find work. He told some of the faculty/staff that he was having difficulty completing job applications – a task most assumed he would have been able to complete on his own – and eventually resumed a job he had held previously as a luggage carrier. William had recently moved to another state, where he had more friends and family.

Participants discussing this case wondered whether the institution had done William a disservice. Jakala felt that the situation was 'very, very, very sad' and suggested that there was 'liability' on the part of the college. Janet found it particularly 'problematic' that William could not find work, since he had likely accumulated high amounts of student debt. Rebecca, who had also worked closely with William, was concerned that his English had not improved over his time at NESC: 'he still was not able to be understood by people who didn't know him', she said, and as a result, 'he never got promoted – never'. Referencing the support William had received for his nonprofit initiative, Rebecca said, 'it's very sweet, and probably has made a big difference in [William's] life, but, it creates an inflated sense of worth or self, you know? He left here feeling like he was able to do more than he really is'. She went on to suggest that this effect was exacerbated by grade inflation: 'There's no way that he could have gotten an A in an upper-level business course and then taken another course at a lower level with someone else and barely squeezed by'.

The examples above suggest that in an attempt to recognize the difficulties that RB students have faced in the past, faculty may make pedagogical choices that could be detrimental to those students' success in the future. This finding is echoed in other studies which have shown that calls for greater sensitivity to the needs of refugee students (e.g. Hannah, 1999; McBrien, 2005) may be interpreted by educators as justification for low academic expectations (e.g. Bigelow, 2010; Keddie, 2012; Shapiro, 2014), inconsistent grading procedures (e.g. Hirano, 2011; Vásquez, 2007) and other educational practices that emphasize students' deficits and ignore their strengths (e.g. Roy & Roxas, 2011; Shapiro, 2014).

These anecdotes also raise questions about fairness to non-RB students, who might not have received the same level of support and flexibility from NESC faculty and staff, despite having similar academic and financial challenges. Janet expressed concerns that the college might be on a 'slippery slope' ethically by making certain accommodations available only to RB students. While she recognized that such students faced a number of difficulties, she pointed out that 'in many ways it's not more of a struggle than for our other students'. Jakala said US-born students were aware that RB students were sometimes treated differently, describing one conversation in which a US-born student asked him why the 'African' students were 'being graded on a totally different standard'. Similar tensions around fairness and accommodation have appeared in other discussions of RB students (e.g. Hirano, 2011; McBrien, 2005; Roy & Roxas, 2011).

Implications and Conclusions

This analysis provides a brief snapshot of the ethical considerations that faculty and staff take into account in determining what comprises effective and appropriate support for RB students. One key finding is that institutional lore plays a major role in shaping the beliefs and practices of faculty/staff. NESC's aim to promote social mobility through career preparation influenced how participants conceived of success for their graduates. Cases such as William's, in which a graduate took (or returned to) a job for which a college degree was not necessary, were perceived as 'failure', because they implied that students were not benefitting from their investment in higher education.

However, further conversations with students may complicate this narrative. Although I was unable to contact William, I interviewed another student, Najib, who had been mentioned by several participants as a similar case. Najib had left NESC several years prior, after completing an associate's degree, and resumed a restaurant job he had held in high school. Participants who had worked with Najib were disappointed that he had not returned to finish his bachelor's degree, and seemed to view him as a case of unmet potential. Yet, when I spoke with Najib, he characterized himself not as a 'dropout', but as a college graduate: 'I just wanted to... be the first guy from my family that has a degree', he said. Najib did hope to finish his bachelor's degree eventually, but wanted to transfer to a larger and more prestigious university. For the time being, he said, he was happy working full time at a job where 'everybody knows me and I know everyone'. Najib's story suggests that longitudinal analysis is needed for a more complete understanding of how RB students define and pursue their own visions of success, and what role higher education plays (or could have played) in helping them achieve that vision. Pedagogical practices aimed at supporting RB students may be ineffective if they are based on inaccurate assumptions about students' goals, needs and resources (Bigelow, 2010; Roy & Roxas, 2011; Sharkey & Layzer, 2000).

Another key finding from this analysis is that faculty/staff may have divergent conceptions of fairness, which impact their beliefs and decisions around academic support for RB students. Some participants, such as Kate, Janet and Jakala, seemed to conceive of fairness in universalist terms. While they were willing to offer individual support to students who need it, they felt it was fundamentally unfair to grade a student according to a different set of standards, or to make other accommodations only for RB students. Other participants, such as Henry, Joy, Rebecca and Sandra, seemed to see fairness as a more dynamic construct, and felt that support and assessment should be tailored to each student. They would not characterize such an approach as a lowering of standards, but rather as a way to level the playing field for disadvantaged students. This second conception of fairness was articulated by one RB student in a study by Hannah (1999: 163), who said, 'treating everyone the same can be discriminatory'. More research is needed, therefore, to understand how faculty and staff negotiate divergent conceptions of fairness, and how those conceptions are shaped by prevalent discourses about refugees.

In terms of pedagogical practice, these findings highlight the importance of explicitness among faculty, staff and students. This study suggests that RB students need more opportunities to discuss their goals and expectations with faculty/staff, and should be informed when special accommodations are being made on their behalf – especially if they are being graded or promoted based on a different standard. College faculty and staff also need opportunities for honest dialogue about their experiences working with RB students. Such dialogue is probably rare at most institutions – not just because of logistical barriers, but also because faculty may fear judgment from colleagues who associate support with a decrease in academic rigor (Hirano, 2011). Campus-wide conversation about the issues raised in this study would be useful to elucidate not only points of divergence, but also points of consensus. At NESC, for example, there was widespread agreement about the importance of career preparation. Centering the conversation on the question, 'Are our students prepared to achieve their career goals?' might be one entryway into discussions about the effectiveness of institutional policy and pedagogical practice. More consideration of students' aspirations for the future might also create the discursive space for new stories about RB students – stories that foreground not only these students' needs and challenges, but also their contributions to our academic communities and to society at large.

Notes

(1) Throughout this chapter, I use the term *refugee-background* (RB) rather than simply 'refugee' in recognition of the fact that many students do not see the label *refugee* as an accurate representation of who they are in the present, and some feel that the label also has a deficit connotation (Shapiro, 2014; see also Keddie, 2012).
(2) See the introduction to this volume for more on refugees as a distinct group within educational research.
(3) While I am most interested in the literature on students considered 'at risk' or 'underprepared', it is important to note that concerns about expectations for support have emerged in discussions of undergraduates in general – particularly with the so-called 'millennial generation' (e.g. Levine & Dean, 2012).
(4) Pseudonyms are used for the institution and for all faculty/staff participants, as well as for students.
(5) In the interviews, participants often used the term *English language learners* (ELLs) as a stand-in for RB students, because NESC had few if any ELLs who were *not* of refugee background. This parallels the demographics in the state at large, where the vast majority of ELLs enter through refugee resettlement programs, rather than through other immigration pathways.
(6) This was prevalent throughout the state – particularly in the two districts with the largest numbers of ELLs. A number of initiatives are underway to try to address the issue of underpreparation among all high school graduates, but especially among RB students.
(7) Henry claimed that he would make the open-book option available to any student who requested it – including to non-RB students. It is unclear, however, whether the other students knew that this was an option they could request.
(8) This was ironic, because Jakala had immigrated to the US from Tanzania many years prior, and other participants claimed that he was the staff member who best understood the needs of RB students, many of whom had relocated to the US from other countries in Africa.

References

Adams, J.B. (2005) What makes the grade? Faculty and student perceptions. *Teaching of Psychology* 32 (1), 21–24.

Andrade, M. (2006) International students in English-speaking universities: Adjustment factors. *Journal of Research in International Education* 5 (2), 131–154.

Auerbach, E.R. and Burgess, D. (1985) The hidden curriculum of survival ESL. *TESOL Quarterly* 19 (3), 475–495.

Bastedo, M.N. and Gumport, P.J. (2003) Access to what? Mission differentiation and academic stratification in US public higher education. *Higher Education* 46 (3), 341–359.

Bigelow, M. (2010) *Mogadishu on the Mississippi: Language, Racialized Identity, and Education in a New Land*. New York: Wiley-Blackwell.

Bowen, W.G., Kurzweil, M.A. and Tobin, E.M. (2005) *Equity and Excellence in American Higher Education*. Charlottesville, VA: University of Virginia Press.

Curry, M.J. (2001) Preparing to be privatized: The hidden curriculum of a community college ESL writing class. In E. Margolis (ed.) *The Hidden Curriculum in Higher Education* (pp. 175–192). New York: Routledge.

DeCapua, A. and Marshall, H.W. (2010) Students with limited or interrupted formal education in US classrooms. *The Urban Review* 42 (2), 159–173.

Delpit, L.D. (1988) The silenced dialogue: Power and pedagogy in educating other people's children. *Harvard Educational Review* 58 (3), 280–299.

Fox, T. (1999) *Defending Access: A Critique of Standards in Higher Education*. Portsmouth, NH: Boynton/Cook Publishers.

Harris, M. and Silva, T. (1993) Tutoring ESL students: Issues and options. *College Composition and Communication* 525–537.

Hirano, E. (2011) Refugees negotiating academic literacies in first-year college: Challenges, strategies, and resources. *Applied Linguistics and English as a Second Language Dissertations*, 18.

Johnson, V.E. (2003) *Grade Inflation: A Crisis in College Education*. New York: Springer.

Kanno, Y. and Harklau, L. (2012) *Linguistic Minority Students Go to College: Preparation, Access, and Persistence*. New York: Routledge.

Keddie, A. (2012) Pursuing justice for refugee students: Addressing issues of cultural (mis)recognition. *International Journal of Inclusive Education* 16 (12), 1295–1310.

Kibler, A.K., Bunch, G.C. and Endris, A.K. (2011) Community college practices for US-educated language-minority students: A resource-oriented framework. *Bilingual Research Journal* 34 (2), 201–222.

Kumsa, M.K. (2006) 'No! I'm not a refugee!' The poetics of be-longing among young Oromos in Toronto. *Journal of Refugee Studies* 19 (2), 230–255.

Levine, A. and Dean, D. (2012) *Generation on a Tightrope: A Portrait of Today's College Student*. San Francisco, CA: Jossey-Bass.

MacDonald, M.T. (2013) Emissaries of literacy: Refugee studies and transnational composition. Unpublished doctoral dissertation, University of Wisconsin.

Matthews, P.R., Anderson, D.W. and Skolnick, B.D. (1987) Faculty attitude toward accommodations for college students with learning disabilities. *Learning Disabilities Focus* 3, 46–52.

McBrien, J.L. (2005) Educational needs and barriers for refugee students in the United States: A review of the literature. *Review of Educational Research* 75 (3), 329–364.

Mechur Karp, M. (2012) 'I don't know, I've never been to college!' Dual enrollment as a college readiness strategy. *New Directions for Higher Education* 158, 21–28.

Nelson, J.R., Dodd, J.M. and Smith, D.J. (1990) Faculty willingness to accommodate students with learning disabilities: A comparison among academic divisions. *Journal of Learning Disabilities* 23 (3), 185–189.

Ortmeier-Hooper, C. (2008) English may be my second language, but I'm not 'ESL'. *College Composition and Communication* 389–419.

Pitts, J.M., White, W.G. and Harrison, A.B. (1999) Student academic underpreparedness: Effects on faculty. *The Review of Higher Education* 22 (4), 343–365.

Rachal, J.R. (1984) Community college and university instructor consistency in the evaluation of freshman English themes. *Community/Junior College Quarterly of Research and Practice* 8 (1–4), 127–140.

Ramanathan, V. and Kaplan, R.B. (1996) Audience and voice in current L1 composition texts: Some implications for ESL student writers. *Journal of Second Language Writing* 5 (1), 21–34.

Roberts, F. and Cimasko, T. (2008) Evaluating ESL: Making sense of university professors' responses to second language writing. *Journal of Second Language Writing* 17 (3), 125–143.

Rodriguez, G. and Cruz, L. (2009) The transition to college of English learner and undocumented immigrant students: Resource and policy implications. *The Teachers College Record* 111 (10), 2385–2418.

Rose, M. (1985) The language of exclusion: Writing instruction at the university. *College English* 47, 341–359.

Roy, L.A. and Roxas, K.C. (2011) Whose deficit is this anyhow? Exploring counter-stories of Somali Bantu refugees' experiences in 'doing school'. *Harvard Educational Review* 81 (3), 521–541, 618.

Shapiro, S. (2014) 'Words that you said got bigger': English language learners' lived experiences of deficit discourse. *Research in the Teaching of English* 48 (4), 386–406.

Sharkey, J. and Layzer, C. (2000) Whose definition of success? Identifying factors that affect English language learners' access to academic success and resources. *TESOL Quarterly* 34 (2), 352–368.

Soliday, M. (2002) *The Politics of Remediation: Institutional and Student Needs in Higher Education.* Pittsburgh, PA: University of Pittsburgh Press.

Song, B. and Caruso, I. (1996) Do English and ESL faculty differ in evaluating the essays of native English-speaking and ESL students? *Journal of Second Language Writing* 5 (2), 163–182.

Townsend, B.K. and Wilson, K. (2006) 'A hand hold for a little bit': Factors facilitating the success of community college transfer students to a large research university. *Journal of College Student Development* 47 (4), 439–456.

Vásquez, C. (2007) Comments from the classroom: A case study of a generation-1.5 student in a university IEP and beyond. *Canadian Modern Language Review* 63 (3), 345–370.

Zhang, D., Landmark, L., Reber, A., Hsu, H., Kwok, O.M. and Benz, M. (2010) University faculty knowledge, beliefs, and practices in providing reasonable accommodations to students with disabilities. *Remedial and Special Education* 31 (4), 276–286.

8 'Talk English!' Refugee Youth and Policy Shaping in Restrictive Language Contexts

Daisy E. Fredricks and Doris Warriner

Introduction

This chapter explores the choices made by refugee youth in selected English language development (ELD) and mainstream classrooms and how certain interactional choices reflect their understandings of the ideologies, policies and discursive practices of the moment. With a focus on their everyday interactions, we analyze several classroom exchanges in which refugee youth engage in conversation about language(s), language learning or language 'rules'. The analysis demonstrates that the refugee youth responded in a variety of complicated ways to deficit discourses about multilingualism. In some cases, they ventriloquated (Bakhtin, 1981) what they believed others valued and in other cases, they contested deficit discourses about languages other than English that are dominant in the Arizona context. A close examination of policy as practice in a restrictive language policy context reveals a level of metalinguistic awareness (and metadiscursive practice) that helps refugee youth comment on local language ideologies and shape classroom language policies. By examining instances of 'language policing' (Androutsopoulos, 2009; Blommaert *et al.*, 2009; Foucault, 2007) and language sharing (Paris, 2011), we show how refugee youth use available linguistic resources to invent new discursive positions for themselves within the interactional moment. The analysis demonstrates how individuals make sense of, use and transform the local restrictive language policies in place through socially and historically situated practices.

Language Ideologies and (Restrictive) Language Policies

Drawing from Ruiz's (1984) notion of language orientation, language ideologies (Silverstein, 1979; Tollefson, 1991) and (language education) policy as practice (Hornberger & Johnson, 2007; Sutton & Levinson, 2001; Tollefson, 2002), we analyze the relationships between language ideologies, (restrictive) language policies and classroom practices taken up by the refugee youth in a local context.

Broadly defined, ideologies of language are 'sets of beliefs about language articulated by users as a rationalization or justification of perceived language structure and use' (Silverstein, 1979: 193). Tollefson (1991: 10) argues that language ideologies affect areas of language planning and policy, noting that (language) ideologies can be used to 'justify exclusionary policies and sustain inequality'. This study operationalizes the notion of ideologies of language in order to examine the ways in which (restrictive) language policies in educational contexts influence the discursive practices of refugee youth living in complex social and political contexts (Tollefson, 2002).

Ricento and Hornberger (1996: 402) note that there are many 'language planning agents, levels, and processes...that permeate and interact with each other in a variety of ways and to varying degrees', which comprise and operationalize language policy. In this chapter, we examine 'the everyday contexts in which policies are interpreted and negotiated in ways that reflect local constraints and possibilities' (Ramanathan & Morgan, 2007: 447) by refugee youth as they engage with restrictive language policies to help shape such policies and to act as policymakers (and sometimes policy breakers) in their own right. Here, we examine the connections between language ideologies and (restrictive) language policies with a focus on how such connections affect the teaching, (language) learning and the discursive practices of refugee youth living in situated contexts.

Restrictive language policies in Arizona: English only

After Proposition 203 was passed in the state of Arizona in 2000 (see Wright, 2005), most schools and government offices adopted explicitly English-only language policies. Starting in 2008, all schools (public and charter) implemented policies which resulted in segregating students designated as English language learners (ELLs) from those who were considered English 'proficient' for four hours of ELD instruction a day. Known locally as 'the four-hour block', the stated goal is to provide the targeted instruction that students need to learn English through an approach known as sheltered English immersion (SEI). To transfer out of this ELD classroom and into a mainstream classroom, students need to score 'proficient' on the Arizona English Language Learner Assessment (AZELLA) test.

The 'four-hour block' mandated by the state, and the SEI methods used within it, have been controversial among practitioners and researchers, in large part because they emphasize instruction in language forms and functions over instruction in meaningful communication and in the content-area knowledge that will provide credentials that the students need and want. While growing numbers of ELLs are studying the forms of English with the goal of becoming proficient enough to transfer into the mainstream environment, they fall farther behind in content-area knowledge needed to make it after they demonstrate that proficiency by 'testing out' of the four-hour block.

There has been a great deal of discussion and debate in public and academic contexts about the constraints of such policies and practices (e.g. Arias, 2012; Faltis & Arias, 2012; Fredricks, 2013; Lillie *et al.*, 2010; Wiley, 2012). Many researchers argue that SEI and the restrictive language policies behind it encourage linguistic discrimination (Gándara *et al.*, 2010) and ethnic and linguistic segregation (Gándara & Orfield, 2010; Rios-Aguilar *et al.*, 2010), and that learning English in segregated environments often impedes (language) learning (Garcia *et al.*, 2010; Rumberger & Tran, 2010) and creates physical, emotional and social isolation (Gándara & Orfield, 2010; Lillie *et al.*, 2010). Yet, many legislators and policymakers argue that this approach is better than not attending to the language learning needs of the large and growing population of ELL students in Arizona's public schools.

Within this complex and increasingly restrictive language policy context, we examine the ways that refugee youth in ELD and mainstream classrooms interact with each other with a focus on how the learners themselves are making sense of, taking up and responding to restrictive language policies and practices that value English language learning over multilingualism and that position ELLs as a 'problem' that needs to be 'fixed' (Ruiz, 1984).

Language Policy as Practice through Language Policing

Located in an urban context in Arizona, where anti-immigrant sentiment and legislation is strong and on the rise, we examine the interactions between six fifth-grade refugee youth while they were engaged in small-group-work activities assigned by the teacher. Specifically, we examine how they were talking about and negotiating ideologies of language and language learning as well as restrictive language policies that value English language learning over multilingualism and characterize the multilingual speaker as deficient. In and through talk, and while engaged in forms of everyday storytelling (Ochs & Capps, 2001), refugee youth from different ethnic and language backgrounds demonstrated their awareness of the local ideological landscape as well as an ability to reflect on, and sometimes contest, what is often taken for granted in that landscape.

The interactions we examine demonstrate the students' awareness of the taken-for-granted language policies, their attempts to regulate each other's practices through different forms of language policing and their creative reappropriations of existing practices, understandings and discourses. Like Androutsopoulos (2009), we are interested in the tension between overt language policies and the practices that emerge in actual language and discourse practice. And, like Androutsopoulos (2009), we view many of the emerging practices as a form of language policing, influenced and shaped by language policies dominant in local and national contexts. We are interested in the potential for change offered by such tension. We view the restrictive language policies that have been implemented in Arizona schools in recent years as examples of an intentionally rigid language policy (Lillie *et al.*, 2010; Wiley, 2012; Wright & Sung, 2012) and the interactions between youth from distinct ethnic and language backgrounds as offering spaces in which agency, dynamism, change and fluidity are not only tolerated, but are also promoted (Ramanathan & Morgan, 2007). While 'policing' practices impose order, other practices push the boundaries of that order so that additional practices, ideologies and discourses are made possible.

Following Blommaert (2009: 204), we view youth as 'mediating actors in contemporary multilingual, globalized contexts' as well as 'actors of language policing'. We are particularly interested in the situated (and sometimes contested) ways that interaction 'regulates' language behaviors. To examine the struggles that accompany 'the production of particular identities' (Blommaert, 2009: 204), we examine the role of 'polycentric multilingual environments' in the production of national sentiment, memory, belonging, membership and learner agency. By looking closely at the role of language choice and language use in creating and negotiating policy, we show that policies are situated, emergent, dynamic and discursively shaped (Blommaert, 2009; Blommaert *et al.*, 2009; Ricento, 2006). As Leppänen and Piirainen-Marsh (2009) remind us:

> Language policy is an evolving phenomenon shaped and reshaped by discursive practices, which in turn are embedded in the multiple contextual and semiotic resources available in specific social activities and environments. (Leppänen & Piirainen-Marsh, 2009: 263)

Taking into account how local norms, frameworks and practices might be created, maintained or challenged, the analysis shows how such policies and practices are 'made and remade in social activities' (Leppänen & Piirainen-Marsh, 2009: 262) with the end result being a sort of 'informal language policing' and the 'production of a regimented subject' (Blommaert *et al.*, 2009: 244). In these ways, we hope to demonstrate our belief that language is more than a set of linguistic structures; it is also a 'densely loaded ideological package' (Blommaert, 2009: 245) that allows, facilitates and mediates 'access to particular types of social trajectories'. Drawing on such frameworks, we use the term *language policing* to refer to comments or directives about what languages should or should not be used in a classroom and at a school that has been subjected to restrictive language policies that are directed at the ELLs who are in ELD classrooms, as well as 'English proficient' ELLs who have recently been moved from ELD classrooms to 'mainstream' classrooms.

Interactional Narrative

With a view of storytelling and narrative as situated social practices that are shaped by a range of material and discursive influences, we examine how the first-person accounts that occur during more mundane or everyday conversation might influence particular constructions and performances of identity for speakers from certain social groups. As Wortham *et al.* (2011) note, language use always involves more than conveying representational meaning. It also involves taking a stance in relation to widely circulating, commonly understood positions and identities available in local discourses: 'speakers adopt interactional positions within emergent interactional events and with respect to larger social struggles in ways that may have little to do with the events being narrated' (Wortham *et al.*, 2011: 41).

This analysis of interactional data relies on an assumption that meaning is 'jointly constructed by the participants but with differentiated actions and contributions from each of them' (Georgakopoulou, 2007: 91). The exchanges examined provide evidence of the multiple and varied ways that identities are not just performed for strategic purposes but are also shaped by one's membership in local communities, the beliefs and practices recognized in those communities, and ideological influences:

> ...the identities that people display, perform, contest, or discuss in interaction are based on ideologies and beliefs about the characteristics of social groups and categories and about the implications of belonging to them. (De Fina, 2006: 353–354)

Our examination of interactional data highlights the complex relationships between language, identity, social structures and ideologies of language and language learning. The exchanges reveal the creative ways that individuals might use talk and interaction to emphasize, hide, refashion or contest various accounts of what is going on, what counts and what is at stake:

> In many years of studying the way structured variation in language reflects the social structures of the community, it has become clear

that language can serve to mark a number of kinds of identity. The way individuals situate themselves in relationship to others, the way they group themselves, the powers they claim for themselves and the powers they stipulate to others are all embedded in language. (Lippi-Green, 1997: 31)

Assuming that everyday talk plays a significant role in the construction and representation of social life (Erickson, 2004), the analysis focuses on how performances of identity are actually accomplished in and through interactional narrative, especially while making use of locally relevant and locally recognized metapragmatic discourses. The exchanges examined here shed light on the relationship between language in use and the organization of groups in society:

Self-representations are, therefore, the basis for ideologies, and for this reason their investigation is of primary importance for an understanding of the constitution and functioning of social groups. (De Fina, 2006: 356)

Drawing on the notions of metapragmatic discourse (Silverstein, 1993, 1981/2001; Silverstein & Urban, 1996) and interactional narrative (De Fina, 2006; Wortham, 2001), we show how the situated communicative practices of multilingual refugee youth in two specific classroom contexts are able to reflect and resist ideologies of language and language learning that are dominant in this ideological context. As Silverstein and Urban (1996: 6) note, ideologies and metadiscourses that foreground and devalue particular identities, social categories and practices can be taken up and strategically reconstituted in and through interaction.

Research Context

New Frontiers Elementary School (NFES) is a K-6, Title I school located in an urban neighborhood in Phoenix, Arizona. Up until 2005, the residents in this community were largely of Mexican origin. However, during that year, the Office of Refugee Resettlement began placing refugees from the Congo, Kenya, Rwanda, Somalia, Sudan and Tanzania in a neighborhood apartment complex. The school district identified and registered all refugee youth for school services, and such youth were designated as refugee based on particular required registration documents (i.e. I-94 forms). At the time of this study, the principal and the teachers of NFES used the label *refugee* to distinguish these youth from other (reclassified) ELLs (i.e. US citizens and documented and undocumented youth).

According to the principal, by the 2010–2011 school year, 40% of the 691 students in this school were designated as refugee – with most learning

English as an additional language. Schoolwide, refugee youth came from Burundi, Colombia, the Congo, Egypt, Kenya, Mexico, Rwanda, Somalia, Sudan and Tanzania – with many different languages spoken by the students. The most commonly spoken languages included Arabic, Dinka, English, French, Kirundi, Maay Maay, Somali and Swahili.

Drawing on data collected from two classroom-based studies conducted during 2010–2012, this chapter focuses on the narratives and daily classroom interactions of refugee youth in Mrs Williams' fifth/sixth-grade ELD classroom during 2010–2011 and her fifth-grade mainstream classroom during the 2011–2012 school year (Fredricks, 2013). In Mrs Williams' fifth/sixth-grade ELD classroom (during the 2010–2011 school year), out of 21 classified ELL students, 70% of the students spoke Spanish as their first language (and were not classified as refugee); 25% were native speakers of Somali; and the remaining 5% spoke Kirundi (though it is important to note that some of the speakers of Somali and Kirundi also spoke additional African dialects and languages and were designated as refugee learners).

The following school year (2011–2012), in Mrs Williams' fifth-grade mainstream classroom, the linguistic diversity of the students was similar, with 65% of the students speaking Spanish as their first language (and were not classified as refugee); 19% were native speakers of English; 8% spoke Kirundi; 4% spoke Maay Maay; and 4% spoke Somali. The native speakers of Kirundi, Maay Maay and Somali were refugees from a number of different African countries (including Tanzania, Somalia and Kenya) and also spoke additional African dialects and languages.

Methods and Data Analysis

The qualitative data presented in this chapter come from extended participant observation, recorded interviews and document collection that occurred in two phases. During the first phase of data collection (May–September 2011), the authors jointly collected and analyzed over 50 hours of data from students enrolled in Mrs Williams' ELD classroom. During the second phase of data collection (January–June 2012), Fredricks collected data independently from and with students she had observed previously (in the ELD classroom) after they had moved into a mainstream classroom in order to understand the processes and policies of mainstreaming in the Arizona context. During Phase 2 of data collection, Fredricks recorded approximately 150 hours of classroom interaction and observed students outside the classroom on a regular basis (e.g. in the lunchroom, during lunch detentions, during recess) and conducted individual interviews (with students and teachers). Throughout Phase 2 of the study, Fredricks engaged in informal conversations (with students and teachers) in a variety of school contexts. Fredricks and Warriner collaboratively analyzed the data collected during both phases of the study and present some of those findings here – with a focus on narratives and interactional data collected from six of the fifth-grade refugee youth from the ELD and mainstream classrooms.

Findings

In this section, we present student narratives and interactional data from Aasha, Catherine, Kansah, Mishall, Malik and Raija – in addition to their classmates – that demonstrate how these youth conform to, contest and shape local language policies and the ideological context that supports such policies. The first set of examples examines how different refugee youth (i.e. Aasha and Raija) engaged in language policing activities in the classroom. The analysis demonstrates that local practices are often influenced by local policies and by ideologies of language and language learning circulating more widely in US society. The second set of examples examines the creative ways that refugee youth, like Aasha and Malik, were able to reflect on and resist particular ideologies of language that devalued multilingualism. The analysis demonstrates that even refugee youth who were actively engaged in language policing expressed an interest in learning other languages (i.e. Spanish) used in the classroom and local community.

Policy, practice and policing: 'These girls are speaking Spanish!'

Mrs Williams was the fifth/sixth-grade ELD teacher at NFES during the 2010–2011 school year, and she upheld the English-only language policy in her ELD classroom. Though A.R.S. §15-756.0l(F) mandates that restrictive language policies are only for ELD classrooms – and not mainstream classrooms – the following school year (2011–2012), Fredricks (2013) documented that the restrictive language policies continued in Mrs Williams' fifth-grade mainstream classroom and were actively implemented in all classrooms throughout the school. Fredricks observed that when students used languages other than English in the classroom, teachers and students were quick to remind each other of the school's English-only language policy, often through various forms of language policing – i.e. verbal reminders about the type of language that needed to be used in the classroom.

Toward the end of the 2010–2011 school year, Fredricks observed fifth-grade girls Catherine, Kansah, Aasha, Mishall and Jane (a native Spanish speaker) reading a passage about major league baseball and answering multiple-choice questions based on the reading in Mrs Williams' ELD classroom. Native Somali speaker, Catherine, began to tell a story about her brother to the group of girls, but only Mishall, also a native Somali speaker, continued to engage in the story with Catherine. Catherine and Mishall continued talking in Somali until native Kirundi speaker, Aasha, interrupted them:

8 **Aasha**:   Eh! Talk good man!
9 **Mishall**:   [told a story in Somali]
10 **Catherine**:   [in Somali]
11 **Mishall**:   [in Somali] and every time she goes like 'Tsh'.
12 **Aasha**:   (singing a song) *Can you see...*
13 **Kansah**:   Mishall! No more English! (inaudible)
14   ...One more...
15 **Mishall**:   [in Somali]
16 **Aasha**:   (to Mishall) Talk English!
17 **Mishall**:   I AM talkin' in English!
18 **Aasha**:   That's not English.
19 **Mishall**:   Yeah it is.
20 **Aasha**:   (softly stated) No it's not.
21 **Mishall**:   (almost inaudible) Yeah it is.
22 **Kansah**:   [in Somali]
23 **Aasha**:   I'm sick and tired of this ladies!

After listening to Catherine and Mishall converse mostly in Somali, Fredricks overheard Aasha remind Catherine and Mishall that they must speak in English by telling them, 'Eh! Talk good man!'. We interpret Aasha's directive to 'talk good' to mean that she wants her peers to speak in English only. Comments that Aasha made later in the interaction support this interpretation. Although Aasha's initial request (Line 8) is aligned with classroom and school policies, it is interesting to observe that Catherine and Mishall both disregarded Aasha's request and continued talking in Somali. When Aasha directed Mishall to 'Talk English!' (Line 16), Mishall claimed that she was talking in English (Line 17) at which point Aasha clarified her request by restating that Mishall had not been using English (Line 18). The two girls continued to argue the point until Mishall ended the debate by saying, 'Yeah it is'. After this exchange, Kansah began to speak in Somali again and the exchange ends with Aasha saying, 'I'm sick and tired of this ladies!' and turning her attention back to her project.

In this excerpt, the girls' interactions demonstrate their metapragmatic awareness of the value of speaking English in the local context. Their talk, or metadiscursive practice (Silverstein & Urban, 1996), illustrates how robust and pervasive certain ideologies of language are in this institutional context – and how those ideological influences shape interactions between students from a range of cultural and linguistic backgrounds (De Fina, 2006; Lippi-Green, 1997). However, this excerpt also shows that different students are reacting differently to the social context and the emphasis placed on learning English and using English (Blommaert, 2009). While Aasha firmly believes in the importance of speaking only English in this classroom context, the other girls in the group are much more interested in talking to each other in Somali. Although it is possible to interpret Aasha's actions as a request that her classmates use a language of wider communication (more likely to be understood by all participants in the interaction), it is also possible to interpret Aasha's evaluative comments as indexing an awareness of national-level, societal-level and school-level discourses about the value of English relative to other languages. Her metalinguistic awareness combined with her firsthand experiences with being 'policed' by others (i.e. students and teachers) likely shaped the interactional context in which it became acceptable for her to negatively evaluate and attempt to control the practices of others.

During a conversation that Fredricks had with Aasha about a year later (when Aasha was in sixth grade), Fredricks asked Aasha about policing the use of her classmates' language as observed the previous year. Aasha explained that for her, it was important that all students spoke English at school because 'those were the rules'. She also said that it was important for her classmates to speak in English because she was not fluent in other languages that students were using (i.e. Somali and Spanish) and she did not want the other girls to talk about her in a language that she could not understand (Interview, June 8, 2012). During that same conversation, though, Aasha also told Fredricks that she would like to be able to speak her native language at school because it would be easier to communicate with other students who also spoke Kirundi.

Language policing also occurred in the mainstream classrooms that Fredricks observed. On a March day, Fredricks arrived in the classroom as students were working in small groups to prepare their oral presentations (to be given that day during class) and overheard Raija (a native Maay Maay speaker from Kenya) shout out a directive to native Spanish speaker, Calvin, who was conversing with fellow Spanish speaker, Eric, in Spanish:

1 **Raija**:   Hey! Please speak in English. [4] Or I'll start talking
2   in my language to myself.
3 **Mrs Williams**:   You know what? There's a lot of talking in languages
4   other than English in here and it needs to stop.
5 **Raija**:   Me?
6 **Mrs Williams**:   Just because people here get upset when
7   somebody else talks about or talks in their language
8   then they start tattling.
9 **Malik**:   Like you don't get upset when they talk in Spanish.
10 **Raija**:   I know, right? So, if you guys talk in Spanish
11   one more time.

Fredricks had learned from previous conversations with Raija that he often felt uncomfortable when others used languages that he did not know (e.g. Spanish) and that he sometimes worried that people might be talking about him. This excerpt shows how the use of multiple languages in the classroom context might cause certain students to feel excluded. As such, it provides a small rationale for instituting English-only policies in classrooms where students speak multiple languages. This view does not take into account the challenges that face students who are less proficient in English and/or the kinds of exclusion that might result from the imbalance. We learned that like his teachers, Raija tended to view English as a unifying language that allowed for everybody to understand the different conversations taking place in the classroom. Note Mrs Williams' comment that all students should be communicating in English 'because people here get upset when somebody else talks about or talks in their language, then they start tattling'. Other teachers had also told Fredricks that they believed that this was one important way to reduce tensions between their multilingual and multiethnic learners.

Malik's response to Mrs Williams (Line 9) also makes clear that the linguistic ecology that has been established in the classroom is not strictly based on ideologies of monolingualism or English-only sentiments. He draws attention to what he believes to be a contradictory stance or policy by pointing out that the teacher sometimes allows Spanish-speaking students to use their first language in the classroom. His comment signals the existence of a local policy that contributes to a hierarchy of languages where Spanish is afforded a higher status relative to the other non-English languages spoken at the school. Mrs Williams' reminder to the entire class (that they should speak only English) provided an opportunity for Malik to point out that some of the underlying tensions were caused by the fact that a seemingly clear and fair classroom language policy had been enforced unevenly at best, arbitrarily at worst. For Raija and Malik, the problem seemed to be that the agreed-upon English-only language policy was enforced differently for different students, and the language spoken (or the background of the student) was a factor. Although Raija's comments demonstrate a belief that all students should use English for communication purposes in the classroom, they also reveal how particular refugee youth directly responded to certain tensions created by the restrictive language policies used in multilingual and multinational learning spaces.

Although refugee youth in the larger study often voiced and enacted discourses that explicitly devalued multilingualism (i.e. through policing each others' language), a number of refugee learners were also actively engaged in learning additional languages – specifically, Spanish. Despite an awareness of (and an attempt to actively support) the restrictive language policies in place, these students engaged in practices that served to affirm, value and recognize proficiency in (and knowledge of) languages other than

English. This complicates any assertion that refugee youth consistently ventriloquate (Bakhtin, 1981) beliefs and ideologies that privilege English over all other languages. The next section provides a few examples.

Valuing multiple linguistic resources: 'What's sombrero mean?'

The following excerpt is taken from a conversation that took place the same day as Aasha's interaction with Mishall and Catherine. Just before this exchange took place, Daniel (a US-born fifth grader) and Aasha (also in fifth grade at the time) were looking up facts about different states on the computers located at the back of the classroom. As Miguel approached Daniel to inform him that he was done with the work for his assignment, he made a comment in Spanish (a native language for both of them):

228	**Miguel**:	Ya acobé con esto. Perro babosa (inaudible)
229	**Aasha**:	Was that English?
230	**Daniel**:	No, sorry. (to Miguel) Mi mama me compra todo.
231		Una camisa, un sombrero, y unas botas.
232	**Aasha**:	Sombrero? What's sombrero mean?
233	**Miguel**/**Daniel**:	Uh...hat! (together)

In response to Aasha's question, which seems intended to discourage the use of Spanish in the classroom, Daniel initially apologized but then turned back to Miguel and continued speaking in Spanish. His apology in English combined with his continued conversation in Spanish seems to indicate a complicated stance – one which simultaneously accepts and challenges the linguistic norms (and social order) that Aasha attempted to impose (Androutsopoulos, 2009). Daniel seemed aware of the dominant ideologies that devalue Spanish but also seemed unwilling to follow the rules, perhaps because he had completed his academic work and was talking with a friend about something not related to school. After Aasha realized that both boys were not going to switch to English, she asked them to explain what one of the Spanish words meant. As in the other examples, Aasha's first statement serves as a form of metapragmatic discourse (Silverstein, 1993, 1981/2001) whereby 'rules' about talk are conveyed and enacted through a form of language policing (Androutsopoulos, 2009). However, by the end of this very brief exchange, she seemed to follow the boys' lead and to accept that languages other than English have value. As the boys continued on with their conversation in Spanish, a little more loudly than before, Aasha returned to her project and continued working independently.

Another exchange that demonstrates the ways that refugee youth actively engaged in learning other languages occurred in Mrs Williams' fifth-grade mainstream classroom. The students were assigned to play a pirate-themed board game to help them develop a better understanding of context clues. Native Spanish speakers, Anayeli, Juan, Veronica and Jairo, were grouped with Somali speaker, Malik, and Maay Maay speaker, Raija. As the students were rolling the dice and moving pawns, Anayeli and Veronica began to code-switch (or alternate between languages – English and Spanish) during the board game. Overhearing the exchange, Malik responded:

1276	**Malik**:	(to Anayeli and Veronica) Eh! English, man!
1277		(to Anayeli) You know Spanish, right?
1278	**Anayeli**:	(still playing the game) [Number 2]
1279	**Malik**:	How do you say, 'bald white man?'
1280	**Anayeli**:	Pelon? I don't know how to say 'bald' (to Veronica)
1281		How do you say, 'white man' in Spanish?
1282	**Veronica**:	'Hombre blanco'.
1283	**Anayeli**:	(to Malik) 'Hombre blanco'.

Much like Aasha's attempt to discourage her classmates from using Spanish in the classroom, Malik also reinforces the local restrictive language policies (and perhaps attempts to establish social order) by reminding Anayeli and Veronica to speak in English while in the classroom. Again, we see a conflicted stance, as no sooner has Malik reminded the girls to speak in English, then he immediately seeks to confirm if Anayeli can speak Spanish, because he wants to know how to say 'bald white man' (Line 1279). (He requested this particular phrase, as one of the pirates on the board game box was a white, bald man.) Malik's request for this Spanish translation illustrates how particular refugee youth engaged in practices that resisted the rigid English-only language policies in place and created space for multilingualism in the classroom (Ramanathan & Morgan, 2007). Though Anayeli is not certain how to say 'bald' in Spanish, she uses fellow Spanish speaker Veronica as a linguistic resource (Lines 281–1282), and is able to at least provide Malik with a translation for 'white man', which satisfies Malik's curiosity.

A few minutes after this exchange, Fredricks talked with Malik and Raija about their thoughts on learning Spanish. The boys acknowledged that while they actively enforced English-only language policy in the classroom, both were still interested in learning Spanish because they would be able to understand what particular people around them were saying and it could help them to develop stronger relationships with friends who were Spanish speakers. In these ways, the boys seemed to believe that learning Spanish might become an asset for them – in and out of school. Such responses show that these refugee youth had a sophisticated understanding of the value of learning and knowing multiple languages, despite the restrictive language policies in place.

Discussion

In their everyday talk about language, the refugee youth not only demonstrate a sophisticated understanding of the many ideological and discursive forces that devalue their linguistic resources and position them as deficient; they often ventriloquated (Bakhtin, 1981) and perpetuated those deficit discourses. In these ways, their talk about 'rules' reflects their engagement in metapragmatic discourse (Silverstein, 1981/2001). The excerpts demonstrate that these students were aware of restrictive language policies, and that this awareness influenced their interactions with each other. In some cases, students commented on the 'talk' of other students in ways that conveyed particular ideological stances (De Fina, 2006; Wortham, 2001). For example, Aasha, Raija and Mrs Williams all try to get other students to speak English for a variety of reasons, even while observing the contradictory practices that exist and while acknowledging that the English-only policies in place are not always evenly or fairly executed. At the same time, the data from this study also reveal refugee youths' awareness of a hierarchy where both English and Spanish are held in higher regard than the languages they speak. Aasha, for instance, demonstrates an awareness of the English-only policy even while asking her peers to provide a translation for *sombrero*. In addition, the exchange between Malik and two Spanish-speaking peers also reflects an understanding of the dominant and valued role of Spanish in the local linguistic ecology. While the focus of this chapter is on how selected refugee youths' interactional choices reflect their understandings of locally relevant language ideologies and restrictive language policies, it is possible that other factors, like race and ethnicity, might also have shaped the interactions that occurred between the youth in this setting. More research that explores how factors like race and ethnicity might influence interactional dynamics is an area for further investigation (see Ong [2003] for further discussion on race in relation to Cambodian refugees).

Implications

Our analysis of these data shows that refugee youth use language and respond to language policies in ways that both reflect and shape local practices and policies and that create situations in which they can assert their own views and understandings of local linguistic hierarchies and their relationships to them (De Fina, 2006). In this context, restrictive language policies are often directed at Spanish speakers, and ideologies of language that devalue languages other than English influence interactions between students (Spanish speakers and refugee students alike). The interactions examined here show that refugee students living in Arizona understand local language ideologies and policies in ways that place Spanish above the refugee youths' languages. In these interactions, the refugee youth of this study were quite aware of what counted in the local context – English is the dominant language, followed by Spanish, and the African languages are most devalued – even among the African students.

Such students used their growing understanding of local language ideologies and language policies to try to gain advantage by engaging with policy in complicated ways. In some cases, refugee learners tried to improve their own position in the local linguistic ecology by enforcing the restrictive language policies in place. And, in other cases, some students would try to learn additional languages (i.e. Spanish) in order to move up the linguistic hierarchy of the local community. By analyzing the relationship between how local norms and dominant discourses intersect with situated practices, we show that refugee youth are sophisticated readers of the local linguistic landscape as well as burgeoning policymakers of their own – sometimes ventriloquating (Bakhtin, 1981) the words and stances of those around them, sometimes inventing new ways to maintain the status quo and occasionally challenging or resisting what is taken for granted in the local context. This analysis of talk about talk among refugee youth shows how robust deficit discourses are in local policies and local practices, how they might be 'made and remade in social activities' and the role of 'informal language policing' (Leppänen & Piirainen-Marsh, 2009: 262) in the 'production of a regimented subject' (Blommaert et al., 2009: 244).

These findings demonstrate how narratives in interaction 'draw on taken-for-granted discourses and values circulating in a particular culture' (Riessman, 2008: 3) whether they are liberating or not. They also show how individual speakers might respond to, take up or ignore ideologies of language that devalue their linguistic resources and social identities. Our analysis offers a new way to examine and understand how restrictive language policies in a classroom context might influence the talk of refugee learners (in contact with other minoritized learners – i.e. Spanish speakers) in a restrictive language policy context.

References

Androutsopoulos, J. (2009) Policing practices in heteroglossic mediascapes: A commentary on interfaces. *Language Policy* 8 (3), 285–289.

Arias, M.B. (2012) Language policy and teacher preparation: The implications of a restrictive language policy on teacher preparation. In M.B. Arias and C. Faltis (eds) *Implementing Educational Language Policy in Arizona: Legal, Historical and Current Practices in SEI* (pp. 3–20). Bristol: Multilingual Matters.

Bakhtin, M. (1981) *The Dialogic Imagination: Four Essays.* Austin, TX: University of Texas Press.

Blommaert, J. (2009) A market of accents. *Language Policy* 8 (3), 243–259.

Blommaert, J., Kelly-Holmes, H., Lane, P., Leppänen, S., Moriarty, M., Pietikainen, S. and Piirainen-Marsh, A. (2009) Media, multilingualism, and language policing: An introduction. *Language Policy* 8 (3), 203–207.

De Fina, A. (2006) Group identity, narrative and self representations. In A. De Fina, D. Schiffrin and M. Bamberg (eds) *Discourse and Identity* (pp. 351–375). Cambridge: Cambridge University Press.

Erickson, F. (2004) *Talk and Social Theory: Ecologies of Speaking and Listening in Everyday Life*. Cambridge: Polity Press.

Faltis, C. and Arias, M.B. (2012) Research-based reform in Arizona: Whose evidence counts for applying the Castañeda test to structured English immersion models? In M.B. Arias and C. Faltis (eds) *Implementing Educational Language Policy in Arizona: Legal, Historical and Current Practices in SEI* (pp. 21–38). Bristol: Multilingual Matters.

Foucault, M. (2007) *Security, Territory, Population*. London: Palgrave.

Fredricks, D.E. (2013) Policy as practice: The experiences and views of learners and teachers in restrictive language contexts. Unpublished doctoral dissertation, Arizona State University.

Gándara, P. and Orfield, G. (2010) A return to the 'Mexican room': The segregation of Arizona's English learners. *The Civil Rights Project at UCLA*. See http://civilrightsproject.ucla.edu/research/k-12-education/language-minority-students/a-return-to-the-mexican-room-the-segregation-of-arizonas-english-learners-1/gandara-return-mexican-room-2010.pdf (retrieved 7 July 2015).

Gándara, P., Losen, D., August, D., Uriarte, M., Gómez, M.C. and Hopkins, M. (2010) Forbidden language: A brief history of U.S. language policy. In P. Gándara and M. Hopkins (eds) *Forbidden Language: English Learners and Restrictive Language Policies* (pp. 20–36). New York: Teachers College Press.

Garcia, E., Lawton, K. and Diniz de Figueiredo, E. (2010) The education of English language learners in Arizona: A legacy of persisting achievement gaps in a restrictive language policy climate. *The Civil Rights Project at UCLA*. See http://civilrightsproject.ucla.edu/research/k-12-education/language-minority-students/the-education-of-english-language-learners-in-arizona-a-legacy-of-persisting-achievement-gaps-in-a-restrictive-language-policy-climate/garcia-az-ell-gaps-2010.pdf (retrieved on 7 July 2015).

Georgakopoulou, A. (2007) *Small Stories, Interaction, and Identities*. Amsterdam: John Benjamins.

Hornberger, N. and Johnson, D. (2007) Slicing the onion ethnographically: Layers and spaces in multilingual language education policy and practice. *TESOL Quarterly* 41 (3), 509–532.

Leppänen, S. and Piirainen-Marsh, A. (2009) Language policy in the making: An analysis of bilingual gaming activities. *Language Policy* 8 (3), 261–284.

Lillie, K.E., Markos, A., Estrella, A., Nguyen, T., Peer, K., Trifiro, A., Arias, M.B. and Wiley, T.G. (2010) Policy in practice: The implementation of structured English immersion in Arizona. *The Civil Rights Project at UCLA*. See http://civilrightsproject.ucla.edu/research/k-12-education/language-minority-students/policy-in-practice-the-implementation-of-structured-english-immersion-in-arizona/lillie-policy-practice-sei-2010.pdf (retrieved 7 July 2015).

Lippi Green, R. (1997) *English with an Accent: Language, Ideology, and Discrimination in the United States*. New York: Routledge.

Ochs, E. and Capps, L. (2001) *Living Narrative: Creating Lives in Everyday Storytelling*. Cambridge: Harvard University Press.

Ong, A. (2003) *Buddha is Hiding*. Berkeley and Los Angeles, CA: University of California Press.

Paris, D. (2011) *Language Across Difference: Ethnicity, Communication, and Youth Identities in Changing Urban Schools.* New York: Cambridge University Press.

Ramanathan, V. and Morgan, B. (2007) TESOL and policy enactments: Perspectives from practice. *TESOL Quarterly* 41 (3), 447–463.

Ricento, T. (ed.) (2006) *An Introduction to Policy: Theory and Method.* London: Blackwell.

Ricento, T. and Hornberger, N. (1996) Unpeeling the onion: Language planning and policy and the ELT profession. *TESOL Quarterly* 3 (30), 401–427.

Riessman, C. (2008) *Narrative Methods for the Human Sciences.* Thousand Oaks, CA: Sage.

Rios-Aguilar, C., González-Conche, M. and Moll, L. (2010) Implementing structured English immersion in Arizona: Benefits, costs, challenges, and opportunities. The Civil Rights Project at UCLA. See http://civilrightsproject.ucla.edu/research/k-12-education/language-minority-students/implementing-structured-english-immersion-sei-in-arizona-benefits-costs-challenges-and-opportunities/AZ-ELC-Study-7-7.pdf (retrieved 7 July 2015).

Ruiz, R. (1984) Orientation in language planning. *NABE Journal* 8 (2), 15–34.

Rumberger, R. and Tran, L. (2010) State language policies, school language practices, and the English learner achievement gap. In P. Gándara and M. Hopkins (eds) *Forbidden Language: English Learners and Restrictive Language Policies* (pp. 86–101). New York: Teachers College Press.

Silverstein, M. (1979) Language structure and linguistic ideology. In P. Clyne, F. Hanks and C. Hofbauer (eds) *The Elements: A Parasession on Linguistic Units and Levels* (pp. 193–247). Chicago, IL: Chicago Linguistic Society.

Silverstein, M. (1993) Metapragmatic discourse and metapragmatic function. In J. Lucy (ed.) *Reflexive Language: Reported Speech and Metapragmatics* (pp. 33–57). Cambridge: Cambridge University Press.

Silverstein, M. (1981/2001) The limits of awareness. In A. Duranti (ed.) *Linguistic Anthropology: A Reader* (pp. 382–401). Malden, MA: Blackwell.

Silverstein, M. and Urban, G. (1996) The natural history of discourse. In M. Silverstein and G. Urban (eds) *Natural Histories of Discourse* (pp. 1–20). Chicago. IL: University of Chicago Press.

Sutton, M. and Levinson, B. (eds) (2001) *Policy as Practice: Toward a Comparative Sociocultural Analysis of Educational Policy.* Westport, CT: Ablex Publishing.

Tollefson, J. (1991) *Planning Language, Planning Inequality: Language Policy in the Community.* London: Longman.

Tollefson, J. (2002) *Language Policies in Education.* Mahwah, NJ: Lawrence Erlbaum Associates.

Wiley, T. (2012) Foreword: From restrictive SEI to imagining better. In M.B. Arias and C. Faltis (eds) *Implementing Educational Language Policy in Arizona: Legal, Historical and Current Practices in SEI* (pp. xiii–xxii). Bristol: Multilingual Matters.

Wortham, S. (2001) *Narratives in Action: A Strategy for Research and Analysis.* New York: Teachers College Press.

Wortham, S., Mortimer, K., Lee, K., Allard, E. and White, K.D. (2011) Interviews as interactional data. *Language in Society* 40, 39–50.

Wright, W. (2005) The political spectacle of Arizona's proposition 203. *Educational Policy* 19 (5), 662–700.

Wright, W. and Sung, K. (2012) Teachers' sheltered English immersion views and practices. In M.B. Arias and C. Faltis (eds) *Implementing Educational Language Policy in Arizona: Legal, Historical and Current Practices in SEI* (pp. 86–106). Bristol: Multilingual Matters.

9 The US Refugee Resettlement Process: A Path to Self-Sufficiency or Marginalization?

Nora Tyeklar

Introduction

Social institutions such as mainstream media, governments, non-governmental organizations and voluntary agencies involved in the refugee resettlement process have largely been the agents responsible for the production and dissemination of discourses surrounding the representation of refugees, their identities and resettlement. Researchers have focused on the analysis of refugee narratives as told by refugees (Blommaert, 2005) and the analysis of the discursive construction in the media of the social representations and political policies surrounding how refugees in European societies are impacted (see Baker & Garbielatos, 2008; Baker & McEnery, 2005; Steimel, 2010). This study will focus instead on the discursive mechanisms used in the self-representation of voluntary agencies acting as supportive social and bureaucratic structures in the refugee resettlement process in the US, specifically in Massachusetts.

Through an examination of several texts on websites presenting the services of Massachusetts resettlement organizations, I question whether self-sufficiency is a realistic outcome of the assistance such organizations provide. For instance, given the constraints under which such organizations operate, is it possible for resettlement assistance provided through underfunded and under-resourced faith-based organizations that must rely heavily on the work of volunteers to ensure the self-sufficiency of their clients? While open borders to persons fleeing either conflict or a well-founded fear due to persecution in their country of origin are absolutely essential to the resettlement process, they are not enough on their own. The apprenticeship (including linguistic resources and material support) that is necessary for resettlement that truly leads to self-sufficiency in US society must take into consideration refugees' backgrounds (not only linguistic and cultural knowledge, but also ideological positions), US military (and other state forces) involvement in their country of origin, the political and cultural climate which refugees face upon arrival in the US, the foundation of the US as a nation of immigrants, as well as the precepts upon which US ideals, such as democracy and the American dream, are based. Additionally, I will incorporate some ethnographic findings as a volunteer English as a second language (ESL) teacher at one voluntary agency in Massachusetts throughout my analysis to further contextualize and support my arguments.

Since federally funded voluntary agencies play such a significant role in the resettlement process in the US, this chapter will focus closely on how their positive discursive self-representations and the negative (or, more specifically, 'needy') representations of refugees serve to sustain the unequal power relationships between those individuals and organizations that provide resettlement assistance and those who must rely on such services in order to navigate and build a new life in an entirely unfamiliar culture that is often extremely different from the culture of their country of origin or the country into which they were initially displaced. Drawing from the work of Jan Blommaert and James Gee in discourse studies as well as Norman Fairclough's dialectical-relational approach and Ruth Wodak's historical-discourse approach to critical discourse analysis (CDA), I will strive to synthesize a unique approach to analyzing the texts promulgated, specifically the operationalization of the keyword *self-sufficiency*, through the websites of two voluntary agencies working in Massachusetts. It is my goal to make explicit how power relationships and inequalities are generated and sustained through linguistic mechanisms within the particular historical contexts and existing social structures of US refugee resettlement.

This leads to the research questions of this study: Is the refugee resettlement process in the US actual resettlement (i.e. one that leads to so-called *self-sufficiency*) or is it in fact a process of marginalization? If so, why? How does the use of the term *self-sufficiency* work to construct a very particular understanding of the experience that recently arrived refugees face and what might a deeper analysis index about the structural constraints of the resettlement process as it currently exists? Do the discursive mechanisms operationalized by these voluntary agencies work to reproduce marginalization and perpetuate existing social structures that hamper rather than facilitate social integration? And, finally, what constitutes resettlement that can lead to actual self-sufficiency?

Refugee Status Within a Global Historical Context

To begin, I want to historically contextualize the refugee who is ultimately resettled in the US as well as the discursive constructions surrounding the US refugee resettlement process with a brief genealogy of the work of the United Nations High Commissioner for Refugees (UNHCR) and some of the criticisms that have been levied against its ability to effectively respond to and manage large humanitarian crises. By providing such contextualization, I want to show that several scales of context must be considered for a more capacious interpretation to be made of the texts appearing on the websites of voluntary agencies in Massachusetts. Since the outbreak of the Syrian civil war in March 2011, the UNHCR (2014) has been faced with the largest refugee displacement it has had to manage in the course of its brief history. In this era of rapid globalization, it is therefore imperative to keep in mind that such global institutions and countries are embedded and inextricably linked more than ever within a world system in which communicative events do not exist only inside single societies, but influence and are influenced by actors and events beyond them (Blommaert, 2005).

As a result of the refugee crisis at the end of World War II, the UNHCR was formed in 1949 by the United Nations General Assembly to address the plight of Europeans displaced by the war. Originally mandated to commit to assisting refugees for only three years and then disband, the 1951 Refugee Convention was adopted. In the decades following the establishment of the UNHCR and the adoption of the 1951 Refugee Convention, the UNHCR's role began to change as major displacements of people continued to occur. Not long after coordinating the response to its first major refugee crisis, the UNHCR was soon faced with numerous large refugee movements with little possibility of permanent solutions due to much instability within the countries in which these new refugees sought asylum. In 1967, a protocol to the convention was drafted and adopted (UNHCR, 2005) in order to widen both the temporal and geographical scope of the UNHCR's role. At the turn of the century, the UNHCR remains involved in major refugee crises in Africa, such as Sudan and Somalia, in the Middle East and Asia, such as Burma, Bhutan and Syria, and countries in which the US has been or is currently engaged in war, namely Afghanistan and Iraq (UNHCR, 2014).

While the UNHCR has been awarded two Nobel Peace Prizes for its work since its inception, it has been confronted with criticism for its inability to effectively handle large-scale human displacements. As a non-political entity (UNHCR, 2010b: 6), how can the UNHCR also 'reduce situations of forced displacement [and encourage] states and other institutions to create conditions which are conducive to the protection of human rights and the peaceful resolution of disputes?' (UNHCR, 2014). In other words, how can an organization claiming to be non-political resolve the 'refugee problem' that often stems from political turmoil within a country, while simultaneously refraining from being involved in a political manner? After all, the 'UNHCR is often at the mercy of its donors and host governments...[and] can only carry out its enormous emergency and maintenance programmes if it receives funding from the industrialised states' (Loescher, 2001). Therefore, it is difficult not to question the neutrality of the actions of the UNHCR once the sources of its funding, which are often from states responsible for wars leading to massive displacements, are taken into consideration.

In fact, since its inception, the role of the UNHCR has shifted from being primarily a protective one to one in which the ultimate goal is the delivery of material support in emergencies (Loescher, 2001: 29). As a global humanitarian organization, the UNHCR is thus relegated to the position of an ineffective agent that is either incapable or unwilling to get at the root causes for the generation of more and more refugees and displaced peoples (Bauman, 2004) and local solutions must be sought instead. Such 'solutions' include refugee resettlement, repatriation and local integration – all part of the UNHCR's durable solutions program for refugees. Nevertheless, oftentimes such 'durable solutions' are durable not for refugees, but for the status quo that upholds the positions of dominant institutions and ideologies already in place. If the necessary support does not exist, the promise of rebuilding in 'dignity and peace' (UNHCR, 2014) risks becoming an unrealistic and difficult one to keep.

US involvement in the refugee resettlement process

Resettlement in a third country is one part of the three-pronged mandate of the UNHCR's durable solutions program. Nevertheless, 'of the 10.5 million refugees of concern to UNHCR around the world, only about 1 per cent are submitted by the agency for resettlement' (UNHCR, 2014).[1] The US plays an integral role in the refugee resettlement process as it 'is by far the largest of the 10 "traditional" resettlement countries, in that it has historically accepted more refugees for resettlement than all other countries combined' (Patrick, 2004) and welcomes more than half of all refugees eligible for resettlement in a third country (US Department of State [DoS], 2012). Through cooperative agreements with the State Department, 10 domestic voluntary agencies provide resettlement assistance to refugees upon their arrival to the US. Most of the agencies are either religious or community-based organizations providing goods, resources and services, including housing assistance, medical care, English language instruction, vocational services and interpreters and translators of various languages.

The length and differences in services provided varies state by state, so a refugee who is being resettled in Oregon will more than likely have a somewhat different experience than someone who is resettled in Texas. Typically, refugees are assigned a case manager who works closely with them not only to provide assistance in negotiating their new cultural surroundings, but also to obtain the necessary support in order to build a foundation for their new lives. In Massachusetts, refugee resettlement state-funded cash assistance programs typically come to an end after about six to eight months (sometimes sooner in other states), so it is imperative and urgent that refugees improve their English language skills and find employment before their funding runs out. Again, while this varies on a state-by-state basis, some exceptions to the six to eight months' rule are made for the elderly, refugees who have been physically disabled and those who are responsible for dependents. In these cases, such refugee clients may be eligible to receive other social services.

Method

Data collection

The texts covered in this study comprise the websites of two voluntary agencies, specifically Catholic Charities Archdiocese of Boston (CC) and Lutheran Social Services of New England (LSS), responsible for assisting with the US resettlement process in Massachusetts. Additionally, the legal definition of the term *refugee* as defined in the UN's 1951 Refugee Convention will be considered in its larger historical context and in the way in which the term is employed in the self-representations of the two voluntary agencies examined here. Within those self-representations, a goal of the resettlement process that surfaces repeatedly in the texts is the word *self-sufficiency*. It is a term that is not explicitly defined and, therefore, this study will eventually attempt to also uncover its possible definitions and consider its uses within the discourse surrounding the US refugee resettlement process.

The choice to focus on two voluntary agencies in New England stems from the fact that my work as a volunteer ESL teacher at a voluntary agency located in Massachusetts will be incorporated into the data and their analysis. I began working as a volunteer ESL teacher in the spring of 2011 in order to gain more language teaching experience while a graduate student. I sought out an ESL classroom comprised of refugees to gain that experience with little prior knowledge about how the US refugee resettlement process worked. At the voluntary agency where I was placed, ESL classes were offered Monday through Thursday for three hours per day with each hour designated for advanced, intermediate and beginner English proficiency levels. Because the ESL teacher welcomed all students no matter their proficiency to each hour since there was a lack of human resources available to provide more hours of instruction with individualized attention, it became all the more challenging to coordinate and deliver lessons in a meaningful, student-centered manner. Most days, the intermediate class that fell during the middle of the morning was at full capacity. The students were predominantly adult males in their twenties who had been in the US for less than six months. Many of them came from countries such as Sudan, Iraq, Myanmar, Eritrea, the Central African Republic and Afghanistan. At first, my responsibilities entailed working one-on-one with students during the two times per week I attended the ESL classes. Later on, as I gained more experience and the ESL teacher's availability decreased considerably, my responsibilities grew. Occasionally, I was responsible for leading classes and making decisions about the content of those classes, and I eventually increased my weekly attendance to four times per week. I worked at that particular voluntary agency for about a year and a half before that branch closed. Since then, I have continued my work in refugee resettlement at other agencies, assisting in developing ESL curriculum and resources at each.

The material conditions and the lived experiences of the refugees with whom I worked are taken into consideration in my analysis because of how they diverge from claims made by voluntary agencies on their websites regarding the services they provide and how they are provided. My contention is that material conditions determine linguistic resources, not only in terms of language acquisition development, but also how recently arrived refugees are able to gain literacy in the social practices of their new culture.

Data analysis

The analysis of linguistic production and competence must encompass more than and exceed Noam Chomsky's notion of what that constitutes (Bourdieu, 1977) because 'when people mean things to each other, there is always more than language at stake' (Gee, 2011). Therefore, the way in which the meanings of texts or other semiotic forms are created, decoded and negotiated is dependent on the resources that members of a given society have available to them. Additionally, if we understand semiosis (Fairclough, 2012) as a process of situated meaning-making (Gee, 2011), then it can be said that such processes play a large part in shaping the sort of situated social practices (i.e. literacies) that different social actors in society develop. Ultimately, as Blommaert (2005) asserts, a speaker's access to linguistic resources is 'socially consequential' and a great determinant of how much say and power that person has in certain contexts. Moreover, certain groups may assert their dominance and wield their power to silence and implement exclusionary tactics in order to deny others access to cultural capital as a way to maintain the status quo that serves the more powerful group's interests. In fact, 'among the most radical, surest, and best hidden censorships are those which exclude certain individuals from communication (e.g. by not inviting them to places where people speak with authority, or by putting them in places without speech)' (Bourdieu, 1977).

Conversely, language can also be used as a tool by which subordinated groups may produce the solidarity crucial to protect their own 'distinctive ways of acting, interacting with others, believing, valuing, dressing, and using various sorts of objects and tools in various sorts of distinctive environments' (Gee, 2011). It is a mode through which groups can potentially re-'colonize' (a slightly different take on Fairclough's [2012] point that recontextualization has an ambivalent character) language in order to reclaim and infuse words and discourses with new meanings and ultimately change the social structures that sustain them. Blommaert (2005) makes a similar point when he writes, 'the way in which discourse is being represented, re-spoken, or re-written sheds light on the emergence of new orders of discourse, struggles over normativity, attempts at control, and resistance against regimes of power'. I argue that such struggles can only take place and be taken up if certain discourses and linguistic resources are present in the first place.

Language and social practices work in tandem through a dialectic construction:

> On the one hand, the situational, institutional and social settings shape and affect discourses, and on the other, discourses influence discursive as well as non-discursive social and political processes and actions. In other words, discourses as linguistic social practices that can be seen as constituting non-discursive and discursive social practices and, at the same time, as being constituted by them. (Wodak, 2001: 66)

Therefore, it is necessary to understand not only the context in which certain texts, discourses and social practices are situated, but also the history from which they stem (among others, see Blommaert, 2005; Fairclough, 2013; Gee, 2011; Wodak, 2001). By making apparent how those in control use discursive mechanisms to make present or leave absent certain lived experiences, CDA can be used to expose those ideologies that are privileged and made to seem invisible while simultaneously creating a new space for those discourses that are left out. 'Discursive control of public perceptions consists of the complex interplay of the language that is chosen and sanctioned by the listeners, the power dynamics around who has access to public discursive space and the denial of access to the information, its construction and the location of its dissemination' (Gunn, 2011). When critical discourse analysts raise questions regarding matters of interpretation of texts, they simultaneously raise issues of access to linguistic resources (do subjects of the texts, refugees themselves, have the sort of literacies needed to decode the text the way that they are intended to be read?); and discursive spaces (do subjects of the texts have a say in how they are construed before the public?). Refugees who have never used a computer, are not familiar with the internet or have low levels of computer literacy may not even know that such texts exist let alone the ideologies which brought them into existence. CDA's intertextual contribution to the contextualization of the texts being examined is that it points out the numerous ways in which texts can be understood depending on who is doing the interpreting.

The discourse that surrounds refugee resettlement risks the perpetuation of a lack of awareness concerning the under-resourced and underfunded material conditions with which refugees must negotiate their new lives. Such obstacles in newly arrived refugees' lives impair their ability to ensure they acquire the numerous literacies, or situated practices, needed in a new language and culture. If we accept the claim that 'language in use always performs actions in the world' (Gee, 2011) and, as a result, language has transformative power, then it is possible to use discursive mechanisms not only to control silences so as to minimize resistance against certain social practices, but also conversely to create democratic spaces in which previously absent experiences can take part in the co-construction of publics that ultimately function to create inclusive social practices.

Discussion of Data

Refugee as a legal term

The decision to include the UNHCR's definition of refugee as part of the data is so that its situated meaning(s) in the US refugee resettlement process can be uncovered through hermeneutic interpretation. The term refugee is defined in the legal discourse of the written text establishing the UNHCR, a text that can be assigned to an institutional genre of legislation and is primarily situated in the field of law-making political procedure. It is important to keep the UNHCR's legal definition in mind while considering the agency of refugees, the power relationships between refugees and voluntary agencies, the ways in which refugees are represented by government agencies and how the roles of voluntary agencies are represented to the general public. In the 1951 Refugee Convention, under Article 1(A)2, refugee is a legal term that applies to any person who

> ...owing to a well-founded fear of being persecuted for reasons of race, religion, nationality, membership of a particular social group or political opinion, is outside the country of his nationality and is unable or, owing to such fear, is unwilling to avail himself of the protection of that country; or who, not having a nationality and being outside the country of his former habitual residence as a result of such events, is unable or, owing to such fear, is unwilling to return to it. (UNHCR, 2010a)

It is important to consider the nuances of such a legal definition because they raise questions such as: who defines under what circumstances someone qualifies as a refugee? For whom, by whom and for what purpose is this definition determined and used to direct the trajectories of the lives that fit into it?

For the purposes of this chapter, I want to briefly consider one aspect of the above definition: religious persecution is the second principal reason listed in the UNHCR's legal definition of a refugee for why a person may have a well-founded fear for not returning to his or her country of origin. Many of the largest and most active voluntary agencies that receive funds from the State Department in order to assist in the US resettlement process are religious organizations, such as Catholic Charities, Lutheran Social Services and Jewish Vocational Services. While they are not allowed to proselytize and they claim their intent is to assist recently arrived refugees safely away from persecution, it is difficult to remove these religious groups themselves from their own histories, many of which have also been, at some time, responsible for some form of persecution. Additionally, how is a refugee who is fleeing religious persecution to feel safe in his or her new, and supposedly protective, home when the organization providing its assistance (or 'charity') is faith based and fraught with its own particular religious ideologies and agenda?

The UNHCR definition of *refugee* does not explicitly index any sense of power in its description of the people given such a protective status, nor does it directly acknowledge their often permanently transient state (Bauman, 2004). 'Refugee' is a deeply political issue, not only because it has to do with social, political and economic circumstances that force migration from a country, but additionally because the host country is also a political choice[2] and because these are individuals who will claim a share of the cultural and economic capital in the resettlement country. In short, a lot is at stake for the multitude of different groups involved in resettlement.

Yet, when many refugees languish for multiple years, sometimes upward of a decade, in refugee camps that are not always best equipped to handle varying and sometimes large influxes of people, does that also constitute protection? The psychological and physical toll that such a 'transitional' period can have on a person, especially after he or she has already fled persecution in his or her country of origin, can leave severe, if not permanent, and debilitating imprints on a person's life. When a person is finally granted permission to be admitted into a third country to be resettled, is it a realistic expectation that he or she should be able to learn an entirely new language and get and hold down a job in a culture which is entirely unfamiliar in order to become 'self-sufficient' within six months? Research shows (Cummins, 1999) that it takes approximately one to three years for second language learners to acquire conversational skills in a language and it takes even longer for the acquisition of academic language to a level of proficiency similar to that of native speakers. The potential for acquiring conversational skills in a second, third or fourth language becomes all the more challenging when the learners have not only faced constant instability, trauma and/or physical violence in their past, if not for most of their lives, but may also be preliterate in their native languages. Especially for those whose English language proficiency is at a complete beginner's level and when interpreters are not readily available, how is it possible to effectively advocate for themselves within an unfamiliar support system comprised entirely of strangers who they are unsure whether or not to trust?

> The efficacy of discourse, its power to convince, depends on the authority of the person who utters it, or, what amounts to the same thing, on his 'accent', functioning as index of authority. Thus, the whole social structure is present in the interaction (and therefore in the discourse): the material conditions of existence determine discourse through the linguistic production relations which they make possible and which they structure. (Bourdieu, 1977)

This is exemplified when the material conditions necessary to refugees' gaining literacy in a social practice are lacking and failing to be effectively supportive. While many refugees gain employment by the time their cash assistance runs out, it is uncertain whether they ultimately acquire the literacies[3] necessary to navigate the multitude of discourses present in US society. Frequently, the employment that refugees gain, often dubbed 'survival jobs', consists of jobs that are low wage, entry level, without benefits, sometimes part-time and often do not pay enough to support a family. Furthermore, refugees who have higher levels of education must take jobs for which they are overqualified not only because of their lower English proficiency but also due to restrictions on transferrable credentials, such as professional certifications or educational degrees that are not accepted forms of documentation in US society.

Should not truly supportive resettlement ultimately include the development of those particular literacies necessary beyond just survival, so that refugees are able to maintain and sustain their language development even after their allotted cash assistance runs out? Whether the assistance provided to them through voluntary agencies funded by the US government actually guides them to self-sufficiency thus becomes questionable. Without the knowledge vital to exhibit resistance and self-advocacy, is it possible for such goals to be realized?

Representations: The positive self and the 'needy' other

Upon a close examination of the texts that appear on the websites of several voluntary agencies responsible for providing support in refugee resettlement in the US, a discursive construction of a dichotomous 'us' and 'them' becomes evident. Both Catholic Charities Archdiocese of Boston (CC) and Lutheran Social Services of New England (LSS) construct positive self-representations of the way in which they provide their services while the representations they develop of the refugees they claim to assist are based largely on that of the negative, and in this case more specifically the 'needy' other. 'The discursive construction of "us" and "them" [are] the basic fundaments of discourses of identity and difference' (Wodak, 2001). My contention here is that it is also that of a discourse of marginalization.

For each of the voluntary agency–generated, web-based texts I have chosen, I focus only on the portion of their websites that presents the resettlement services (usually titled 'Refugee and Immigrant Services') for which they receive funding. Each website has information to visitors on the services they offer, with Catholic Charities also listing links to current, local news articles in a column on the right-hand side of the page and Lutheran Social Services of New England providing a much more robust entry point into their resettlement services with direct links to statistics, refugee stories, an FAQ section and information on how to get involved. The rationale in including the websites of CC and LSS is that they are two of the largest charitable organizations and providers of social services in Massachusetts (ccab.org (CC), 2014; LSS, 2014). Given the magnitude of people they serve and that they are non-profit organizations, they rely heavily on contributions from community members whether it is through monetary donations or the work of volunteers. As such, their websites are one channel through which they are able to reach members of their community and spread the word about their work.

The Refugee and Immigration Services section of their website boasts, 'Catholic Charities has the ability to fill job openings quickly' (CC, 2012). Yet, at the voluntary agency where I worked, the one employment services coordinator position – a position that required assisting in job searches, resume creation and preparing and transporting refugees to job interviews – stood vacant for four months. When voluntary agencies are already faced with tight budgets and staffed with the bare minimum of employees, the responsibility of the employment services coordinator falls on either the case managers or the ESL teacher who are also maxed out in terms of the needs they must address for over 50 refugee clients and their families to whom employment services are provided.

There are several more reasons why such claims to '[filling] job openings quickly' are misleading. First, the assumption is that there are job openings to be filled at all. Since the US recession hit in 2008, the unemployment rate has remained higher than normal, which means that there is a larger than normal pool of job applicants seeking work and fewer positions available due to the downsizing that inevitably occurs during a recession. Secondly, due to the combination of the recession and the unfilled employment services coordinator position, many of CC's refugee clients did not find employment until days before their cash assistance allowance terminated. While in a larger context this may be considered 'quick', in the lived experience of a newly arrived refugee who is very much cognizant of the pressures to find a job before the cash assistance ends, it is not. In fact, it places further undue stress upon refugee clients and inevitably makes it difficult to focus on their other new and equally (if not more) important goal: to acquire a level of English proficiency that eases their ability to navigate their new culture. And finally, a third reason why the phrase is misleading is because often many of the refugees were inevitably directed toward Walmart's online application. While a job at Walmart may open new social possibilities (more opportunities to speak English with native speakers on the job), it also acts as a system of exploitation as shown through documentaries exposing Walmart's dubious business practices (Greenwald, 2005). Walmart is not, in fact, 'Making Better Possible' – at least not for those whom it claims to. Therefore, while their job openings may in fact be filled quickly, does such job placement lead to actual self-sufficiency when oftentimes a minimum wage does not constitute a living wage?

In the very first few paragraphs on the Refugee and Immigrant Services page of LSS, another voluntary agency providing social services to refugees in Massachusetts, LSS describes the refugees they assist as 'among the earth's neediest' and 'the stranger in our midst' as shown here:

> Lutheran Social Services views refugees as among the earth's neediest populations and affirms our call to welcome and offer aid to the stranger in our midst by providing new Americans with the resources they need to adjust to their new culture and become self-sufficient and productive citizens. (LSS, 2014)

While 'the stranger in our midst' is not outright discriminatory – in fact, it is part of a religious genre often associated with the Bible – it nevertheless does set up the dichotomous relationship of a charitable 'us' who come from a 'tradition of caring' and a deficient 'them' who are lacking in the economic means for their self-sufficiency and 'need' to obtain them from the voluntary agency. Here, viewed from an angle of intertextuality, a religious genre is recontextualized (Fairclough, 2012) in an institutional text that is used to present to its public through the channel of a website the social services they provide to their clients. The operationalization of a religious genre through an institutional genre becomes slightly more complex when we remember that, as part of their agreement with the federal government, it is illegal for such institutions to proselytize. Furthermore, when describing refugees as 'the stranger[s] in our midst', how can a sense of belonging be truly fostered when refugees are depicted as the other within our normalcy from the start? Why not, instead, describe refugees as the new members of our community, rather than using a literary term such as 'midst', which gives a mystifying air to what is really just a community or neighborhood?

The sentence eventually shifts to the more inclusionary descriptors 'new Americans' and 'self-sufficient and productive citizens' but only after first identifying their clients simply in exclusionary terms ('refugees' then 'the earth's neediest populations' and 'the stranger in our midst'). The way in which refugees are successively positioned in one ideologically laden sentence so summarily and heavy-handedly indexes the transformation that the persecuted refugee supposedly undergoes through his or her displacement and subsequent resettlement process into a US citizen. The implication is that refugees are productive citizens only once they become 'self-sufficient' through voluntary agencies since they have little choice but to be reliant on such agencies to apprentice them into their new lives. Thus, one conclusion that may be drawn from the series of renderings of the refugee experience as 'view[ed]' by LSS is that refugees evidently come from powerlessness with few skills due to the displacement they face in their country of origin and inevitably face more powerlessness in the country in which they find asylum and then additionally in a third country where they may eventually resettle. Decisions are made about them, for them, but certainly not by them. Without the LSS aid and resources they need in their new culture, refugees may not 'become self-sufficient and productive citizens' otherwise. In other words, if LSS is not there to welcome them, then what do they become instead?

How does *self-sufficiency* become a realistic expectation?

Before I begin my analysis of the term *self-sufficiency* as it is used in the context of refugee resettlement, I want to make note of the meaning of *self-sufficiency* as a concept on a larger scale. According to the *Oxford English Dictionary*, to be self-sufficient means to be 'sufficient in or for oneself (itself) without aid or support from outside; able to supply one's needs oneself. Not now of persons'. In our ever-globalizing world, it is becoming less and less possible to be entirely independent of any aid or support from outside as we grow more alienated from the sources and processes involved in the production of our most basic needs (i.e. food, water, shelter). The term *self-sufficiency* appears repeatedly in the discourse used by voluntary agencies, particularly as the ultimate goal of the social services provided to refugees. However, *self-sufficiency* as a process and a goal is not explicitly defined on their websites. Moreover, the term is not contextualized within the material constraints of the resettlement process. In my analysis, I will first examine the descriptions of *self-sufficiency* contained on the websites of several agencies involved in the resettlement process, and then I will show examples of its usage within the texts examined.

While it is not a voluntary agency, the Massachusetts Office of Refugees and Immigrants (ORI) is the state agency in charge of coordinating the services provided by voluntary agencies through the Massachusetts refugee resettlement program. The ORI's website is dotted with the term *self-sufficiency* and it appears on its homepage as part of its mission statement (ORI, 2014). The ORI provides a glossary section for the terms used in its documents and on its website and includes definitions of the terms *durable self-sufficiency* and *self-sufficiency*. *Durable self-sufficiency* is defined as when a 'family's gross income exceeds 450% of the Federal Poverty Level for the state' and the definition given for *self-sufficiency* reads as when a 'family's gross income exceeds 150% of the Federal Poverty Level for the state' (ORI, 2014). Here, *self-sufficiency* is defined as independence in purely economic terms and can be understood as high enough levels of income that allow for a family to subsist without government cash assistance and benefits such as food stamps. These definitions do not treat the term as a hyponym that might take into account and subsume other ways in which refugees may or may not be self-sufficient. Overcoming a lack of language proficiency in English and mental and physical health issues resulting from past traumas that may prove to be obstacles in achieving an income above the poverty level are left out of the definitions provided by the ORI. Such conceptualizations of self-sufficiency make the assumption that finding employment, usually at a job (or jobs) that pays little more than a minimum wage, is its main constitutive factor.

Without any explicit definition, *self-sufficiency* appears in two sections of Catholic Charities' Refugee and Immigrant Services website: Refugee Resettlement and Adult Education as Second Language (ESOL) classes. In the Refugee Resettlement section, *self-sufficiency* is coupled with the word *independence* as something that their staff helps in attaining *for* refugees: 'Along with this critical assistance, refugees receive compassion, understanding and positive reassurance from our staff to help in the attainment of independence and self-sufficiency' (CC, 2012). By not providing an explicit definition of the term, voluntary agencies cannot be held strictly accountable when their refugee clients do not meet the goal of self-sufficiency, whatever that may be – a goal that should encompass more than just obtaining employment that pays a minimum wage and acquiring a level of English language proficiency that may never progress beyond a conversational level. Furthermore, if self-sufficiency is considered in terms of the two main support services provided by voluntary agencies – that is, vocational services and English language instruction – is self-sufficiency a realistic goal when the prospects of competing for a job without a high level of English language proficiency create additional difficulties that further compound the challenge for refugees of transferring their professional skills into an American job market mired in a global recession?

On the LSS website, the term *self-sufficiency* appears numerous times, including in the sentence quoted in the previous section of this chapter. Throughout their Refugee and Immigrant Services section, it is frequently used in a variety of contexts in which the achievement of economic independence, getting health and vocational services, and English proficiency are discussed. In other words, LSS's version of self-sufficiency might be implicitly understood in a variety of ways, depending on which of their services for 'new Americans' is being considered. Nevertheless, in none of its uses is a definition of the term made explicit.

Here, in an attempt to uncover other connotations, I will focus on two of its uses, namely those instances in which the term is used in contexts similar to those of other voluntary agencies or governmental organizations with respect to English language acquisition and employment. On the page delineating their English for speakers of other languages (ESOL) services, LSS uses *self-sufficiency* in the following way:

> The ESOL curriculum is a competency-based model and focuses on helping students reach early self-sufficiency by incorporating community and societal orientation with an emphasis on job-related ESOL instruction. (LSS, 2014)

Again, language learning and employment are coupled together as the formula for how students may reach what LSS calls 'early self-sufficiency', which can be interpreted as their term for a quick route to acculturation. In the refugee resettlement context, the length of time for which refugees receive resettlement assistance is an important factor when considering how and when self-sufficiency takes place. As pointed out in earlier sections of this chapter, it seems unrealistic to expect refugees dealing with past and current traumas and then simultaneously entering a depressed job market into which their job skills may or may not be transferrable to find gainful employment in less than six months' time; reach a high enough level of English proficiency that will not only help them find employment but also maintain that job; and know to advocate for themselves should their employer have questionable labor practices or if they are not a member of a union. Moreover, the overriding assumption again is that self-sufficiency is something that results from assistance provided by LSS in the short time during which refugees are receiving services from them rather than something with which refugees already arrived considering their success at gaining refugee status through the UNHCR's often labyrinthine bureaucracies.

In another section of the Refugee and Immigrant Services section of their website, called 'Frequently Asked Questions about Refugee Resettlement', in answer to a question that asks 'Can refugees afford their apartments?' *self-sufficiency* is used in the following way:

> While it is certainly very difficult to start over again, the majority of refugees transition to self-sufficiency within a short time after arrival. Like others with limited income who are just getting on their feet, setting priorities is crucial for refugees. LSS New American Services assists refugee families with applying for subsidized housing when appropriate. (LSS, 2014)

Although the question is framed in a manner that should elicit a yes or no response, it does not directly include either as part of it. Instead, an answer indirectly implying that once refugees 'transition to self-sufficiency' with the assistance of LSS, 'the majority' are able to do so. Again, *self-sufficiency* is used in an ambiguous sense. A refugee's ability to afford an apartment seems to connote that it is constitutive of the sort of self-sufficiency LSS assists refugees in achieving. Nevertheless, it remains unclear as to whether self-sufficiency is to be equated only with the survival skills necessary to meet basic needs such as food, water and shelter or if it should be understood as merely the separation from the voluntary agency that inevitably occurs when the allotted assistance runs out.

Concluding Remarks

Although the analysis contained within this chapter is not exhaustive, I have attempted to begin to unveil through a CDA the negative representation of the refugee as the 'needy' other by certain voluntary agencies. The omission of the lived experiences of refugees as well as their service providers from their representations in the texts of voluntary agencies responsible for providing resettlement services serves to sustain existing unequal footings that risk further marginalizing refugees. Moreover, it was through my work with one particular voluntary agency that raised my own awareness and identification of what Fairclough (2012) calls 'social wrongs' which 'can be understood in broad terms as aspects of social systems, form or orders which are detrimental to human well-being, and which could in principle be ameliorated if not eliminated, though perhaps only through major changes in systems, forms or orders' (Fairclough, 2012). It is understood that the task of voluntary agencies is to address a social wrong. Nonetheless, via the same institutional process of providing assistance, such agencies end up risking the creation of new social wrongs when they are unable to function to their full capacity because of a lack of sufficient funding. In a sense, it can be argued that the original social wrong (marginalization of certain groups of people) is recontextualized in a new setting as another, new social wrong (the continued marginalization of certain members of those original groups). The voluntary agency then risks becoming an obstacle in addressing it. After all, voluntary agencies must present themselves as successfully providing their services in order to continue to get federal funding. And finally, the inclusion here of some ethnographic observations, as Fairclough points out, allows for 'the relationship between reality and discourse— the reality and the discourses of the "global economy" and of its impact, implications and ramifications' (Fairclough, 2012) to be more directly questioned. In this case, the 'global economy' that Fairclough alludes to manifests as the positive self-presentations of voluntary agencies provided through their websites to the public. In reality, they do not always have the power to assist their clients in the ways that they claim to. As critical discourse analysts claim that language has a dialectical relationship with social structures and if language truly can have transformative effects, then it is imperative that it be used as a tool and a resource in ensuring equitable access to the discursive spaces and resources for the people directly affected by such discourses.

In this chapter, I hoped to emphasize what implications the material conditions with which refugees are faced have in their ability to acquire the necessary language skills and literacies in order to effectively negotiate their new cultural surroundings and achieve the seemingly ever-elusive self-sufficiency that is widely asserted as the ambiguous end goal of the services provided through the US refugee resettlement process. Moreover, to readers who have less familiarity with how voluntary agencies do or do not conduct their work and meet the needs of their clients, I want to stress that my singular experiences at the one voluntary agency I described in this chapter should not be taken as indicative of how voluntary agencies and other resettlement assistance providers generally operate. To do so, would be to risk essentializing them. Nevertheless, as I have continued working with other refugee resettlement organizations, it is very common to see struggles in obtaining funding and other resources to ensure the 'self-sufficiency' of those they serve. And, finally, I also want to acknowledge the risk of essentializing refugees as a monolithic whole, which gives the impression that they arrive in the US with the same experiences and needs. In fact, outside of being under-resourced, that is one of the myriad reasons that work in refugee resettlement can be so challenging.

Through the adoption of an approach to teaching literacy practices that builds upon their daily lived experiences (Freire, 1998) and acknowledges the ideological positions they may hold, refugees can be further enabled to develop vital agencies in order to intervene in their realities as subjects capable of proficiently availing themselves of their symbolic and material circumstances. One such practice is building refugees' metalinguistic awareness and continually emphasizing that even once their support from the voluntary agency they have been placed with is over, they must continue their English language development. Refugees who are denied such a necessary resource or opportunity to practice it will have greater difficulty in adeptly navigating the contexts in which they are expected to so quickly acculturate. It is undeniable that language is a communicative resource used by human beings to relay messages and interact with one another, but its role in our realities transcends such a narrow definition. Language is a social and cultural force. It has the power to shape social practices but can also be pushed and pulled at by those very practices.

Notes

(1) The other 99% of persons with refugee status who are not submitted to an agency for resettlement in a third country are either repatriated to their country of origin once the UNHCR has deemed it safe to return, local integration into the country to which they fled through that country's asylum-seeking process, migration to another country or waiting (often in a refugee camp) for reunification with family. It should also be noted that there are many people who are displaced as a result of the same crises, but are not documented by the UNHCR and thus are not reported in official statistics.

(2) If we consider 'political' in terms of James Gee's definition, that is 'any situation where the distribution of social goods is at stake' (Gee, 2011: 31) with 'social goods [being] anything a social group or society takes as a good worth having' (Gee, 2011: 31) and, therefore, are 'ultimately what give people power and status in a society (or not)' (Gee, 2011: 32), then the UNHCR's actions and responsibilities mandated by the 1951 Refugee Convention are certainly political despite the fact that it also mandates that the UNHCR remain strictly non-political. Moreover, once resettled, refugees are afforded the same rights as nationals are (UNHCR, 2014) and, therefore, are allotted equal access to the same social services. Nevertheless, debates over post-crisis responsibility and negative representations of refugees as 'criminals' and so on often circulate through the media. Such posing in the media of refugees, immigrants and asylum-seekers makes integration into their country of resettlement that much more challenging as it significantly shapes the political and cultural climate that they enter. And, finally, for Iraqi or Afghan refugees who are fleeing their countries of origin as a result of US-led wars, resettling in the country for which they worked as translators/interpreters or the country that played a large role in the devastation of Iraq's or Afghanistan's infrastructure, is deeply political as their association with the US is often construed as traitorous by certain groups in their countries of origin.

(3) As previously noted in this chapter, I am using the term *literacy* as a form of situated social practice. The types of literacy necessary just for survival by refugees in their country of resettlement include but are not limited to: vocational skills (navigating the job market, creating resumes, understanding the job search process, effective interview demeanor); metalinguistic awareness to ensure their continued language development beyond the initial instruction they receive; computer literacy; financial literacy (such as banking in general, saving money,

using credit); navigating the US healthcare system (including mental health counseling); tenant's rights; if they are parents, understanding the school system; grocery shopping (making both nutritionally sound and informed consumer choices); and so on.

References

Baker, P. and McEnery, T. (2005) A corpus-based approach to discourses of refugees and asylum seekers in UN and newspaper texts. *Journal of Language and Politics* (4) 2, 197–226.

Baker, P. and Garbielatos, C. (2008) Fleeing, sneaking, flooding: A corpus analysis of discursive constructions of refugees and asylum seekers in the UK press, 1996–2005. *Journal of English Linguistics* 36 (1), 5–38.

Bauman, Z. (2004) *Wasted Lives: Modernity and Its Outcasts*. Malden, MA: Polity Press.

Blommaert, J. (2005) *Discourse*. New York: Cambridge University Press.

Bourdieu, P. (1977) The economics of linguistic exchanges. *Social Science Information* 16 (6), 645–668.

Catholic Charities Archdiocese of Boston (2012) See http://www.ccab.org (accessed 4 July 2014).

Cummins, J. (1999) BICS and CALP: Clarifying the distinction. See http://isulead2010.wikispaces.com/file/view/Jim+Cummins+2+-+Bics+and+Calp%5B1%5D.pdf (accessed 10 July 2015).

Fairclough, N. (2013) *Language and Power*. New York: Routledge.

Fairclough, N. (2012) A dialectical-relational approach to critical discourse analysis in social research. In R. Wodak and M. Meyer (eds) *Methods of Critical Discourse Analysis* (pp. 162–186). Thousand Oaks, CA: Sage.

Freire, P. (1998) *Pedagogy of Freedom: Ethics, Democracy, and Civic Courage*. Lanham, MD: Rowman & Littlefield.

Gee, J.P. (2011) Discourse analysis: What makes it critical? In R. Rogers (ed.) *An Introduction to Critical Discourse Analysis in Education* (pp. 23–45). New York: Taylor & Francis.

Greenwald, R. (Producer and Director) (2005) Wal-Mart: The High Cost of Low Price [Motion Picture]. Culver City, CA: Brave New Films.

Gunn, A.M. (2011) Discourses that silence and deflect attention away from the interests of low-wage workers experiencing job loss. *Critical Discourse Studies* 8 (1), 31–44.

Loescher, G. (2001) UNHCR and the erosion of refugee protection. *Forced Migration Review* 10, 28–30.

LSS Lutheran Social Services of New England (2014) See http://www.lssne.org (accessed 4 July 2014).

Massachusetts Office for Refugees and Immigrants (2014) See http://www.mass.gov/ori/ (accessed 4 July 2014).

Patrick, E. (2004) Migration Policy Institute. 'The US Refugee Resettlement Program'. See http://www.migrationinformation.org/Feature/display.cfm?ID=229 (accessed 4 July 2014).

Steimel, S.J. (2010) Refugees as people: The portrayal of refugees in American human interest stories. *Journal of Refugee Studies* 23 (2), 219–237.

'self-su'fficient, adj.'. (2014) *OED online*. Oxford University Press. See http://www.oed.com.ezproxy.lib.utexas.edu/view/Entry/175462.

UN High Commissioner for Refugees (2005) An introduction to international protection: protecting persons of concern to UNHCR. See http://www.unhcr.org/refworld/docid/4214cb4f2.html (accessed 4 July 2014).

UN High Commissioner for Refugees (2010a) Convention and protocol relating to the status of refugees. See http://www.unhcr.org/3b66c2aa10.html (accessed 4 July 2014).

UN High Commissioner for Refugees (2010b) Statute of the Office of the United Nations High Commissioner for Refugees. See http://www.unhcr.org/3b66c39e1.html (accessed 4 July 2014).

UN High Commissioner for Refugees (2014) See http://www.unhcr.org (accessed 4 July 2014).

US Department of Homeland Security (2012) Refugees and asylees: 2011. See http://www.dhs.gov/xlibrary/assets/statistics/publications/ois_rfa_fr_2011.pdf (accessed 4 July 2014).

US Department of State (2012) Bureau of Population, Refugees, and Migration. See http://www.state.gov/j/prm/index.htm (accessed 4 July 2014).

Wodak, R. (2001) The discourse-historical approach. In R. Wodak and M. Meyer (eds) *Methods of Critical Discourse Analysis* (pp. 63–94). Thousand Oaks, CA: Sage.

10 Language as a Fund of Knowledge: The Case of Mama Rita and Implications for Refugee Policy

Cassie D. Leymarie

Introduction

This chapter focuses on how language is a resource, and a *fund of knowledge* (FoK; González *et al.*, 2005), by highlighting the case of Mama Rita, an exceptional Somali refugee woman in Clarkston, Georgia. The data originate from a larger research project and my time working with a community-based, refugee-serving organization. By sharing Mama Rita's case, I aim to underscore that policies for refugee language education are inadequate and that they neglect to acknowledge that language is a powerful precondition for community participation. Additionally, I aim to challenge local and societal discourses about refugees, in particular, Somali refugees.

Somali refugees began resettling in Clarkston in the early 1990s and despite a prominent community of refugees and refugee service providers, they along with other refugee groups continue to face obstacles in integrating into and participating in their new community. Several studies suggest that language is a primary and complex challenge of refugee resettlement (Fong, 2004; Martin, 2004; McBrien, 2005). Despite language as a primary challenge, current policies vary in terms of how long refugees must attend English classes. Most refugees attend classes between 30 and 90 days before entering the workforce. This chapter explores the practices of Mama Rita in order to shed light on how her language practices support her agency, or the socioculturally mediated capacity to act (Ahearn, 2001), and in turn assist her to participate in the community.

Additionally, Mama Rita's case points out that, at times, refugees are misrepresented and face misperceptions. They are subject to the media discourses that are propagated about refugees and more specifically Somalis. Oftentimes, Somali refugees are presented as cunning crooks or vulnerable victims (Horst, 2007) and are portrayed in the media as warlords and pirates. Such portrayals reproduce discourses and contribute to social realities (Van Dijk, 2005). In the small community of Clarkston, Somali refugees are subject to mass mediated and local discourses. In addition to the media and discourses surrounding Somalis, local residents are influenced by discourses that are anti-refugee or that portray refugees as draining local resources.

Given the context-specific factors surrounding refugee language policies, this research study aims to demonstrate that more emphasis must be put on language pedagogy to enhance the lives of not only the refugees but also their greater community. Although several studies have investigated Somali immigrants' educational experiences, identity and ability to acquire print literacy (Hopkins, 2010; McBrien, 2005; Oikonomidoy, 2009; Tarone *et al.*, 2009), few have explored language as an FoK that might contribute to the language socialization of refugees and their ability to participate communally.

Funds of Knowledge

The present research project has been developed using the concept of FoK (González *et al.*, 2005). FoK as a construct provide a meaningful method for researchers to observe and investigate the daily practices of marginalized people. Simply defined, FoK are people's daily practices that educators and policymakers may fail to notice. The FoK conceptualization facilitates 'a systematic and powerful way to represent communities in terms of resources, the wherewithal they possess and how to harness these resources [...]' (González *et al.*, 2005: x). In essence, FoK help to bridge the gap in knowledge and understanding between people and their communities at large.

FoK include language practices, social relationships and strategies that have been developed and accumulated; the bodies of knowledge integral to the functioning and well-being of people and their households. For example, understanding ways in which refugees participate and interact within their community can inform educational activities and policies that are geared toward progressing their language socialization and integration into their community. Or, one may find that an individual greatly values one-on-one conversation rather than a small-group format for exchanging knowledge. For the purposes of this study, I will identify the practices that put Mama Rita's language use in context and demonstrate how language is a factor contributing to her active participation in the community.

The FoK approach allows for theorizing based on 'the lives of ordinary people, their everyday activities, and what has led them to the place they find themselves' (Gonzalez, 2005: 1). Thus, the concept

[...] opens up spaces for the construction of new fields wherein students are not locked into an assumed unilineal heritage [...] allows for variability within populations rather than only between populations. More importantly the funds of knowledge of a community occupy that space between structure and agency, between the received historical circumstances of a group, and the infinite variations that social agents are able to negotiate within a structure. (Gonzalez, 2005: 43)

The FoK perspective emphasizes theorizing based on practices and acknowledging that 'practices do not emerge from nowhere; they are formed and transformed within sociohistorical circumstances' and 'constructed by and through discourses' (Gonzalez, 2005: 1). The FoK research model aims to discredit the view that culturally and linguistically diverse minorities lack knowledge or have a deficit for learning. In this sense, using FoK to conceptualize practice is a deliberate reactive choice to go against deficit views of refugees' linguistic and cultural resources.

FoK and Bourdieu's capital

The FoK approach may seem to have some commonality with Bourdieu's notion of cultural capital. Bourdieu defines capital as something that is

[...] in its objectified or embodied forms, takes time to accumulate and which, as a potential capital to produce profits and to reproduce itself as in identical or expanded form, contains a tendency to persist in its being, is a forced inscribed in the objectivity of things so that everything is not equally possible or impossible. (Bourdieu, 1986: 15)

Bourdieu describes three different forms of capital and suggests they contribute to the reproduction of inequality in society. They are

[...] economic capital, which is immediately and directly convertible into money and may be institutionalized in the form of property rights; [...] cultural capital, which is convertible, in certain conditions, into economic capital and may be institutionalized in the form of educational qualifications; and [...] social capital, made up of social obligations ('connections'), which is convertible, in certain conditions, into economic capital and may be institutionalized in the form of a title of nobility [...]. (Bourdieu, 1986: 16)

Bourdieu (1991) discusses the notion of linguistic capital as a form of cultural capital. Cultural capital may be in the form of dispositions of the mind and body, cultural goods and/or educational qualifications and membership in professional organizations. He goes on to say that the value and influence of cultural and social capital are often overshadowed by analyses of economic capital. Going back to the FoK approach, which focuses on resources within households, the cultural capital notion of Bourdieu suggests that the passing on of cultural capital in the home reproduces inequality of educational achievement, and because it is less visible than economic capital, it may not be as readily recognized as capital and may be seen as legitimate competence. Bourdieu emphasizes that cultural capital is not inherently valuable but is given value by the dominant class. Thus, the concept of cultural capital challenges dominant discourses and cultural hegemony.

Oughton (2010) discusses an important distinction. She suggests that FoK is not a subset of cultural capital. First, as pointed out by Coben (2002), who applied the economic metaphors of use values and exchange values to domains of adult numeracy practice, numeracy and literacy practices that may include budgeting or cooking may have a high use value in the household but a low exchange value elsewhere. In contrast, an academic certification may have a low use value and a higher exchange value. Oughton contends that

> Practices encompassed by the term 'funds of knowledge' tend to be *dismissed as low-status, or common-sense, possessed in some form or other by everyone, and often regarded as having little exchange-value, though a high use-value.* Contrast this with Bourdieu's cultural capital, exchangeable for symbolic and economic capital, and privileged and legitimated by a dominant elite. (Oughton, 2010: 69, my emphasis)

FoK, then, can be seen as cultural capital if legitimized and privileged through a dominant group or discourse. Not all FoK may be privileged, thus by their nature, FoK are overlooked practices.

Another distinction between capital and FoK is in the orientation to the term *culture*. The FoK approach does not necessitate the use of the term *culture* as the term may lead to 'expectations of group norms and often-static ideas of how people view the world and behave in it' (Gonzalez, 2005: 10). Instead, FoK research focuses on individuals and households and provides an alternative to generalizing about peoples' lives and backgrounds based on their *culture*, looking at individual lived experiences as resources. As noted by González (2005: 43), the examination of individuals' practices rather than the examination of *culture* 'supplies us with a panorama of activities that may or may not coincide with normative cultural behavior'. Thus, FoK contribute a more precise lens to investigate language and the practices of Mama Rita because current refugee education policies tend to dismiss language as common sense or possessed in some form or other by everyone, while in fact it is not.

Study Context

Clarkston

The population of Clarkston, Georgia, is approximately 7500, and it is located about 10 miles northeast of Atlanta. The city has been in existence since the 1830s as it was a connection point for the Georgia Railroad rail line that provided transport for merchants of Athens and Augusta, Georgia, as well as various locations in South Carolina. It was a typical Southern Christian community. In the 1980s, Clarkston consisted of a 90% white-only population which now stands at less than 14% (Rossenwasser, 2012). Contributing to the change of population was the decision in the early 1990s for Clarkston to become a refugee resettlement site. Since then, the population has dramatically shifted from a small community consisting of native-born American citizens to half of the current residents being foreign born. Somalis are not the only group that have resettled in Clarkston; among others, Burmese, Bhutanese, Iraqi, Eritrean and Sudanese populations are also present. Today, Clarkston is home to refugees from more than 40 nations. Clarkston was chosen as a resettlement site by agencies based on factors such as the metro-Atlanta job market, highways, access to public transportation and affordable housing. Clarkston can be characterized as what Vertovec (2007, 2010) has described as 'superdiverse'. Superdiversity is characterized by population complexity or the 'dynamic interplay of variables among an increased number of new, small and scattered, multiple-origin, transnationally connected, socio-economically differentiated and legally stratified immigrants' (Vertovec, 2007: 1).

Clarkston as a site for policy change

Clarkston was highlighted as a case study in a report given to the members of the Committee on Foreign Relations in the US Senate, entitled 'Abandoned Upon Arrival: Implications for Refugees and Local Communities Burdened by a US Resettlement System that is not Working' (S. Rep. No. 111-52, 2010). The report outlines several findings and recommendations that have implications for refugee education and policy. It documents Clarkston as a place of tumult and includes stories of prejudice and police brutality against refugees. The actions and discourse of the general Clarkston population do not convey a welcoming, understanding community.

The attitudes among the Clarkston community are in part due to the reality of resettlement. After three months, resettlement agencies no longer serve their refugee clients. While there are many services that refugees need in order to become acclimated to their new communities, English language education is integral. Many of these new residents have not fully integrated and their tribulations are left for the local community to handle. A greater emphasis on language and learning and pedagogy may resolve some of the issues. For example, refugee residents experience problems with housing. The report notes that refugee residents often caused apartment fires, one time leading to the tragic death of four refugee youth in 2008 (S. Rep. No. 111-52, 2010). Housing was not the only problem cited, but also access to and understanding of the legal system as well as the strain on the education system. Though the case study is brief, it touches on some of the issues that are still evident in present-day Clarkston, issues that generally disturb the greater community.

The report finds that resettlement locations 'burden' local governments, schools, police, hospitals and social services (S. Rep. No. 111-52, 2010). It states that in the case of Clarkston, 'resources for language instruction are inadequate. Unlike migrants in search of economic opportunities, who can access extensive friend and family networks, to navigate language or other cultural barriers, new refugee populations lack this type of community resource upon arrival' (S. Rep. No. 111-52, 2010: 2). Findings include the fact that 'efforts to address the special needs of refugee students are ad hoc, adding strain on local education funding' (S. Rep. No. 111-52, 2010: 2) and that 'each refugee is initially afforded one-size-fits-all assistance' (S. Rep. No. 111-52, 2010: 3). These findings progress the already burgeoning negative perceptions of refugees in the community.

The following suggestions are offered to alleviate the burden. First, a recommendation for the restructuring of the Bureau of Population, Refugees, and Migration's (PRM) process of consulting with state and local leaders about the backgrounds and quantities of refugees to be resettled and both qualitative and quantitative input from local communities. Another recommendation given in the report was to increase access to English as a second language (ESL) courses which includes finding ways to 'incentivize proficiency' through some conditional public assistance programs (S. Rep. No. 111-52, 2010: 4). The other major suggestions include investing in education (K-12), discarding the one-size-fits-all approach to refugee resettlement and education, improving accountability, exploring innovative models and promoting community engagement. This chapter will begin to offer further support for increased access to ESL courses in order to support community engagement.

Somali refugees and the Clarkston community

Mama Rita, whose case is the focus of this chapter, is a Somali refugee. In the 2012 report on the state of the world's refugees, the United Nations High Commission for Refugees (UNHCR) characterizes Somalia as a microcosm of the state of the world's refugees (United Nations High Commission for Refugees [UNHCR], 2012). It asserts that the crisis in Somalia and among Somali people represents the entire range of issues plaguing refugees and that the unpredictable nature of the Somali conflict coupled with drought has severely strained host countries and resulted in few durable solutions for Somali refugees. Somalis fled their native lands in response to a civil war which broke out after the collapse of General Mohammed Siyaad Barre's regime in 1991. In 1992, the year after the regime collapsed, 45% of Somali people were displaced and many others died due to the conflict, disease and famine that occurred (Putnam & Noor, 1993). The region has since been characterized by clan warfare, military activity and political conflict, and dozens of failed peace initiatives and external interventions (UNHCR, 2012). In 2011, a drought once again displaced a large number of Somalis, creating yet another wave of migration (Muhumed & Van Kemenade, 2011).

At the end of 2011, there were approximately 1 million Somali refugees registered in countries in the Horn of Africa: 520,000 in Kenya, 202,000 in Yemen, 186,000 in Ethiopia, 18,700 in Djibouti and within Somalia itself an estimated 1.4 million internally displaced peoples (UNCHR, 2012). In 2011, the Census Bureau's American Fact Finder estimated that there are over 127,000 Somali-born persons living in the US.

Statistics from the UNHCR (2012) show that 90,000 Somalis were resettled as refugees during the period of 1991–2010 principally to the US, Canada and a few Nordic countries. The UNHCR sought resettlement sites for 35,000 Somalis in 2011 in spite of the reluctance of the resettlement countries. Resettlement countries cite integration challenges and security issues as reasons for their disinclination to settle Somalis although it is duly noted that the Somali diaspora is very strong in North America and Europe. Given that Somali refugees represent a large portion of refugees in the US and given recent crises, it is important to expand the knowledge of this community and its people.

Public Perceptions of Somali Refugees

A major impetus for this research project was to contest the negative and subtractive discourses about refugees, and Somalis in particular, in the media. Assuming discourse is a social practice, media portrayals as discursive practices have ideological effects based on the representation and positioning of people (Fairclough, 2003). These ideas that persist throughout society have an effect on the daily lives of refugees (Horst, 2006). Looking to movie, television, print and musical discourses surrounding Somalis, then, is useful because they represent technologically and institutionally based, mass-produced and distributed discourses (Gerbner, 1972). Take the critically acclaimed movie, *Black Hawk Down*, as an example. This film misrepresents Somalis and has been criticized for doing so. Mitchell (2001) wrote

> In "Black Hawk Down," the lack of characterization converts the Somalis into a pack of snarling dark-skinned beasts, gleefully pulling the Americans from their downed aircraft and stripping them. Intended or not, it reeks of glumly staged racism. (Mitchell, 2001: 1)

Anecdotally speaking, whenever talking with someone about the community I work with, I have often heard in reply something along the lines of 'Oh, you work with pirates?' This is not surprising though, as the Somali pirate is a commonly recurring character in media discourse.

The animated series *South Park* provides an example of the discursive representation of Somalis as pirates. In the episode 'Fatbeard', one of the characters, Eric, decides he is destined to be a pirate, and promises his friends that if they join him in his travels to Somalia they will reap the benefits. Eric and his entourage go to Somalia to meet Somali pirates (Parker & Stone, 2009).

K'naan, a Toronto-based musician, uses music to discuss the plight and reality of the Somali people and such discourses. K'naan's career began when he performed a spoken word piece criticizing the UN for its failed attempts to help in Somalia in front of the United Nations High Commissioner for Refugees (Takiff, 2010). In his song, 'Blues for the Horn', (K'naan, 2005) he acknowledges the way that the media creates a certain image of Somalis as warlike. He poses a series of questions through his lyrics about Somali practices, asking if the youth still create poetry and if the nomads' herds are grazing well. He then notes that he does not know the answer, at least not based on what the media reports. His lyrics reflect his disapproval of the discourses of Somalis and the gap in knowledge between this discursive ideology and the realities of Somalis' practices.

These 'standardized discursive and representational forms' of Somalis as 'cunning crooks' create a sustained image of refugees (Horst, 2006). Refugees are also often portrayed as 'vulnerable victims' (Horst, 2006) depicted by images of masses of people, vulnerable women and children, and a rudimentary humanity. These media representations 'both influence and are part of the policies and politics that determine the lives of refugees' (Horst, 2006: 14).

Research Methods

This chapter presents a small part of a larger research project focusing on Somali refugee women. I have used a life story approach (Linde, 1993) as much of the data were collected from the multiple accounts and retellings of Mama Rita's life. Additionally, data were collected using semi-structured interviews, three years of participant observation, field notes and the collection of artifacts when relevant. After analyzing and coding the data for themes, I used member checking to ensure that I was accurately representing the voices and agendas of the participants with which the research was being conducted.

The research project uses the principles of participatory action research (PAR) to inform the study because the overall goal of the project is to bring about change in the participants' social situations, generate theoretical and practical knowledge about the situation and collaborate with participants to affect change in the community (Burns, 2010). PAR emphasizes building community partnerships and utilizing knowledge from immigrant and refugee communities in order to accomplish more for the common good (Auerbach, 2002).

My positionality in this research is that of a participant-observer. Over the past few years, I have volunteered at a small organization started by a group of Somali refugee leaders. Since first meeting with the executive director three years ago, I have served as a teacher, volunteer coordinator, after-school program director, refugee advocate, curriculum developer and grant writer. I worked alongside the executive director on whatever matters needed to be attended to. My influence in policymaking is significant as I help write grants to develop and carry out educational programming in the refugee-serving community. The description of language as an FoK in the case of Mama Rita will help me to frame English language education as a priority for local and national refugee education policies.

The first time I met Mama Rita was early in 2013 and it was at the apartment community where the organization's after-school program was held. Mama Rita had met with an Eritrean man who was homeless and staying on the streets and had brought him to the program. This meeting with her and the way that she brought people together to help one person was just a preview of what I would come to learn is one of her strengths. I would see her often in the community and at the grocery store, helping newcomer refugee families. When I was just about to officially launch my research project, Mama Rita fit my criteria and eagerly agreed to help me.

Since that time, Mama Rita and I have formed a very close and special relationship. She helps me 'write my book' (that is what she calls my research), and I help her with whatever she needs whether it be taking her to a doctor's appointment, helping with groceries or reading a ticket or bill for one of her friends. In this way, our relationship is mutually beneficial. We also meet regularly in the city's various retail plazas. Mama sits in her friend's store and helps her sell goods. She has an 'office' set up in front of one locally owned grocery store. There, she talks to everyone, sometimes finding out who is a new refugee, helping people find jobs, medicine, food or whatever they need.

Mama Rita

Mama Rita was born in Mogadishu, Somalia, in 1928 (her immigration documents say she was born in 1950). She came from an affluent family who was in the business of farming and selling cattle. She, along with her husband, brothers and sisters would follow suit and also become involved in the business. Mama Rita went to school until she was about 12 years old and was married shortly after. She recounted to me that when she was married, she went to her father and asked why he was trying to sell her like one of his cattle. Nonetheless, she was married. Over the years, she gave birth to and raised 10 children. She had five sets of twins. Each set came as a boy and a girl.

It was years later in the early 1990s when her children were grown that the civil war broke out in Somalia. This is when Mama Rita and her family were attacked. The story of the attack is told in fragments – I've never tried to pressure Mama Rita into telling me what exactly happened. She told me that her family was killed right in front of her eyes. She was also attacked, tortured and left for dead. She spent three days in the morgue when an American Red Cross worker saw her throat move. She was taken to Kenya and was in the hospital, in a coma, for one year and seven months. She stayed an additional eight months in the hospital while healing after she regained consciousness. From there, she moved to Burundi as a refugee. In Burundi, she worked as a storekeeper for the Red Cross. She lived there for 15 years and made many friends. She lived in a house with a single mother and two boys who she adopted as her family. She said that during her time there she made many friends and was even friends with the Burundian president and his wife. Mama Rita was resettled in the US in 2009. She said she started out working as a housekeeper in the home of some Somalis and she also volunteered at a local community center. Shortly after her arrival, she also began to participate in local government campaigns. After only one year, she had made many friends and had started to participate in various ways in the community.

Mama Rita's FoK

This section will feature a selection of Mama Rita's FoK. The practices described below are in part based on Mama Rita's knowledge of and ability to use English. Mama Rita does not recall exactly how she came to be proficient in English, but she believes her English has improved since living in Clarkston. She is also proficient in several other languages, enabling her to interact with a diverse group of people in the Clarkston community. The practices described below are ones that I have noted and that I believe the community should be aware of. They accentuate how language is one prerequisite to participation in a community. These practices also demonstrate Mama Rita's agency and effectiveness as a refugee and what she views as valuable for her own well-being and the well-being of her community. These FoK include her abilities to gather and disseminate information, participate in politics and participate in various worship groups.

Mama Rita as a purveyor of information

One of Mama Rita's most significant FoK includes her ability to access, evaluate and share information. This type of information literacy is often overlooked in the discussion of refugee resettlement. As noted by Lloyd *et al.* (2013), there is often discussion about access to services in the refugee literature rather than information literacy practices. In their study on refugee information literacy practices, Lloyd *et al.* (2013) indicate that three phases of resettlement exist. The first stage, the transitioning phase, begins before refugees arrive and includes refugees seeking information about their new country. During this phase, caseworkers and service providers are primary information sources. The primary type of information during this phase includes information on compliance, rules and regulations of society in general and the community in particular as well as immediate information needs related to food, clothing, shelter and medical care.

The second phase, the settling phase, is characterized by less reliance on caseworkers and the development of networks and skills. This phase generally occurs after the first six months. In this phase, refugees are aware of their personal information needs and have been able to select and identify aids that help them to meet their needs.

The final stage, the settled stage, is characterized by the refugee's understanding of the information landscape and his or her ability to see that he or she has progressed through the previous stages. Refugees in this stage are ready and able to share what they have learned with others. Lloyd *et al.* (2013: 130) suggest that new refugees need to 'identify and establish relationships that support their transitioning into a new community by connecting them with people who can mediate and interpret the new information landscape for or with them'.

Mama Rita falls into the third stage. She has identified and established networks and relationships with people who are able to mediate the new information landscape. More importantly, she shares information and networks with other refugees and has become a navigator of information for refugees in the first and second settlement phases.

Mama Rita is a very good communicator. She speaks, reads and writes Somali and English. She is also very proficient in Swahili and various languages spoken in Burundi. I have observed her speaking with Ethiopians, Burmese and Nepalis in their mother tongues and she also knows some

Arabic and French. In a diverse community like Clarkston, her ability to communicate in various languages is especially useful when it comes to the gathering and dissemination of information. I categorize her ability as an FoK because it has a high use value, and less of an exchange value (Coben, 2002; Oughton, 2011). One would suspect that multilingualism would be cultural capital (Bourdieu, 1986) in a diverse community like Clarkston, at least in the refugee-serving community. This is not the case, as many of the refugee-serving organizations do not utilize refugees who have this sort of linguistic capital.

When I had my first interview with Mama Rita, I asked her how she got her information. She mentioned watching the local news reports, Al Jazeera and CNN and attending local community meetings, adding:

> I get from, I get information let me tell you, I have my own office there in front of Shoptown [grocery store], Rita information center, (laughs) That is the place I get all information. Talking to people, because people they love me they have to tell me everything, what happened here… I sit there outside, I sit, I smoke there, my cigarette, everybody come and give me information. They give me resume, to look job for them. There, outside.

Mama Rita hands out her own business card to people, sharing her telephone number and the profession of community outreach. She has recognized that having a business card is a type of cultural capital (legitimized and privileged by dominant groups) and helps facilitate the exchange of personal information. It offers her an expedited method of sharing her information and a way to participate in the dominant class. She has a collection of hundreds of business cards that she keeps in order to assist people in finding the services they need. This is another example of a practice that has an extremely high use value but a lesser exchange value (Coben, 2002). In addition to her business cards, Mama Rita has an email address and a Facebook account, and she uses her telephone frequently to get in contact with people. If she can't text message or email you, she will have someone else do it for her. This practice is an example of 'the learning of the use of language in such a way as to maintain and appropriately and progressively change one's position in society' (Fischer, 1970: 107).

It is in her 'office space' that Mama Rita informally and effectively shares knowledge. Her strategy of 'setting up office' and informally discussing everyday obstacles with her peers is a FoK. She knows where to get information for people. If you need a job, she knows that there is a small internet café that on Thursdays helps refugees find jobs with local companies. If you need help reading a traffic citation or other type of ticket, she knows that she can go to the police station and ask directly. Everyone in the city government and city council knows her very well, and she isn't afraid to take them up on their open-door policies. If you can't pay rent one month, Mama Rita has the number of several foundation and agency leaders that will make a donation.

Although Mama Rita wants the refugee community to be informed, she wants the flow of information to be two way. She knows that refugees need to know about Americans and the American way of life just as much as Americans need to understand the refugee situation. This knowledge practice exemplifies what Lloyd *et al.* (2013: 130) suggest as the highest level of information literacy – the ability to 'identify and establish relationships that support their transitioning into a new community by connecting them with people who can mediate and interpret the new information landscape for or with them'. Her ability to connect with people to gain and provide information exemplifies language socialization as a two-way street (Ochs, 2000).

Mama Rita as a political participant

Aside from her information center, Mama Rita uses her 'office' as a site for political participation. She has campaigned for two different city council members (one in her first year of residency and one in her fourth), both of whom had successful elections. She passes out fliers (one candidate told me that she passed out over 2000 for him). She also helped campaign for the local sheriff election in 2014 as well as for a congressman. In these instances, Mama Rita's literacy includes the discussion of important issues with the candidates and their teams. She then compares candidates' stances and decides which platform seems the best for the refugee community. I have observed her meeting with these politicians in her 'office' and asking them their stance on issues affecting the refugee community. If she supports the candidate, she will take fliers and informational materials and then discuss them with and distribute them to new American citizens who were previously refugees. These acts of campaigning enable Mama Rita to participate despite the fact that she is not yet a citizen.[2] Her ability to navigate and compare the various political discourses surrounding refugees is a literacy practice that is overlooked and that could potentially be used for pedagogical purposes, and it also demonstrates how she has been socialized into the political community and how she helps to socialize others as well.

Mama Rita participates in every single community meeting to which she is welcomed. She attends all of the city council meetings, town hall sessions and other community dialogues. It is at these venues that Mama is able to advocate for her refugee community and influence the local government officials and community members and in turn the misconceptions about refugees in Clarkston. The meetings are forms of cultural and social capital and give Mama Rita the opportunity to participate in the dominant class (Bourdieu, 1986). They are also one way that through language use and participation she is able to 'challenge and transcend the existing social categories' (Garrett & Badequeno-Lopez, 2002: 349).

At the beginning of 2014, I observed Mama Rita's political engagement when I joined her at the Capitol in Atlanta. She signed up to participate in New American day, which, in part, was aimed at informing state representatives and asking them to support the resettlement of refugees in Georgia. Although the state of Georgia does not directly contribute funding to refugee programming (all of the funding is from federal sources), the governor of Georgia is openly against the resettlement of refugees in his state, and so is the general political discourse about refugees. On this day, Mama Rita, other refugee advocates and myself met and distributed information to the state representatives' offices. Mama Rita and I even called a representative out of a session in order to discuss the economic benefits that refugees bring to Georgia. This event is significant because refugees' voices are rarely heard in politics, rather it is often others talking about them or for them. In this way, they become *dis-citizens*; they are not allowed to participate fully (Ramanathan, 2013). Generally, citizenship is viewed as the holding of a passport and the right to vote rather than the capacity to participate fully in various realms of society (Devlin & Pothier, 2006). Citizenship is not just status but practice that locates individuals in the larger community. Thus, any context that does not allow for full participation creates *(dis)citizenship* (Devlin & Pothier, 2006). Mama Rita's case is significant because she is participating in politics as a refugee although she is technically not yet a citizen. Dominant discourses and ideologies would not consider her to be a citizen; her acts of participation can help to expand the idea of *citizenship* as *practice* rather than *status* (Devlin & Pothier, 2006) and help refugee political participation become a form of capital that is observed by the wider community. Mama Rita is not yet a citizen and so her participation in politics is an FOK; it pushes the envelope on the meaning and definition of citizenship.

Mama Rita as a participant of multiple religions

For Mama Rita, worship is a valued practice and a proven resource because it brings her not only peace but also friends and social networks. Mama Rita is a Muslim and she goes to a masjid (mosque). She has a few different masjids that she attends, one near her home in Clarkston and a larger one in Atlanta that her friends take her to. She networks with the leaders of her faith community to help her refugee friends who need rental assistance and other forms of aid. Mama Rita not only attends a masjid and has many strong relationships from her participation, but she also attends church and bible study and frequents a local interfaith group meeting. Mama Rita's faith brings peace to her, but she has also found that faith organizations are a good source for networking and gathering resources. She has created a close relationship with a pastor and the congregation of a rather large church. This church's leaders call her on a weekly basis to offer volunteers and various donations. She helps them to identify the newest and neediest families. Her participation in this church community is also a source for growing and maintaining friendships.

In addition to church, Mama Rita attends local bible study sessions and frequents an interfaith meeting with Clarkston elected officials and community leaders. It is in these more intimate group exchanges that Mama Rita is able to once again become a messenger, or a bridge, between the various communities in Clarkston. Considering that Mama Rita is Muslim, and wears the hijab in the predominantly conservative, Christian, South, her social network of faith and interfaith organizations is a very successful FoK. Her practices can help us to revise the notion of 'integration' (Blommaert, 2012). If we expand the notion of 'integration' to include the ability to make oneself understood in a vast variety of social environments (not just the dominant culture, but various subcultures), then Mama Rita's ability to integrate into the various religious groups that are fundamental to the dominant and subcultures of Clarkston is remarkable. It is especially remarkable if we consider the anti-Muslim discourses and sentiments of Clarkston and the South.

Religious involvement may help Mama Rita integrate because it is a type of involvement associated with having influential friends (Wuthnow, 2002). Membership in religious congregations is consistently associated with friendships with elected public officials, corporation executives, scientists and persons of wealth, and acts as a method of 'status-bridging' (Wuthnow, 2002). Her participation in religious activities is yet another way that she combats existing social categories created for refugees and Muslims in the community through participation and language use (Garrett & Baquedano-López, 2002) and is an example of how language helps her to create and maintain 'a sense of shared understanding, drawing on those assumptions members share and negotiating others' (Schiefflin & Ochs, 1986: 168).

Conclusion

I will begin my conclusion by stating that Mama Rita's FoK are not desirable to everyone. As a Somali woman, although she is respected as an elderly member of the community, many Somalis see her political and religious participation as unacceptable or odd. In this way, sometimes Mama Rita struggles with interacting in the Somali community. She does not let it bother her, and her eagerness to interact and build relationships with all people may be a key to her success.

Mama Rita's case shows that refugees can become active, contributing members in their communities and need not be seen as a 'cunning crook' or a 'vulnerable victim' (Horst, 2006). The report to Congress claims that resettlement locations 'burden' local governments, schools, police, hospitals and social services. It states that refugees, 'Unlike migrants in search of economic opportunities, who can access extensive friend and family networks, to navigate language or other cultural barriers, new refugee populations lack this type of community resource upon arrival'. I show that there are refugees who can serve as navigators to new refugees, and Mama Rita exemplifies this. New refugee communities do not lack this resource, but local refugee-serving agencies do not efficiently tap into these resources. Mama Rita has FoK and they are not being utilized because they are not seen as capital (Bourdieu, 1986) within the larger community.

A suggestion based on this case is that integrating refugees into resettlement communities a process of relationship building. Language is a key part of this process. Mama Rita is not a passive recipient of sociocultural knowledge in her language interactions, but rather an active contributor. Refugee education policies must acknowledge language socialization as an interactive process that relies on informal relationships among refugees, more established refugees and long-time residents. Building intercultural understanding, understanding different faiths and identifying the shared values among members of Clarkston, a resettlement community, are synonymous with the language socialization of refugees, the building of community and the combating of negative dominant discourses about refugees. Educational policies are needed that acknowledge the extent to which language plays a role in community participation and that also recognize that language learning and social and cultural adjustment belong together in pedagogy.

I have utilized the findings of my research to create an educational program model that utilizes established refugees as community mentors to newcomer refugees for a type of extended cultural orientation. After six months, refugees should be falling into the second phase of resettlement, the 'settling phase' and have less reliance on caseworkers and a greater ability to navigate the information landscape in their local community (Lloyd et al., 2013). Six months is very little time to be able to navigate information by oneself. At this stage, an established refugee can show a newcomer refugee the methods of participation and different social practices that may be relevant to his or her integration into and participation in the local community. Mentors can socialize their mentees to and through language in the community. I have written this model that utilizes refugees' FoK into a grant that would benefit the community organization with which I work. The model is an attempt to have a localized rather than a 'one-size-fits-all' approach to refugee education and an approach that utilizes refugees' FoK and help their practices become capital in the community at large. It acknowledges that language competence, in part, is a matter of participating effectively in the community (Garrett & Baquedano-López, 2002).

Mama Rita's language proficiency, in English and other languages, is an integral part of her ability to participate so widely in her community. The implications of English language proficiency for community participation cannot be overlooked, but often is. Mama Rita's case illustrates how refugee resettlement policy must place more emphasis on English language education. The 'burden' will be less on the resettlement location if community leaders and policy makers open up spaces for refugees to participate more fully in all aspects of society and to truly become citizens.

Notes

(1) Pseudonym chosen by participant.
(2) Mama Rita was not yet eligible to apply for citizenship at the time of writing this chapter. She was very near to the five-year anniversary of her arrival, which is when she would become eligible to apply for citizenship.

References

Ahearn, L.M. (2001) Language and agency. *Annual Review of Anthropology* 3, 109–137.
Auerbach, E. (2002) Shifting roles, shifting goals: Integrating language, culture, and community. In E. Auerbach (ed.) *Community Partnerships* (pp. 1–12). Alexandria, VI: TESOL.
Blommaert, J. (2012) Citizenship, language, superdiversity: Towards complexity. *Working Papers in Urban Languages and Literacies* 95, 1–5.
Bourdieu, P. (1986) The forms of capital. In J.G. Richardson (ed.) *Handbook of Theory and Research for the Sociology of Education* (pp. 241–258). New York: Greenwood Press.
Bourdieu, P. (1991) *Language and Symbolic Power*. Cambridge: Harvard University Press.
Burns, A. (2010) Action research. In B. Paltridge and A. Phakiti (eds) *Continuum Companion to Research Methods in Applied Linguistics* (pp. 80–87). New York: Continuum.
Center for Health Disparities (2010) Somalis, Sudanese, and other refugees from East Africa. See http://www.iowahealthdisparities.org/documents/somalissudanese.pdf (accessed 3 October 2013).
City of Clarkston (2013) Clarkston facts. See http://www.clarkstonga.gov/index.php/about/interesting-facts (accessed 3 October 2013).
Coben, D. (2002) Use value and exchange value in discursive domains of adult numeracy. *Teaching, Literacy, and Numeracy Studies* 11 (2), 25–35.
Creswell, J.W. (2012) *Qualitative Inquiry and Research Design: Choosing Among Five Approaches*. Thousand Oaks, CA: Sage.
Devlin, R. and Pothier, D. (2006) Dis-citizenship. In Law Commission of Canada (eds) *Law and Citizenship* (pp. 141–175). Vancouver: UBC Press.
Fairclough, N. (2003) *Analysing Discourse: Text Analysis for Social Research*. London: Routledge.

Fischer, J.L. (1970) Linguistic socialization: Japan and the United States. In R. Hill (ed.) *Families in East and West* (pp. 107–119). The Hague: Mouton.

Garrett, P.B. and Baquedano-López, P. (2002) Language socialization: Reproduction and continuity, transformation and change. *Annual Review of Anthropology* 31, 339–361.

Gee, J.P. (1986) Orality and literacy: From the savage mind to ways with words. *TESOL Quarterly* 20, 719–746.

Gee, J.P. (2008) *What Video Games Have to Teach Us About Learning and Literacy* (revised and updated). Basingstoke: Palgrave Macmillan.

Gerbner, G. (1972) Mass and human communication theory. In D. McQuail (ed.) *Sociology of Mass Communications* (pp. 35–58). Harmondsworth: Penguin.

González, N. (2005) Beyond culture: The hybridity of funds of knowledge. In N. González, L. Moll and C. Amanti (eds) *Fund of Knowledge* (pp. 29–46). Mahwah, NJ: Erlbaum.

González, N., Moll, L. and Amanti, C. (2005) *Funds of Knowledge: Theorizing Practices in Households, Communities, and Classrooms.* New York: Routledge.

Hopkins, G. (2010) A changing sense of Somaliness: Somali women in London and Toronto. *Gender, Place & Culture* 17 (4), 519–538. doi:10.1080/0966369X.2010.485846

Horst, C. (2006) *Transnational Nomads: How Somalis Cope with Refugee Life in the Dadaab Camps of Kenya.* New York: Berghan.

Muhumed, M. and Van Kemenade, L. (July 10, 2011) Somali drought is 'worst humanitarian crisis: UN. *Huffington Post.*

Lloyd, A., Kennan, M.A., Thompson, K. and Qayyum, A. (2013) Connecting with new information landscapes: Information literacy practices of refugees. *Journal of Documentation* 69 (1), 121–144.

McBrien, J.L. (2005) Educational needs and barriers for refugee students in the United States: A review of the literature. *Review of Educational Research* 75 (3), 329–364.

Ochs, B. (2000) Socialization. *Journal of Linguistic Anthropology* 9 (1–2), 230–233.

Oikonomidoy, E. (2009) The multilayered character of newcomers' academic identities: Somali female high school students in a US school. *Globalisation, Societies and Education* 7 (1), 23–39.

Oughton, H. (2010) Funds of knowledge: A conceptual critique. *Studies in the Education of Adults* 42 (1), 63–78.

Putnam, D.N.M. (1993) The Somalis: Their history and culture. *Refugee Fact Sheet 9,* 1–34.

Ramakrishnan, S.K. and Espenshade, T.J. (2001) Immigration incorporation and political participation in the United States. *International Migration Review* 35 (3), 870–909.

Ramanathan, V. (2013) *Language Policies and (Dis)Citizenship: Rights, Access, Pedagogies.* Bristol: Multilingual Matters.

Rosenwasser, M. (2012) *Need to Know: America by the Numbers, Clarkston, Georgia.* The Corporation for Public Broadcasting, September 21.

Schiefflin, B. and Ochs, E. (1986) Language socialization. *Annual Review of Anthropology* 15, 163–191.

S. Rep. No. 111-52 (2010) See http://www.gpo.gov/fdsys/pkg/CPRT-111SPRT57483/pdf/CPRT-111SPRT57483.pdf (accessed 1 January 2013).

Street, B. (2005) The new literacy studies. In E. Cushman, E.R. Kintgen, B.M. Kroll and M. Rose (eds) *Literacy: A Critical Source-Book* (pp. 430–442). Boston, MA: St. Martin's.

Tarone, E., Bigelow, M. and Hansen, K. (2009) *Literacy and Second Language Oracy.* Oxford: Oxford University Press.

United Nations High Commissioner for Refugees (UNHCR) (2012) *The State of the World's Refugees: In Search of Solidarity* (p. 288). Oxford: Oxford University Press.

Van Dijjk, T.A. (2005) *Racism and Discourse in Spain and Latin American*. Amsterdam: John Benjamins.

Vertovec, S. (2007) Super-diversity and its implications. *Ethnic and Racial Studies* 30 (6), 1024–1054.

Vertovec, S. (2010) Towards post-multiculturalism? Changing communities, contexts and conditions of diversity. *International Social Science Journal* 199, 83–95.

Wuthnow, R. (2002) Religious involvement and status-bridging social capital. *Journal for the Scientific Study of Religion* 41 (4), 6669–6684.

Index